D1520081

CEO Mastery Journey

Sudhir Chadalavada

CEO MASTERY JOURNEY

7 Breakthrough Practices That Propel Successful Leaders to Greatness

Sudhir Chadalavada

HIGHPOINT
EXECUTIVE
PUBLISHING

This edition published by Highpoint Executive Publishing. For information, write to info@highpointpubs.com.

First Edition
ISBN: 978-1-64467-751-3

Library of Congress Cataloging-in-Publication Data

Chadalavada, Sudhir
CEO Mastery Journey: 7 Breakthrough Practices
That Propel Successful Leaders to Greatness
Includes index.

Summary: "CEO Mastery Journey is packed with insightful nuggets of practical wisdom and breakthrough practices in personal and organizational effectiveness, appealing to every leader's quest to build a purposeful, high-performance, and high-trust organization." – Provided by publisher.

ISBN: 978-1-64467-751-3 (hardcover)
1.Business 2.Leadership

Library of Congress Control Number: 2018960135

Design by Sarah Clarehart

Manufactured in the United States of America

10 9 8 7 6 5 4 3 2 1

Endorsements

"Sudhir digs deep and makes a compelling connection between mastery and business performance for the CEO in search of greatness. CEO Mastery Journey *delivers a practical how-to filled with insights and makes profound concepts easy to grasp and applicable in a direct, inspiring way."*

– Marshall Goldsmith, *Thinkers 50* **#1 Executive Coach and only two-time #1 Leadership Thinker in the world. Bestselling author of** *Triggers and What Got You Here Won't Get You There.*

"Sudhir has mastered the art and science of inspiring and effective leadership. CEO Mastery Journey *provides a compelling "How to" blueprint for building high trust and high-performance teams and organizations. This process has delivered exceptional results for us."*

– Ash Patel, President & CEO, Commercial Bank of California

"Sudhir Chadalavada has the ability to see the deeper reasons why we are the way we are and seems to know what stage we're at in our growth, and what's the best thing to do at this stage. His methods at Golden Hippo have led to more thoughtful, calmer, and happier leaders who are able to create conditions for their teams to thrive and grow."

– Mark Clemens, CEO Golden Hippo

*"*CEO Mastery Journey *inspires business leaders to become role models for inclusive and purposeful growth. Sudhir presents a comprehensive roadmap to develop conscious leadership and build a conscious organization. This framework will be the new normal for measuring business and leadership excellence."*

– Raj Sisodia, Professor of Global Business, Babson College and Co-Founder and Co-Chairman, Conscious Capitalism, Inc.

"Very seldom do I meet someone who really 'speaks my language.' Sudhir gets it—he correctly emphasizes the importance of leadership behavior and skill in building a purposeful and profitable business organization. This outstanding book provides life-tested examples, frameworks and practical steps to make this happen. I have seen it work."

**– Paul Folino, Chairman Commercial Bank of California &
Chairman Emeritus, Emulex Corporation**

"Business leaders have the most influence and impact in the world today. CEO Mastery Journey *inspires them to become role models and build organizations where everyone is engaged and inspired to unleash their talents, gifts and creative genius."*

– Jagdish Sheth, Professor of Marketing, Emory University

"I have been blessed to have found Sudhir along my journey; it is rare that you find someone who can be so helpful and so selfless. CEO Mastery Journey *guides, me, my leadership team, and our current and future leadership development in each of our portfolio companies. Through insights and tools gained from reading and practicing the teachings, we have transformed our business and our lives on our journey to be our best selves. We are more self-aware, perform at a higher level, achieve greater business results, and have a lot more fun working with one another."*

– Anand Gala, President & CEO, Gala Corporation

"If you are looking to be an elite CEO or leader and want your organization to be considered one of the greatest places to work, treat yourself to Sudhir's work and allow it to be your playbook! This book guides you to your own awakening, expansion and realizations that will help you quickly transform yourself, your leadership quotient, your team and your organization's capacity to thrive and prosper in these changing times. If you are ready to move past being successful to living a life of significance, fulfillment and service, then dig deeply into yourself through the pages that follow!"

**– Kevin Rafferty, Executive Coach, CEO, and Author of the book
*Wake Up, Get Real, Be Happy—Becoming Your Authentic Self***

"Promises made and kept. Sudhir Chadalavada set the bar high for himself and his readers by stating he'd answer three questions. Indeed, by the end of the book, we do have answers to: 1. How can being more personally aware, evolved, or conscious make me a more effective professional and better business leader? 2. How do I know how conscious I am? Can we measure and track personal development and consciousness? And 3. How can I become more conscious? How do I accelerate my growth? One can ask no more of an enlightened and skillful author than to make and keep promises. Sudhir is that author."

– David Kinnear, CEO dbkAssociates, Inc., Vistage Chair, Center for Credentialing, and Education Board Certified Coach and Certified Veteran Development Coach

"Sudhir not only talks the talk…he walks the walk! Human capital and conscious leadership are concepts that are foreign if not downright esoteric to most business leaders. Sudhir has a deeper understanding than most and an uncanny ability to deliver the methodologies to successfully help organizations transform from the old paradigms of business to become, as he has coined it, 'the change they want to be'. I have personally experienced two of those successful journeys with him."

– Jay Jannise, Executive Vice President, CITO/ISTO, Commercial Bank of California

Book Overview

Table of Contents

Acknowledgements

This book is an inspiration from many years of intense practice, study, observation, self-inquiry, introspection, learning, teaching and coaching. I have been influenced by regular men and women, seekers of truth and wisdom, friends, family, teachers, leaders, coaches, mentors, spiritual giants, and enlightened masters from a diverse and universal group. Together they represent the omnipotent, omnipresent, and omniscient force which we can call "universal intelligence" or as Emerson put it the "great intelligence." The yogis in India from thousands of years ago referred to this as *Mahat*, the cosmic intelligence.

I am thankful to Michael Roney for patiently going through the arduous task of pouring through my writings, articles, blogs and streams of consciousness. I wouldn't have been able to do this without his enthusiastic and expert guidance.

I spent a lifetime living, learning, and practicing these principles, and it is time to share my story. I owe Professor Jagdish "Jag" Sheth a big thank you for his efforts in this journey of mine. He would constantly urge me to discipline myself to write regularly, encourage me to not let go of the momentum, and set deadlines and milestones for completion. I am grateful to Marshal Goldsmith for sage advice to keep my message simple, not to take myself too seriously, and to stay humble.

Authoring this book has been a long road. It has been worth the wait since this is my intense and passionate personal journey. Jag saw back then what became obvious to me much later. Besides, as he points out in the best-selling *Firms of Endearment: How World-Class Companies Profit from Passion and Purpose*, which he co-authored with

David Wolfe and Rajendra Sisodia, the practical process of developing "great" or "enlightened leaders" for the age of transcendence has not been explored by any other authors.

My wife Usha and our three kids Suhas, Bhavna, and Ketana, have been troopers in this journey. They were willing participants and guinea pigs in testing these practices and were happy to challenge me and give me a dose of my own medicine. They enthusiastically accepted a life of simplicity and uncertainty while I was pursuing this unusual path and career choice. Everyone sacrificed and bore the challenges with calm courage.

Preface

Are great leaders born or made? Is it nature or nurture? If we say leaders are born, then we are ignoring one of the fundamental natural laws of being human. We are intelligent, self-reflecting beings who are capable of feeling, learning from our mistakes, and growing. It would be self-defeating and inaccurate to say we cannot change for the better or worse. On the other hand, if we say leaders are made, we are ignoring another important fact. We are all born with specific and unique gifts, talents, weaknesses, and blocks. Leaders are both born *and* made.

Some of us by our innate nature are emotionally stronger, more balanced and spiritually more purposeful than others, or other individuals just like some athletes and artists who are more gifted genetically. However, a gift or talent is useful only when you harness that potential. Some of us have to work harder to develop those emotional and spiritual muscles to lead an inspired life and to become inspiring leaders. But all of us have the opportunity for greatness. Some of the best leaders are not necessarily very naturally gifted; they just find a way to overcome serious obstacles and adversity and constantly stretch themselves to unleash their full potential. Adversity can be our ally. Our innate ability certainly matters, but curiosity, openness, and consistent practice can improve leadership qualities and effectiveness as many great leaders have repeatedly demonstrated.

We all have the opportunity to be better than we are currently by making the most of the deck of cards were dealt. Leadership starts with self. We are the captains of our ship of life and have the capacity to direct our destiny. The journey is more important than the end game. We do not pursue happiness; it is a by-product of a meaningful life. The same is true with inspiring, conscious, and enlightened leadership; it is a by-product of a purpose that is larger than self and transcends personal ambition.

The CEO Mastery Journey is a "how to" journey from success to greatness. I define successful leaders as those that are pursuing professional mastery. Unleashing your greatness requires you to add two other critical dimensions: personal mastery and organizational mastery.

Personal Mastery is the ability to stay positive, present, and grateful independent of external circumstances. This is being an inspired person and living an inspired life.

When you master your ego and emotions and release subconscious fears, you are on purpose. You are inspired to give your very best, and therefore are a lot more effective. Personal mastery is being in this state of inspiration consistently where you align your personal passion with professional vision.

Organizational Mastery is the ability to inspire everyone to give their heart, mind, and spirit to pursue a common purpose. This is being an inspiring leader and leading an inspired organization.

Success = Professional Mastery

A successful leader achieves very good financial results. He motivates with a carrot and stick or rewards and punishment approach, with a primary focus on self-centered achievement.

Greatness = Professional + Personal + Organizational Mastery

A great leader achieves exceptional financial results that are sustainable. She inspires by appealing to the innate drive for purpose, to make a difference and to be of service.

The Seven Practices in this book detail these aspects of Personal and Organizational Mastery along with practical real-life examples to help you understand and take your own journey. We will deep dive into those practical methods that have worked well for me and for many other successful leaders who are on this journey.

Professionals and business leaders have several years of extensive experience and training to hone and master their craft—this involves functional skills such as finance, engineering, marketing, operations. However, they have much less, if any, training in pursuing Personal and Organizational Mastery. This is a significant gap. The functional and analytical skills along with a solid work ethic and strong intellect that contributed to your success are no longer sufficient. Personal and organizational mastery is about mastering human motivations and emotions, and integrating them with organizational operations and practices. Leadership training should result in behavioral change, mere intellectual understanding is not sufficient.

Environment and Experience: Some of us get lucky and grow up in environments where sacrifice and sharing is part of life. That helps us to experience empathy and connect with others. Experience is a very good teacher. Over time we naturally get better by repetition of similar situations. There is no guarantee, though. All of us know people who have had the benefit of environment and experience but did not take advantage of it.

Inner Development: A large portion of what it takes to demonstrate inspiring leadership is inner development. For training to be effective, we have to dig deeper to understand the source of the behavior; the beliefs, values, mental models, and frameworks that shape our behavior. Understanding and intervening at the source results in a more impactful, lasting, and consistent transformation. Many experts and researchers have defined the characteristics and behaviors of such peak performing business leaders and organizations, but a practical process to develop them has largely remained a black box. Decoding this black box and bridging the execution gap between intent (to be a great leader) and impact (how a leader actually shows up) has been my lifelong passion.

CEO Mastery Journey: Seven Breakthrough Practices That Propel Successful Leaders to Greatness helps you master all of the steps needed to become an inspired conscious leader. This book is divided into two parts:

Part 1 begins with my personal journey of how I unraveled the secrets and practical steps to Personal and Organizational Mastery.

I then detail the unique socioeconomic inflection point we are in—
the paradoxical juxtaposition of remarkable progress made and dire
crisis taking us to the precipice of disaster. I identify the root cause
for the situation we are in and call business leaders to action to claim
the next level of leadership and usher in a new era of conscious and
inclusive growth and prosperity.

We will then explore the uplifting journey of a successful CEO
who is courageously transforming himself and his financial institution into a purposeful $1 billion organization.

Part 2 contains the practices and practical steps that every successful business leader can take to achieve personal and organizational
mastery and unleash his or her greatness to build an exceptionally
purposeful and profitable organization. These practices include mastering human motivations; mastering your own behavior; inspiring
noble purpose in you, your leadership team, and your organization;
accurately assessing current reality within your organization; bridging
the gap between intent and impact; engaging in action leadership to
effect change; and baking mastery into your organization's DNA, so
the lofty vision and goals match the reality of tactical operations and
execution.

With the following stories, steps, examples, and tools, I hope to
inspire you to embrace the journey from success to greatness, accelerate the socioeconomic shift that is taking place, and be the change
you wish to see.

PART I:
The Journey to
CEO Mastery

From Brink to Breakthrough

"Everybody can be great ... because anybody can serve."
— Martin Luther King, Jr.

I am an ordinary man with an extraordinary dream. Over the years, as the dots got connected, I can say with conviction that many of my dreams and goals boiled down to one thing—how to lead a self-actualized life and build an organization that achieved the same level of full potential! My primary tools and skills in making progress in this pursuit have been an insatiable thirst and an intense passion to seek, to know, and to understand. That is all I had to do. The universe, the cosmic intelligence or *Mahaat*, as the Vedas say, took over and conspired to make it happen. I could say that I did it or I pursued my passion. However, I have to declare with all honesty and humility that I was led and shown the way. I was thrust into experiences which forced me to learn, grow, fall, get up, learn more, and grow more.

As I stayed on the journey, something remarkable happened—the answers came, solutions unfolded, and I discovered the keys to leading a self-actualized life and building a self-actualized organization. This included understanding the keys to physical fitness, mental soundness, emotional maturity, and spiritual wisdom. One of the greatest lessons I learned was to recognize that meditating and living consciously doesn't prevent or even solve problems magically. It allows you to deal with problems more effectively. Pain is essential for progress but suffering delays or stops progress. Your goal should not be to avoid pain or problems. You should equip yourself to deal with any problem business or life throws at you confidently and consciously. My mistakes and failures were painful but necessary for growth. I kept at it and persisted even when it seemed impractical and foolish. With practice, I realized that pain is inevitable, but suffering is optional. The journey got better when I found a way not to suffer or get down even when the obstacles and problems got bigger and bigger. Solutions always followed!

Our modern life is one-dimensional and is heavily focused on intellect. The successful business leaders I work with have this attribute in abundance. I call this professional mastery. They have a solid work ethic and have mastery over their core functions such as finance, engineering, marketing, sales, or operations.

However, to lead a self-actualized life and to build a self-actualized organization, two other dimensions are crucial: personal and organizational mastery. You have to learn and practice the diet, exercise, rest, and sleep patterns that will optimize your physical fitness. You have to always naturally be in a present and balanced mindset, independent of positive or negative external events and circumstances to deal with life's ups and down with equanimity. You have to work on unleashing your inherent genius, expressing your natural gifts and strengths while overcoming the blocks that come in the way. This is personal mastery—you are living an inspired life.

Further, you have to evoke excited, energized, and enthusiastic commitment from the people you lead and serve and provide inspirational leadership by bringing out the best in them. This is *organizational mastery*. While this may sound intimidating and seem like a lot to learn and practice, it is not. They are all connected and mutually reinforce each other. There is a natural flow which makes it rewarding and fun. A self-actualized state is to lead an inspired life and demonstrate inspiring leadership. Everything boils down to discovering how to reach a self-actualized state.

If I can do it, anyone can. You do not have to compromise the way you lead your life and build your career. I believe it is your birthright to show up fully with heart, mind, and spirit everywhere, every time. Life can be lived fully only when you integrate personal, professional, and spiritual pursuits. You do not have to artificially separate and compartmentalize them.

I know this may sound preposterous to some. You may have plenty of questions and doubts. Seek answers for them with an open and inquiring mind. This approach is a lot more productive than being sure and suspicious about things. I went all in and, in the process, discovered the secrets of personal and organizational mastery practiced by the best and the brightest leaders. I say to my friends and clients, "I love to work with people who are skeptical and open, but there is nothing I can do when you are closed and cynical."

All the practices and examples I share in this book are based on personal experience, which was followed by repeatedly demonstrating the same processes with several successful CEOs and leaders. I feel humbled, stunned, and proud of the exceptional results we achieved. I am grateful for the trust and confidence these brave men and women had in me. To protect their privacy and confidentiality, I have used composite characters everywhere except for one: my partner in crime in this remarkable journey, Ash Patel, the passionate and courageous CEO of Commercial Bank of California. Ash took the plunge by trusting my process and continues to grow remarkably as a conscious leader.

How did I discover the secrets and practical steps to achieving personal and organizational mastery? How did I integrate them with business processes, strategy, and execution so we can lead a conscious, evolved, and inspired life and provide conscious, enlightened, and inspiring leadership? It has been a journey that began with innate curiosity, then professional disconnect and discontent, followed by intense personal and professional exploration, and finally, the cosmic gift of a breakdown. Then the dots connected, and answers began to emerge.

Innate Curiosity

I was born into a secular Hindu family and grew up in multicultural, cosmopolitan India. My mother taught in the local high school; she was my teacher in fourth grade. My father was a successful executive in a national pharmaceutical firm, which he eventually ran. The leaders and managers of this organization came from all over the country. My friends were from a variety of states, religions, and ethnic backgrounds and spoke different languages. I studied in a Jesuit school, and some of my close relatives were Christians. My paternal grandmother was a proselytizing Christian preacher; she never lost an opportunity to share stories from the Bible and the power of forgiveness exemplified by Jesus Christ. My maternal grandmother was a devout Hindu. My first close friend was a Sikh; the second one had a white American mom and an Indian dad. My two best friends in high school were Christian and Muslim, respectively. I grew up in a unique, secular, and diverse environment, and I thrived in it.

My family was not particularly religious or ritualistic. Growing up, I was fascinated by the warrior heroes and kings Ram, Arjuna, Karna, Dharma Raj, and their enlightened masters from the two great epics of India: Ramayana and Mahabharata. I also deeply admired the more recent wise warrior-kings, Ashoka, Maharana Pratap, and Akbar. Their demonstration of noble values such as courage, sacrifice, generosity, loyalty, righteousness, and commitment to truth and justice made an indelible impression on me and became the foundation for my life. I was touched and impacted by their universal outlook: treating all human beings with fairness and justice in spite of superficial differences, while living a balanced, well-rounded life. These leaders and kings had great skill and expertise in their profession (archery, weapons, administration, and governance). They sought counsel from wise enlightened masters on the art and science of living purposefully and leading consciously. They ruled with courage, justice and integrity, and at the same time demonstrated respect, love, and compassion for their subjects, society, and family members.

Their behavior and mindset matched what groundbreaking psychologist Abraham Maslow would call a *self-actualized state*. For example: Simultaneously demonstrating behaviors of humility and courage, open and assertive, self-assured and self-effacing, deep listening and emphatic articulation is a typical characteristic trait of self-actualized people. Mahatma Gandhi also was a major influence, as I was deeply inspired by his will, discipline, and ability to bring about transformation through personal example. These were my heroes, and I truly wanted to emulate their noble characteristics. At the same time, I became aware of the gap in consciousness that existed in the current leaders and society in India. This was disappointing. I was particularly disturbed by rampant corruption and poor ethics, along with a pervasive apathy and inferiority complex in the society.

I wondered what had become of the land which believed in and practiced *vasudhaiva kutumbakam*, an ancient Sanskrit term which translates to "world is one family." Perhaps America, with its inclusive and secular society, would be better equipped to demonstrate these principles. Perhaps I would merge my appreciation of ancient eastern wisdom with modern western practicality. I therefore decided to move to the United States to continue my pursuit of enlightened leadership. I was obsessively driven and crazy enough to risk everything to find the answers—to create a system that could liberate organizations of all sizes from the constraints of left-brain-only approach. I had the love and unconditional support of enlightened masters, family, and friends.

Professional Disconnect and Discontent

I came to the United States from India with a big dream and twenty dollars in my pocket. I earned a master's degree in electrical engineering in New York and then moved west to Silicon Valley, California, to start my professional career. But I had no interest in engineering or in pursuing a career as a technologist. I was an accidental engineer to begin with, and frankly I was not good at it. I had always been more interested and intrigued by the inner human engineering, i.e., engineering of the human mind, human motivation, human spirit, and fulfilling human potential.

I soon discovered that the enlightened leadership environment that I was desperately seeking was not to be found in the business world of mid-1980s and 1990s. I was fortunate to work with some of the best business minds in diverse organizations of all sizes; large

Fortune 500 corporations and as well as small- and medium-size companies, including technology companies in the dotcom era. These bright, knowledgeable, driven, high-IQ professionals and leaders were focused on intellectual stimulation and financial incentives to motivate people to perform. The daily processes, management behavior, and reward systems overwhelmingly favored intellect over emotional maturity, individual contribution over team collaboration, passion over compassion, and bottom-line results over personal fulfillment. They had very little understanding of what it took to inspire people to give their very best. There was no place for managing or mastering emotion and intuitive feeling for people and business. There seemed to be an underlying fear that if people brought emotion and feelings to the workplace, they would compromise their objectivity and make poor decisions. I knew this wasn't true and felt that emotional mastery actually enhances decision-making, objectivity, fairness, and justice.

My friends and colleagues seemed to be satisfied with intellectual stimulation and material comforts that came with work and were willing to put up with inconveniences. A "practical" person would say I should have been, too. In many ways, I had it made. I was single and living in California with a well-paid job. I was the captain of our company's tennis team. I loved the easy and affordable access to a health club and became a fitness fanatic. All of this was fun but only served as a temporary distraction from my quest for mastery. I was seeking more. I wanted to know and learn how to always stay positive and inspired, no matter what the external circumstances were.

My passion had always been in leadership, *right action*, and human inspiration. Right action is action taken in line with one's values and principles, for the good of the team, without a personal desire to be right. As I toiled at these places, I imagined ruefully how much better the team, division, and company would be if only they embraced these principles in their culture. The companies I worked for and the people I knew were doing well financially and intellectually. I knew they could do much better, but I did not know how to articulate it professionally in business terminology. I had a lot to learn about life and was struggling to survive in this alien world of business. I had no passion for this work and felt like a fish out of water. My two bad options seemed to be to quit work or sell out, that is postpone the quest for meaning, purpose, and fulfillment. I took the unconventional third option—I went on a deep personal and diverse professional exploration.

Intense Personal and Professional Exploration

Adversity, they say, is the greatest teacher. I have always been passionately driven by right action, leadership, mastery, and living life to the fullest. I channeled my personal disappointment and professional discontent to an intense inner and outer journey of personal and professional exploration. I left my corporate job to set out on this adventure with my wife Usha and three young kids, Suhas, Bhavna, and Ketana. I remember a short but distinct conversation within me. "Sudhir, are you sure you want to do this?" The answer was instantaneous and spontaneous. "Yes, absolutely." It was a no-brainer. This is my passion, and this is what I was born to do. I had prepared for this situation: I had been working on myself and made significant lifestyle changes, including regular meditation, to become more conscious. I learned a lot about strategy, marketing, operations, and business processes having worked in successful corporations with passionate leaders. Besides, my unique ideas of organizational leadership, engagement, and alignment were being enthusiastically received by the corporate teams I had been leading.

Since my ultimate goal was to lead a life of professional excellence and personal fulfillment, I had to create this career and path for myself. The first step is the recognition that mastery is about understanding human motivation, human emotions, and human nature. What makes us tick? What makes us angry, grateful, or judgmental? What inspires us to give our very best and be engaged in peak performance? The next step is to remember that whatever needs to be said about human nature was already voiced thousands of years ago.

I plunged into physical fitness, competitive tennis, and personal development. I took a deep dive into self-inquiry, meditation, yoga, and a high-performance vegetarian diet. Meditation had dramatic impact on my life. I became calmer, more confident, less anxious, a much better tennis player, a smoother public speaker and, most importantly, began to develop more clarity in pursuit of personal development and inspirational leadership. I dove into Bhagavad Gita, the 5,000-year-old Indian text, and learned the most profound skills and techniques on leadership, coaching, unleashing human potential, and living a self-actualized life. My search for meaning and purpose, which started in India in my early teens, now took flight in my twenties in California.

Understanding human nature and human potential and integrating that knowledge to improve business performance, organizational effectiveness, employee engagement, productivity, and leadership alignment became my quest and passion. We have teachers and coaches to help us get better and learn faster in school, in college, in sports, in the arts, and practically all aspects of life. Understanding the natural laws of life and leading a self-actualized life, on the other hand, is a lot more complex and confusing. Arjuna, the greatest warrior of his time, had Krishna as his mentor and master coach. Much later, Alexander the Great had the benefit of Aristotle. In modern business leadership, Steve Jobs had Bill Campbell as his coach, and Alan Mulally had Marshall Goldsmith. Doesn't it make sense to learn from someone who has navigated this complex terrain?

The other key issue I was grappling with was how does one develop inspiring, effective, and enlightened leadership? Many thought leaders like Jim Collins defined great leadership as a "paradoxical mix and unique combination of personal humility and professional will." I agreed with this sentiment but none of them had a practical answer for how to actualize it. This uncommon, almost contradictory combination of behaviors represents a higher self-actualized state of operation, which I believe is the key to personal and organizational mastery.

I ultimately realized that enlightened masters held the key to inspiring leadership—they understood human psychology and motivation better than anyone else. I began my mission to find a teacher or master who exemplified these characteristics.

There's an old Indian saying, "When you know what you want, the world conspires to make it happen for you." I feel blessed to have developed poignant relationships and learned from some of the greatest spiritual teachers of our time. They represent the cosmic intelligence wherein resides all wisdom about human nature. They provided me the experience to tap into that omniscient source and unravel the secrets to Personal and Organizational Mastery. I found these masters to be modern versions of the ancient Rishis or Seers who, through self-inquiry and meditation, discovered methods to keep the body, mind, and spirit functioning at peak performance. I ignored the skepticism and controversy that accompanies any pioneering work. Yoga, meditation, and a vegetarian diet, for example, are now commonly accepted as keys to peak performance. This was ancient knowledge and practice in India. I had to leave India (my Janma Bhoomi—place of birth) and discover it in the United States (my Karma Bhoomi—place of action).

I observed some remarkable characteristics in these saints. They never rushed, were always present, and operated in a flow state of execution effectiveness, easily working sixteen-plus hours a day with barely five hours of sleep. They inspired everyone around them to give their very best. They exemplified the epitome of leading an inspired life and inspiring others to do the same. They demonstrated the best of passion and compassion, courage and humility, individual drive and collaborative spirit, as well as masculine and feminine aspects. They demonstrated Personal and Organizational Mastery.

I explored the depths of mind and spirit and diligently practiced everything I learned—martial arts, yoga, meditation, and breathing exercises, while continuously refining my diet and always staying physically active. I did not miss a single sitting of twice-a-day meditation for ten years. Such was my hunger and thirst for learning the secrets of enlightened life and leadership. Spiritual discipline and routine came naturally to me. I treated my mind and body as the laboratory to experiment with peak performance and self-mastery. A pattern was emerging, proving that in order to function at peak performance in business; we have to work holistically on body, mind, emotion, and spirit.

At the time, I was traveling extensively for work and we were raising three young children. I couldn't have done it without my wife, Usha, being a fulltime mom. She continues to be a willing partner in this crazy man's intensely passionate journey of Mastery. The great Indian saint Ramakrishna Paramahansa said, "Do not seek illumination unless you seek it as a man whose hair is on fire seeks a pond." Usha and our children would probably agree that I would pass this test for seeking.

My outer exploration took me from one company to another in search of that ideal environment where we can be ourselves without wearing a mask.

Finally, all the pieces had seemingly come together when I got the dream opportunity to build a $1 billion global organization. I was off to a rocking start, but the universe had other plans. This exciting new adventure was cut short when I was bedridden for most of 2006. This turned out to be a cosmic gift. I had some more lessons to learn—I had to lose ego and judgment and be in a state of gratitude. As the saying goes, "Be careful what you wish for, you just might get it."

Cosmic Gift of a Breakdown

I had to constantly change positions while lying down, shifting from one side to another, and even a faint thought in my mind seemed to cause disturbance and increase physical agony. My only hope to get some physical comfort was to find a way to still my mind. The prescribed treatment was to numb and paralyze the hyperactive muscles in my neck and shoulder with Botox injections every few months. For 40 years, I had lived a robust, healthy life without any medication—not even cold medicine, vitamins, or pain killers, despite a very active lifestyle and many years of competitive athletics and sports. I was sure that I would spend the rest of my life staying healthy. This debilitating ailment was an unexpected jolt that shook me up. I had always intuitively felt that positive thoughts and emotions could play a major role in preventing and healing physical ailments. Could I heal myself by going within, by understanding my thoughts and emotions, and consciously getting into a more positive, fearless state of mind? I resolved to do exactly that.

I had to first still my mind and accept my situation by letting go of disappointment, anger, blame, guilt, or pity. I stayed in the present by not going back and digging up frustrating situations or perceived injustices of the past. I shut down thoughts about possible catastrophic future events involving my health or financial security for my young family. When I was present and stayed in the moment I was able to physically rest and relax. If I could be in a state of gratitude and joy, perhaps I could fully heal.

I dug in to understand how the workings of my mind and emotions determine who I am, what I believe in, and what I stand for. What obstacles have come in the way of leading a life of my choice? What, if anything, is preventing me from doing that? I recognized the power of mind even more intimately. This experience paved the way for me to dive deeper into emotional mastery and make the connection to business execution, leadership effectiveness, and the pursuit of a purposeful life.

Turns out I had one very important lesson to learn on my journey to unlock the secrets to leading an inspired self-actualized life and leading an inspiring self-actualized organization. I had to fully lose judgment of people, be in a state of gratitude, and fully demonstrate empathy and compassion. This required me to overcome my ego and submit to a greater omnipresent, omnipotent, and omniscient force. While my goal was noble and lofty, I had to recognize that I am only an instrument and have to align myself to this universal force. My ego cannot be in the driver's seat anymore; it has to be in service of this force which is my deepest essence. Though it initially didn't seem like it when I was flat on my back, it became obvious that this was a cosmic gift for me to have the time and opportunity to connect the dots, get answers to all my questions, and put all the pieces together! I now had the time and freedom to reflect on the questions that fueled my quest, my drive and my mastery journey:

- Why are qualities and characteristics associated with inspirational leadership not widely and regularly demonstrated at work?
- How can we show up fully with intellect, emotion, and spirit at work and integrate our personal, social, and spiritual lives?
- How can we live life to the fullest, as defined by being present and alive with high energy and enthusiasm during our waking hours?
- Why is stress so high and level of engagement so poor in our business organizations? Why do so many good leadership teams accept high stress and lack of balance as normal?
- Why do even the most successful organizations, leadership teams, and individuals only scratch the surface of unleashing their full potential?
- Why do skilled, hardworking professionals struggle to perform at a high level as a team?
- Who am I? Where did I come from? Where will I go? What is my purpose?
- Is decoding and teaching enlightened leadership my purpose?
- What is the key to being effective, happy and contented?

I am probably not unique in seeking answers to these questions. I was just obsessive, impatient, and maniacal about my pursuit. All of us face these questions at one time or another. Some of us postpone the search for a later date, for some the later date never comes, and many others ponder these thoughts and questions on their deathbeds. I began to feel blessed to have this amazing opportunity to reflect on my life as a ninety-year-old on his death bed would, except it was even better. I had another half a life ahead of me to learn from my mistakes and live the life of my dreams. This was a lovely gift—I relaxed fully, and the healing process got turbocharged. I experienced waves of gratitude.

Dots Connect and Answers Emerge

I made the most of my precious cosmic gift of unlimited and unconditional time reflecting, listening to healing music, engaging in self-inquiry and mediation, and reading inspirational stories. The answers I was seeking and the growth I needed became evident as I delightfully leafed through the biography of the enlightened saint, Sri Ganapathy Sachchidananda Swamiji. This powerful cocktail turbocharged my spiritual growth and healing. Instead of blaming people and circumstances, I let go of the past and experienced remarkable breakthrough. Physical pain melted away magically, emotional turmoil evaporated, and spiritual turbulence shifted to tranquility. I experienced in my own being what it takes to have cognitive understanding of gratitude, followed by emotionally feeling it, and then physically acting on it.

This to me is the essence of mastery—it is not an academic exercise or philosophical theory but involves converting our noble intention to impactful action automatically. Consider this:

Gratitude Practice

Cognitive and intellectual understanding leads to experience, both biologically and emotionally, which then can be expressed in action.

Everyone intellectually understands what living in gratitude means, but very few consistently demonstrate it. Only when you experience the pleasantness of that feeling physically and emotionally can you fully appreciate its power. Then consistent action follows naturally. You don't have to force this behavior. This has been my experience.

The physical pain and mental agony that I endured gave me a deeper insight into the suffering of fellow human beings. I developed greater love, compassion, and gratitude. Sri Swamiji said, "When our heart is filled with love, no one and nothing on this earth can cause unhappiness or discontentment." It was my dream to achieve this state of self-actualized equanimity, independent of positive or negative, triumphant or traumatic situations. Five thousand years ago, Krishna told Arjuna to be in this state of "Sthitaprajna." Through this experience I could biologically (not just intellectually or theoretically) experience that state where gratitude and judgment do not co-exist. I felt a deep sense of peace and liberation. Joy, bliss, ecstasy and contentment followed, and several insights were revealed.

Natural Laws

Just as we have laws for traffic and physics, there are natural laws in life. When we follow them, life is smoother and enjoyable physically, emotionally and spiritually. However, they are not spelled out as clearly or explicitly and are certainly not taught in school. It is on us to figure it out. You can't say *sorry I didn't know.* If you violate the laws knowingly or unknowingly, you will pay a price in terms of peace of mind, physical health, emotional well-being, etc. When we connect with our inner essence or spirit, we discover these natural laws and insights as defined below.

Natural Law #1: No crisis, however serious it is, can cause stress by itself. It is our response to the crisis that causes either stress or allows us to be in a state of equanimity. Stress is caused if we blame the crisis on someone else, including ourselves. Stress is caused when we do not fully accept our situation and instead respond with fear, frustration, disappointment, and disillusionment.

Natural Law #2: When we completely accept ourselves and take full responsibility for our situation, we appreciate what we have and can make the most of our talents. We experience gratitude, liberation and contentment. This is a necessary pre-condition for peak performance.

Peak Performance: Peak performance is possible only when we are not attached to the outcome. Unless we are content, we will invariably be attached to the outcome. This is a paradox because we have to be content before achieving the result. It is possible to get great results—make money, run profitable organizations, win world championships, and Olympic medals—but it doesn't necessarily mean that we utilized our full potential. We may have in some cases, but not necessarily always. In fact, it is entirely possible for some who may not have won any medals or trophies to experience peak performance and experience being in the Zone. This is true of business and life. It is not the external recognition but internal realization that ultimately determines if we are utilizing our full potential at that time. Why is utilizing our full potential so important? It is because contentment and unleashing our full potential go hand-in-hand. And life would be drudgery if we are not content. Who wants that? We always want to be the best we can be, it is the natural state.

This is how the process works:

Acceptance > Gratitude > Liberation > Contentment > Peak Performance

Acceptance leads to gratitude which results in a feeling of liberation and contentment, which in turn drives peak performance.

We have control over our actions alone and not the results—results are lagging indicators that depend on other factors besides our personal expertise and effort. Based on this experience, I developed the concept of spiritual intelligence (SQ) as being critical to leading an inspired and inspiring life and leadership. This is the next logical step of evolution from emotional intelligence (EQ) as I will explain in Practice 1—Master Human Motivations. We cannot achieve the self-actualized state of equanimity by knowing or thinking about it. A higher SQ naturally leads to a state of equanimity, which is the key to peak performance. It typically involves:

Step 1: Set audacious goals—be the change you wish to see.

Step 2: Execute relentlessly with a single pointed focus on action and process.

Step 3: Let go of the attachment to results. Surrender to a higher cosmic force of universal intelligence.

This is how remarkable change agents in human history such as Krishna, Buddha, Christ, Lincoln, Mahatma Gandhi, and Nelson Mandela, to name a few, achieved extraordinary results. Each country, each culture, and each religion has achieved several other similarly evolved souls. I have been inspired by many of these principles in implementing successful change programs in business organizations, which are relatively much less complex than social, political, and religious transformation programs. I have explained this in greater detail in Practice 6, "Engage in Action Leadership," and Practice 7, "Bake Mastery into Your Organizational DNA."

I confirmed that my physical ailment had a deeper spiritual root cause and solution. For example, whenever I passionately talked about inspired and inspiring life and leadership with friends and colleagues, physical problems temporarily vanished. This also happened when I demonstrated tolerance and understanding instead of anger and judgment. Suddenly, magic happened, and I felt my personal power like never before. I realized that if my actions were partially responsible for the problem, then I could act differently and shape my destiny by working toward a different outcome. The outcome wouldn't depend entirely on my actions, but I could significantly influence it. At the very least, I would have the satisfaction of doing my best and taking the right action. This realization was amazingly liberating. I was ecstatic.

Everyone can be great because everyone can be themselves and unleash their gifts, talents, and creative genius.

I realized that I am only an instrument of change. While I am passionate and proud of my work, I cannot take myself too seriously. Why? Because I need to align with the source of universal intelligence in order to make effective progress. I have to allow change to happen through me, not by me. This requires humility and overcoming the ego of "I am doing it" and overcoming judgment of others who are perceptibly "not doing." This shift is necessary for anyone on this journey—we have to ensure that ego is no longer in the driver's seat; rather, it has to be in service of the essence (the spirit, a higher purpose) and there is no judgment of people and situations. The judgment is replaced by intense curiosity which leads to gratitude. All this sounds wonderful in theory but requires an inner awakening to practice consistently.

My state of mind had a direct influence on my physical healing. When I kept my mind still, free from thoughts of disappointment, frustration, and perceived injustices of the past and free from the worries and uncertainty of future, I felt better physically. My doctor at the University of Southern California looked at me in amazement when he saw me after a few months. He said that he had not seen anything like my rapid recovery in over twenty years of practice. He continued, "I don't know what you did, I probably don't understand what that means and how it works. All I can say is that I am delighted to see the physical transformation in you. You obviously don't need any medication. I would like to take a video of you and inspire my patients of the possibility for them."

Looking back, the healing process makes perfect sense. How else could it be? We are not just our body. We are not just our mind. We are not just our spirit. We are all three and true health and healing have to involve all three aspects. Perhaps more so in my case because of the intense passion I carried about right action, purposeful life, and enlightened leadership.

Building an Enlightened Organization

When the health crisis was over, I realized that I had truly prepared myself intellectually, physically, emotionally, and spiritually to build and lead an enlightened global organization. This organization would have these qualities:

- A place where every employee and stakeholder can bring the "whole person" to work and unleash his or her full potential.

- An organization that fosters a culture of professional excellence and personal fulfillment.

- A great place to work where everyone looks forward to coming to work, and leaves at the end of the day invigorated and charged, as opposed to being drained and depleted.

- A company that aligns and balances the interests of all parties and stakeholders and does not make kneejerk "either/or" demands. For example, serving customers doesn't have to be at the expense of overworked, underappreciated, and under-paid employees. Increasing profitability doesn't have to mean driving suppliers out of business, thus affecting the quality of life in their communities. A focus on the bottom line doesn't have to mean an uninspiring work environment.

- An organization that truly practices and promotes empowerment and accountability, autonomy and collaboration, toughness and love, passion and compassion.
- A business where people have fun and give full creative expression to their intellect, emotion, and spirit.
- An organization that becomes a playground for realizing the ultimate dream of living life to the fullest.

People working for such an organization do not have to compartmentalize their lives by using the bulk of their intellect at work, nurturing emotion only with family, and postponing their engagement of spirit until they find time on the weekend or waiting for retirement to engage in a worthy cause. Those working for an enlightened organization don't have to sacrifice personal growth and fulfillment for professional achievement or core beliefs and values for financial security.

Forging Business Mastery with This Book

In this book, I make an objective assessment of current socioeconomic reality, identify the root cause of critical problems, and offer specific solutions that inspire us to take action. As I have done personally, I make a case in these pages for business leaders and organizations to look within and recognize areas where they can improve. For example, there is a general lack of trust in both business and political leadership. Confidence in the direction of our country and economy is low. Business has demonstrated much growth and progress but has also generated many avoidable challenges. Business leaders are very good at directing, commanding, controlling, managing efficiently, and motivating with a carrot and stick, but this approach alone is no longer sufficient.

This book is a result of my journey in transforming organizations to a new level of success, using an approach that has become essential in the competitive, dynamic environment of business today. I began to feel like an instrument for expression of the universal and timeless truth. I even named my consulting practice UniTi Group as an expression of Universal and Timeless Principles of Mastery. The source of this truth is the omnipotent, omnipresent, and omniscient force which we can call "universal intelligence" or, as Emerson put it, the "great intelligence." The yogis in India from thousands of years ago referred to this as Mahat, the cosmic intelligence. Over the years, as I began to understand and appreciate this "intelligence", I found myself to be losing ownership to this work. As I let go of ownership, ironically, the pace picked up. Help started coming from everywhere including from the most unexpected of sources. Inspiration started gushing out from within me in the form of oral and written expression. It was hard to keep up with the flow of information that came at all times. My hand would hurt trying to capture everything that was coming through. My biggest task was to consolidate, organize, and edit all the information that was piling up.

I also discovered, to my delight, that I was not alone in this search. Along the way, I discovered several kindred spirits, all seemingly drawing from the same "source." Ken Wilber is a good example. He is the founder of integral theory and has been called "the Einstein of consciousness." He confirmed my perspective on the root cause for all the business, social, and economic challenges and opportunities we face, including the current social and political divide in our country. His comprehensive approach matches my own "integral" thinking. Many books have sprung from the inspiration of Ken's pioneering work, including *Reinventing Organizations* by Frederic Laloux, *Spiritual Intelligence* by Cindy Wigglesworth, and *Conscious Business* by Fred Kofman. I was on the faculty of Axialent, a wonderful organization that Fred co-founded. There is a rapidly growing list of fellow seekers and cosmic siblings who represent this conscious way of living and leading organizations, embodying the masculine and feminine aspects of life and leadership. Some of the CEOs, business leaders, and thought leaders who embody these attributes are Paul Polman, Satya Nadella, Indra Nooyi, Howard Schulz, Ray Dalio, Jeff Weiner, Mary Barra, Richard Barrett, Robert Kegan, Lisa Lahey, Simon Sinek, Bob Chapman, Charlie Kim, Tony Hsieh, Sheryl Sandberg, John Mackey, Vineet Nayar, Sri Kumar Rao, Chip Conley, Frederic Laloux, Cindy Wigglesworth, Gary Hamel, Craig Hamilton, Dov Seidman, Lance Secretan, and Marshall Goldsmith.

I had several breakthroughs in my journey, and a big one happened during a walk with Marshal Goldsmith. As I was telling my story, he stopped me cold and gave me some tough love. He brought out my concealed arrogance and challenged me to keep my message simple, not to take myself too seriously, and to stay humble. He reviewed one of my earlier drafts and said, "Don't fight battles that you don't have to fight. Speak more in your own voice. It sounds like you are trying to change the world—which is noble but may not sell to a practical buyer." Marshal should know; they call him America's Coach. He was recognized as the world's most influential leadership thinker in the biannual *Thinkers 50/Harvard Business Review* study. His greatest attribute is that he is constantly working on not taking himself too seriously. I call him the master of common sense.

Who Should Read This Book?

This book is intended for CEOs and business leaders who dare to pursue professional excellence and success along with emotional and spiritual fulfillment. You can be practical, hardnosed businessmen and at the same time care for the people, the environment, the society, and the planet. I believe there is a significant and rapidly growing population of people who are seeking enlightened practical solutions to major issues that we face in life and business.

This evolved population is not wedded to any dogma or belief system. They are neither parochial nor fanatic. They may be religious or agnostic, but one thing is for sure: they understand that there are many paths to peace, prosperity, and contentment. Their political affiliation is neither left nor right, their leadership style is neither democratic nor autocratic, and socially they are neither liberal nor conservative. They do not blindly believe anything or blindly disbelieve anything. They are independent, strong willed, and take personal responsibility and accountability for all actions and results. They are practical, open, objective, fair, and inclusive. They are willing to go to great lengths to preserve and fight for what is "right." And, they also clearly see that there is a larger force at play. I represent this population, which is willing to work on a new consciousness-based paradigm that defines leadership, economic models, forms of government, and life itself. This new paradigm involves tweaking our existing capitalistic and democratic models to be more in tune with higher states of human consciousness.

This book reflects the shift in collective consciousness of the society and the stakeholders in business organizations. This shift demands that solid business performance, financial success, and enhancing shareholder value are minimum requirements. The expectation from leadership is to achieve these benchmarks by demonstrating high moral and ethical values without compromising honesty and integrity, while building purposeful organizations that allow us to expand our mind, heart, and spirit. Many believe that the collective business consciousness is now ready to implement the broader, holistic principles of the spiritual dimension.

The next level of effectiveness in business leadership will come from integrating personal and professional excellence. Business leadership that follows the highest principles of honesty, integrity, inclusiveness, and objectivity (practical spirituality) will achieve superior business results. This is a natural progression of growth in business organizations and our socioeconomic institutions.

The quest for personal fulfillment and professional excellence is universal. Those of us who pursue it seriously end up being role models in leadership positions. As inhabitants of this planet, we are not only responsible for ourselves, but for the well-being of the community we live in and the whole planet. Living life in accordance with this natural law is leadership. We are all leaders of our own lives; we have to make critical choices and decisions. Many of us lead our families jointly with our spouses. Some of us take a leadership role in community and civic groups, social, business, political, and spiritual organizations.

To lead effectively, we need to collaborate with the leadership team and connect with all the constituents of the organization. A good leader is a good follower who takes guidance from his or her mentors, advisors, partners, employees, and all the constituents of the organization.

The current global economic malaise—anemic growth, unsustainable debt, inequality, growth fueled by consumerism, exploitation of natural resources, stressed and poorly engaged employees—is only accelerating the shift toward more meaningful and purposeful living, which translates to the need for enlightened business leadership. This is important because, in the last two hundred-plus years, power has shifted from religious to military to political to business leaders. By resolving our business obstacles, we help overcome larger socioeconomic challenges such as economic stagnation, polarized politics, inequality, affordable and quality healthcare, and education. They all have the same root cause and similar solutions. We can make a difference by taking action that is inspired, inclusive, and inspiring! In the process, we help elevate capitalism and democracy to their highest natural capability.

Ultimately, this book is about exploring these next-level methods to further enhance productivity and performance, and therefore leadership effectiveness. It includes experiences and practical insights of personal and business leadership, and the deep connection between the two.

Claiming the Next Level in Leadership

Hardly a day goes by without experts and regular folks alike lamenting the leadership crisis, impending doom, declining values, and a socioeconomic disaster waiting to happen. Is this an accurate assessment of reality? What about the remarkable social, technological, and economic progress we have made since Industrial Revolution powered by the twin engines of capitalism and democracy?

What truly are the business and socioeconomic challenges today and how can we overcome them? Do we have a situation where remarkable progress and dire crisis are both real? Are we struggling with accepting and acknowledging the reality of both situations and therefore unable to collectively focus on resolving the challenges we are facing?

While we can't argue with success, it is obvious for many discerning and conscious leaders that there has to be a better and more effective way to unlock the full value of the organizations we lead. The success we have attained has come with 1) a high risk of not being sustainable in the long-term; 2) poor employee engagement, weak leadership alignment, and high stress; and 3) not feeling purposeful—professional excellence and personal fulfillment do not converge. Only 25 percent of employees give their very best and feel purposeful.

These complex challenges can be resolved by learning new skills and practices to inspire, connect and secure buy-in. Business organizations are the most powerful socio-economic institutions, and global business leaders are the most impactful and influential in the world. By taking this important step of going within and fixing our issues, business leaders and organizations can become role models to solve the broader socioeconomic issues we face today.

Today's World at an Inflection Point

We seem to be at a unique inflection point with the paradoxical juxtaposition of remarkable progress and dire crisis taking us to the precipice of disaster. (See Figure C.1) Since the Industrial Revolution, and especially in the past fifty years, we have made dramatic and exponential advances in poverty alleviation, social (such as race and gender) justice, GDP per capita income, life expectancy, healthcare, and technological innovation. At the same time, there are enough crises to drive us to the edge of disaster: business scandals and corruption, political polarization and gridlock, the growing perception that the income gap is widening, increasing acts of terrorism, and widespread natural calamities and climate change. In business organizations, we are experiencing poor engagement, high stress, and a lack of purpose.

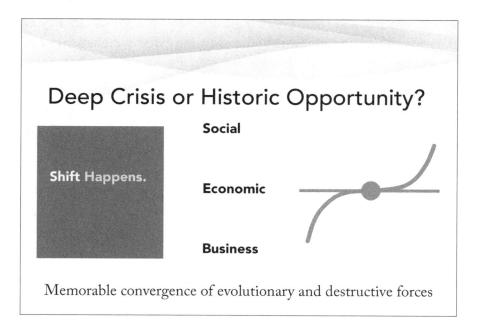

Figure C.1: The world today is at an inflection point.

The Best Time in Recorded History...

By any reasonable benchmarks, we are living in the most prosperous and progressive socioeconomic times in recorded history. Following are some highlights of progress:

- Poverty has declined exponentially in the past fifty years as compared to the previous 500 years. Ninety percent of the population used to live on less than a dollar a day. Now only 17 percent of the population[i] suffers under that kind of poverty.

- GDP Per capita income has been rising dramatically and exponentially: In the past 100 years, the average person is 100 times better off in the United States; 16 times in other developed nations, and 3 times in Africa.[ii]

- Considering the serious concerns about global violence and terrorism, we probably don't realize that this is the most peaceful time ever. According to the Federal Bureau of Investigation (FBI), the rate of violent crime in the United States rate fell 50 percent between 1993 and 2015. Since WWII, there have been no more "great wars," and international conflict has continued to decrease dramatically. The number of people per million (total global population) who have died in armed conflict has dropped steadily since World War II, despite an increase in the number of smaller conflicts.[iii]

- We had slavery 150 years ago, women couldn't vote 100 years back, and colonialism was common 75 years ago. Segregation was a way of life fifty years ago, and apartheid in South Africa ended barely twenty years ago. A callous attitude toward child labor and environmental degradation were prevalent just thirty years ago.

- Feminine values, which are long overdue in socioeconomic structure, are rising. Sixty percent of undergraduates are women and this goes up to 70 percent in graduate studies.[iv]

- We are more connected than ever before. The average person has more access to information at his fingertips than even the U.S. president did fifteen years ago. The United States has more active phone numbers than anywhere else in the world. There are one billion people on Facebook. And, startlingly, the number of Internet users will go up from two to five billion by 2020.

- We have more efficient business and management practices resulting in vastly improved productivity and ability to scale growth. Working conditions have evolved with a lot more autonomy, flexibility, openness, and transparency in communication. There is also an increased emphasis on offering wellness programs and providing a stake in ownership to everyone in the organization.

- We are experiencing an exponential growth and innovation in technology. Thanks to Moore's law, the price performance ratio doubles every twelve to twenty-four months. Smart phones today are a million times cheaper and thousands of times faster than the supercomputers of the 1970s.[v]

...And the Precipice of Disaster

At the same time, we have some serious cause for concern. Political polarization and gridlock have stymied our efforts to solve the most pressing social, economic, and health challenges—both nationally and globally. Headline coverage on incendiary issues such as corruption, scandals, and a widening income gap and income concentration ("the 1 percent") has plummeted trust in business and political leaders to historic lows. Let's take a look back at some of the media headlines and newsworthy events of the recent past:

- Businesses are seen as selfish and exploitative. Trust in big business has plummeted to historic lows as evidenced by polls from Gallup, Roper, Harris, and Yankelovich. The approval ratings for business and the U.S. Congress are at 19 and 17 percent respectively, just above telemarketers and car salesmen.

- Since the Great Recession and global financial crisis, backlash against Wall Street has intensified, with extensive coverage of scandals, corruption and greed. Examples: Enron, WorldCom, Rajat Gupta, and Bernie Madoff, just to name a few. There is the common perception that the income gap is widening and a few are getting wealthy at the expense of the rest.

- Increasing natural calamities and climate change are causing worry. Violence and terrorism have been spreading. We have a health crisis and a food, water, and energy shortage to tackle.

- Social and political divisiveness has become more transparent and obvious with our inability to collaborate and solve serious economic, domestic, and foreign policy challenges.

- People feel less empowered and vested in the democratic process. There is a prevailing sense that democracy has been hijacked by powerful individuals and special interest groups.

- Poor engagement and high stress permeate business organizations. According to Gallup, only 33 percent of employees are engaged, 49 percent are not engaged, and 18 percent are actively disengaged. Approimately 25 percent of employees work at their full potential. Research data indicates that 55 percent have high levels of stress with symptoms of extreme fatigue, while 42 percent experience constant but manageable stress.

- Only 40 percent of Americans feel purposeful, and the number one factor for our well-being and feeling purposeful is professional satisfaction. The ultimate paradox is that many of us would rather work even if we don't have to, but an overwhelming majority can't wait to leave work and go home. Only one in eight employees feel cared for—which probably wouldn't be the case if the environment at work was one of trust, recognition, and respect.

The Current Reality for Leadership

So what is the current reality? Are we regressing? Where are we headed? What is the future of capitalism and democracy?

Do business scandals, political polarization, and distrust in our leaders indicate we are deteriorating and degenerating morally, ethically, and socioeconomically? Do poor engagement, high stress, and not feeling purposeful suggest that work has become less stimulating professionally and not fulfilling personally? Are we getting worse, as some people suggest? While there is no denying that the twin engines of capitalism and democracy have been responsible for creating the most prosperous time in recorded history, how can they best serve us going forward? Do we need to change anything or do anything differently?

While the crises are real, it is inaccurate to make sweeping generalizations that we are regressing, deteriorating, and degenerating. An objective review of the past suggests that life was simpler, not necessarily better. Poor engagement and high stress could be a result of higher expectations from work and leadership. I shudder to think what the engagement levels would be if we had the command and control structure along with a requirement of semi-robotic compliance and conformance from employees like we used to.

The information overload we suffer from creates an *amygdala hijack*—an immediate, overwhelming emotional response to a situation that makes us perceive that we are much worse off than we actually are. Perhaps this perception comes from the fact that there was less transparency before and that we have a tendency for selective memory, where we remember only the "good" about the past while conveniently forgetting the troubling events that took place at the same time.

Lower Transparency in the Past

In past decades, social, financial, political, and business institutions and processes were a lot less transparent than they are today. We were not privy to the internal dysfunction and behind-the-scenes maneuverings. Just because we didn't have an inside view doesn't mean we were better off. Our view of the past is already a lot less rosy as more and more sensitive information gets declassified and becomes publicly available.

As social progress indicators suggest, we are much more respectful of people with different backgrounds and a lot more tolerant of our differences in gender, ethnicity, and religion. Previously, businesses were run in an autocratic, top-down, and exclusive style. The demand for openness, less hierarchical decision-making, and distribution of power in the business world is now obvious and are some of the key reasons for low engagement and high stress.

Information Overload and Amygdala Hijack

We receive way too much information to be processed by the brain alone. Since nothing is more important than survival, the first stop for all data that reaches us is the amygdala, the integrative center of the limbic system. The limbic system is primarily responsible for our emotional life, and amygdala is the early warning detector. It scours through all the data and looks for data that will harm us. Information overload creates a fight or flight amygdala hijack, and we perceive that we are much worse off than we actually are. This experience of amygdala hijack can last from a few seconds to much longer, depending on the perceived risk, before the rational and conscious part of the brain called the prefrontal cortex, the frontal lobe of neocortex, kicks in.

This situation is further exacerbated by the "if it bleeds, it leads" approach to news coverage. No wonder we think that the world is getting a lot worse than it actually is when we hear about violence and terrorism, natural calamities and climate change, food, water, and energy shortages, and health and financial crises. When we are operating in lower states of human motivations such as fight-or-flight survival or self-interest and self-centered achievement, we tend to focus on crisis rather than progress. We are worried, paralyzed, and stressed. Instead of recognizing all the progress we made and the opportunity we have, we get hijacked into dwelling on issues as challenges without taking action. Whereas when we are operating in higher states of awareness, we do not become victims of circumstances. We are grateful, awake, and alive—we take charge and pursue solutions through service, contribution and servant leadership.

Selective Memory

When we glorify the past, focusing only on happy and positive events, we conveniently forget troubling or traumatic events that took place at the same time. As a result, we make sweeping generalizations:

- Things used to be a lot better. We are becoming more violent and more intolerant.

- Our moral and ethical values have degraded. Self-interest and greed are driving our political and business process and institutions.
- Quality of life and healthcare are deteriorating.

An objective review of the socioeconomic benchmarks proves that most generalizations are not true. At the same time, there is an unmistakable fundamental shift that is taking place in our socioeconomic institutions. Let me offer an alternative viewpoint and explore this possibility:

- Life, politics, and business were simpler, not necessarily better. These challenges appear worse than before because of the human nature of latching onto negative contemporary news while glorifying the past. Most socioeconomic and business indicators such as social inclusiveness and harmony, wealth creation, productivity, and health and wellness suggest that we are much better off now than ever before. But we can still improve.
- In the political arena, the divisiveness and ideological differences that we are witnessing is not new. It is the culmination of a pattern and trend that has always been there and building up for the past several years. In fact, our founding fathers understood this aspect of human nature very well and built appropriate checks and balances into our governing system.
- Our challenges are amplified because of the transparency possible through technological innovation. We are also demanding accountability and holding ourselves and our leadership to higher standards. We want economic prosperity without collateral damage, such as a stressful work environment or hurting the environment and the community. We want to create shareholder value without stifling creativity, innovation, or employee engagement.

We need to recognize and celebrate progress while acknowledging and accepting the crises we are in. We are at a stage in history where this reality is dawning upon a larger percentage of our country's population than ever before. Typically this happens because of the convergence of two forces:

1. Existing systems begin to crack and show signs of failing.

2. We the people (the collective consciousness) are more evolved and are unwilling to put up with incomplete, band aid solutions.

Both the current socioeconomic crisis and the rise in human consciousness are forcing us to take a hard look at our accepted models. These two trends are converging to awaken us to the need for a more humanistic, inclusive, and conscious approach to growing business and economy. This also means resolving social, political, and ecological conflicts. This is the way to go forward.

Perhaps at no other time have two powerful opposing forces of creative evolution and destruction come together so forcefully while being balanced so perilously to tip the scales in either direction. The consequence of not transforming has potentially tragic implications, and participating in the shift provides us great opportunity, perhaps the best ever in recorded human history. As philosopher and best-selling author Eckhart Tolle has stated, "The dysfunction of the collective ego (greed, conflict) is taking us to the brink of disaster, and the growth of collective consciousness offers us hope and potential for extraordinary and purposeful growth."

And therein lies the key to leadership and business success in this new millennium. There needs to be *purpose* to what people do professionally and personally. It is up to business leadership to enable and nurture that sense of purpose.

To me, this condition presents an outstanding opportunity to lift capitalism and democracy to their highest natural capabilities and potential.

The Root Cause of Our Troubles

Socioeconomic standards and expectations have gone up. (See Figure C.2.) We want more transparency and authenticity than ever before from our business and political leaders. In business, we no longer seem satisfied with profit without purpose, money without meaning, performance without principles and professional excellence without personal fulfillment. Along with financial and intellectual growth, we are seeking emotional, natural, social, and spiritual opportunities for fulfillment. Self-interest and the bottom line have historically been the drivers for business growth. This creates an environment where employees are driven by survival and a steady paycheck. They learn practical skills to survive instead of unleashing their full potential. As a result, everyone pays a hefty price—we don't feel fulfilled and purposeful, and the organization suffers from low engagement, high stress, and poor productivity.

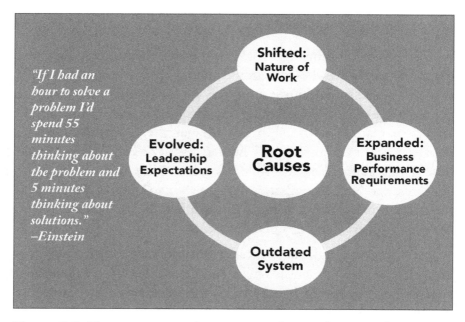

"If I had an hour to solve a problem I'd spend 55 minutes thinking about the problem and 5 minutes thinking about solutions." –Einstein

Shifted: Nature of Work

Evolved: Leadership Expectations

Root Causes

Expanded: Business Performance Requirements

Outdated System

Figure C.2: There are several root causes for our issues today.

Current reality suggests that it is time to rethink that model. We have to create an environment to inspire everyone to give their very best. Most organizations are either focused on the old model or their outdated structures and systems get in the way of implementing the new requirements.

This is also true on a macro level—it is the primary reason for the current disenchantment with politics and poor governance. We want an improved economy and an enhanced quality of life where everyone gets an opportunity to rise to their full capability. Modern societies are comfortable with meritocracy and democracy. We are inspired by individuals who work hard for a good cause and in the process gain power and wealth. However, when the income gap becomes too large and wealth is overly concentrated with a few, when democracy appears to be beholden to special interests, distrust in leadership and disillusionment with the system grows. It thus becomes increasingly difficult to create financial wealth at the expense of other forms of wealth. This is precisely the reason we are at an inflection point. Let us expand on why this is and the fundamental paradigm shift that is taking place socioeconomically and in business in particular.

The Nature of Work Has Shifted

Until about thirty to fifty years ago, work was a place to earn a steady paycheck and make a living. Then came the Information Revolution and we sought professional excellence and an intellectually stimulating work environment in addition to a paycheck. Fast forward to the current times; a rapidly increasing number of professionals are no longer satisfied with only a steady paycheck and intellectually stimulating work. Employees want their business leaders to foster a high-trust and high-performance work environment so they can pursue professional excellence and personal fulfillment.

We are now less willing to accept incomplete solutions: short-term business growth by compromising core values and at the expense of sustainability, professional growth at the cost of personal wellness, and economic progress with social consequences. We are seeking transparency, authenticity, meritocracy, inclusion, reverse accountability, fun, higher purpose, and meaning. A business organization has to create an environment to pursue both professional excellence and personal mastery. We are not satisfied with just financial growth and intellectual stimulation. We are seeking physical, emotional, spiritual, social, and natural prosperity in our lives.

Definitions of Business Growth and Performance Have Expanded

When we talk about growth and performance in business, it has always been defined in financial terms and benchmarks. While customer satisfaction was and is considered crucial, employee engagement, supplier partnerships, and community relationships were not tracked with the same focus, vigor, and discipline. The assumption was that these areas would take care of themselves as long as the business achieved financial growth and profitability

When *Good to Great*, the seminal book by Jim Collins was published in 2001, "greatness" was defined in terms of financial performance. Companies that earned the "greatness" tag outperformed their peers financially. It did not measure how disengaged, stressed, or unhappy employees were or how fragile their supplier and business partnerships were. The perspective today has been evolving from a shareholder- to stakeholder-centric approach. In a more recent book, *Firms of Endearment*, the authors argue that the definition of greatness goes beyond financial performance. A great company, they argue, is one that excels in stakeholder return and earns the admiration of not just shareholders but also employees, customers, suppliers, partners, and the community. We are seeking "and" solutions—personal fulfillment and professional excellence, emotional expansion and intellectual growth, consciousness and technology, purpose and profit, meaning and money, principles and performance.

Leadership Roles and Expectations Have Evolved

With the shift in the nature of work and expansion of the definition of business performance, the role of leadership and expectations from leaders have naturally evolved since the Industrial Revolution. As a result, the leadership paradigm has undergone a significant transformation from a top-down, authoritarian approach, to a hierarchical rules and process-driven model, to a principles- and values-driven, distributed form of authentic leadership. (See the associated sidebar.)

The Evolution of the Leadership Paradigm

- **Autocratic-Command and Control:** Until somewhat recently, a hierarchical, command and control mode of leadership was the norm. A business organization provided employment security and expected employees to check their feelings at the door. In the early twentieth century, Henry Ford went much further than that when he famously said, "Why do I keep getting whole people when all I want is hands?" Employees were expected to take direction and implement predetermined solutions. Bosses had all the right answers, and it was not necessary for anyone else to think about the best possible solution. Organizations sought conformance and compliance from their employees who in turn desired stability. Stability and security served as the primary motivators for employees.

- **Hierarchical, Processes-Driven:** With the advent of information revolution in the 1980s and 1990s, workers sought professional excellence and an intellectually stimulating work environment in addition to a paycheck. This meant that leadership was more open and inclusive in communicating and sharing information, and providing fair compensation and a stake for its constituents in the outcome. This has been an era of unprecedented growth, prosperity, and productivity. Self-interest and self-centered achievement were the primary forms of motivation. However, constant unrealistic growth expectations and the growth-at-any-cost mantra stressed the system. Everyone was expected to keep our values, emotions, and feelings to ourselves. The larger and deeper concerns regarding personal fulfillment and well-being were still separated, which affected employee engagement.

- **Authentic–Distributed, Principles-Driven:** A rapidly increasing number of professionals now are no longer satisfied with only a steady paycheck and intellectually stimulating work. They want an environment where they can pursue professional excellence and personal fulfillment and realize their highest potential. They are also seeking physical, emotional, spiritual, and social prosperity. This requires conscious, enlightened, or authentic leadership that inspires by appealing to the deepest and innermost human yearning for mastery and meaning. Service, contribution, and servant leadership, not personal ambition, are the prime motivators for leaders.

These leaders are transparent and authentic and have the skills to master human motivations and emotions while still being accountable for financial results.

Our System Has Become Outdated

Our socioeconomic systems and institutions were built to motivate us by appealing to our lower states or the deficiency needs of Maslow's hierarchy. For example, in business we motivate and drive performance by reward and punishment. This system produced and still produces results, but it comes with troublesome side effects. As long as leaders disregard the collateral damage, it seems like it is working. However, as we evolve to higher states of awareness, expectations change. We seek autonomy and meaning from work, and transparency and reverse accountability from leadership. Our current systems do not help us to adequately address these requirements.

What makes it worse is that our vision, mission, and values appeal to higher states of human nature, whereas the way we communicate, run meetings and operations, make decisions, evaluate performance, compensate and reward are not in sync with stated aspirations and noble intentions. For example, we talk about teamwork and collaboration but do not reward it. We say we want win-win negotiations but engage in and reward win-lose outcomes. We say that we value openness and transparency but do not practice them. We set long-term goals but sacrifice them in favor of short-term gain. We are not held accountable to values, only to financial performance.

When vision and values are mere statements without any tangible connection to the way business is run, cynicism is a natural reaction. Much of this gap between stated values and the way businesses are run is not intentional. Many simply do not know how. According to a recent Ernst & Young Oxford University study, 87 percent of business leaders believe companies perform best over time if their purpose goes beyond profit. However, only 37 percent say their business model and operations are well-aligned with this purpose.

With wonderful intentions we pursued incomplete solutions in all aspects of our social, economic, political, and business life. This resulted in outstanding progress but also created an avoidable mess and significant collateral damage. We implemented "either-or" solutions and assumed that collateral damage—poor engagement and not feeling purposeful, high stress, short-term transactional relationships, and environmental degradation—were expected and necessary evils.

Now we are demanding transparency, authenticity, reverse accountability, and the distribution of overly concentrated power through an empowered and accountable decision-making process. We are longing, even hurting, for conscious business, servant leadership, truly inclusive economics, and participatory democracy.

The Answer: Personal Awakening and Consciousness

Many leaders now believe that they were successful in spite of, not because of, "either-or" solutions. Business and economic growth have stalled and are anemic at best. As a society, we are polarized socially and politically, unable to solve crises in healthcare, trade, the economy, and many other areas of life. Businesses are suffering from poor engagement, high stress, and a lack of meaning and purpose.

To make matters worse, we are entrenched in two opposing and only partially correct positions. This is obvious in our social and political polarization; the left and right are unable to work together to realize the best of what each approach has to offer. A similar and less obvious situation exists in business. How so? Let's take the case of poor engagement. One solution is to plow ahead with the reward-and-punishment approach to motivation that focuses on self-interest alone. The other approach is to dismantle hierarchy and power structures by empowering and distributing power without ensuring accountability and meritocracy.

We made remarkable material progress and phenomenal technological breakthroughs but have been unable to rise above parochial and partisan self-interest. In fact, we are making it worse in many situations by using advanced technological tools to bolster our respective incomplete solutions. Technology cannot solve problems when we are unable to rise above self-interest and unwilling to be open and inclusive of a different perspective. This is a crisis of consciousness.

With all the tools, resources, technology, and science at our disposal, we need to operate at higher levels of consciousness when performing our functions and responsibilities. When this way of functioning is integrated in the systems and processes of our socioeconomic institutions, everything changes. This doesn't mean that we discredit and abandon what has served us and continues to serve us well; rather, we have to make adjustments by bringing in a higher level of awareness and consciousness.

We have to practice what has been termed by many thoughtful thinkers and leaders as natural, inclusive, enlightened, compassionate, or *conscious* capitalism and democracy. This will help evolve and raise capitalism and democracy to their highest natural capability. In this book, I present what this form of enlightened or conscious capitalism and leadership will look like within business organizations. The same broad principles of governance and leadership can be applied to all socioeconomic institutions, including our political process. By practicing conscious or servant leadership within our business organizations, we earn the right to preach the same to our social and political leaders and become the change we wish to see.

This has been my quest, my passion, and my dream. As an engineer, marketer, strategist, COO, and CEO, I knew intuitively that all of these functions can be improved significantly by operating at higher states of awareness. I followed it up with personal experience. This means that when we combine professional mastery with personal mastery, we not only feel good but produce much better results. These results grow exponentially when it involves groups, teams, organizations, and institutions. This is the domain of organizational mastery.

In this journey, we will answer the following questions:

1. How can being more personally aware, evolved, or conscious make me a more effective professional and better business leader?

2. How do I know how conscious I am? Can we measure and track personal development and consciousness?

3. How can I become more conscious? How do I accelerate my growth?

Pursuing higher states of awakening or consciousness has been the Holy Grail of humanity from time immemorial. When I say *consciousness*, I simply mean mindset or psychological state. When I say *higher level of consciousness*, I mean operating at a higher state or mindset that is characterized by being more present.

Consciousness is not something esoteric; it can be observed, felt, and tracked in people. Many people regard the path to self-actualization as complex and shrouded in mystery, secrecy, and controversy. We now know enough about neuroscience, human physiology, and psychology that we can operate at higher consciousness naturally, systematically, and consistently.

Leadership Mastery and Self-Actualization

Conscious leadership is as important to organizational performance as oxygen is to breathing. Authentic leadership that is in tune with higher states of human consciousness is the acknowledged, dire need of the day! This management imperative—a new attitude toward authentic, conscious leadership—is a direct reflection of a tectonic socioeconomic shift reflecting the natural evolution of human needs, human behavior, and human consciousness. With improved economic prosperity and individual freedom, a significant portion of the population in the United States and many other countries has been moving towards a self-actualized state, a condition described by American psychologist Abraham Maslow in his 1943 article, "A Theory of Human Motivation" Maslow explicitly defines self-actualization to be "the desire for self-fulfillment." Figure C.3 depicts Maslow's model.

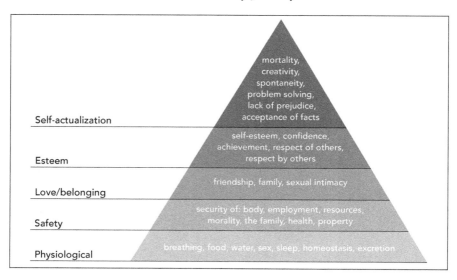

Figure C.3. Maslow's Hierarchy of Human Needs is one way to measure progress toward self-actualization.

Richard Barrett, the British author and thought leader who writes about leadership development and cultural evolution, also has done some remarkable work in this area. Whereas Maslow has four levels of human needs, Barrett has seven as shown in Figure C.4.

Human Needs	Human Motivations	
Spiritual	Service	7
	Making a Difference	6
	Internal Cohesion	5
Mental	Transformation	4
Emotional	Self-Esteem	3
	Relationship	2
Physical	Survival	1

Figure C.4. Barrett transposed Maslow's hierarchy of needs into a complete, seven levels of full spectrum framework of consciousness.

Vedic science, a systematic ancient scientific thought found in early Indian scriptures, the *Vedas*, describes seven states in detail. These have been well captured by Richard Barrett. Barrett transposed Maslow's hierarchy of needs into a complete, seven levels of full spectrum framework of consciousness

Under Barrett's model, once you get to higher states L5-L7, leading a self-actualized life, as well as leading a self-actualized team and organization, becomes second nature. In the highest L7 state, unconditional service and contribution are natural. What's more, they are fully compatible with professional excellence and personal fulfillment.

Barrett has beautifully broken that down. For example, Level 4 is transformation—becoming more of who you really are by aligning ego with soul. This is when you begin to wake up. This happens for most of us in the modern world in our forties, although there are increasing signs that the process is starting much earlier. People have coined the term quarter life (as opposed to mid-life) crisis to capture this phenomenon among the millennial generation. Level 5 follows and is when you begin looking for *meaning* by aligning your passion and purpose to create your vision, whatever that may be. This is basically the internal cohesion of personal and professional journeys. By the time you reach Level 6, you are actually living this in your life in a complete way. When you're at that point, you are fully equipped to lead your organization to a higher level of success, making a difference and serving others.

Robert Kegan and Lisa Lahey have done an exceptional job of defining mindsets and their connection to leadership development and business performance in their book, *An Everyone Culture*. Their three mindsets connect very well with Barrett's mindsets —Socialized (L1, L2), Self-Authoring (L3, L4), and Self-Transforming (L5, L6, L7).

A New Practical Model

At this critical point in history, human evolution and *business* requires a customized, socioeconomic model that expands and adapts Maslow's hierarchy with a more comprehensive consciousness model described in Vedic science. According to Vedic science, there are several higher levels of consciousness beyond the self-actualization state defined by Maslow.

For me and the clients with who I work, the model of socioeconomic evolution illustrated in Figure 5 best explains the evolution of capitalism and democracy in the last 200-plus years. This model has the following components:

1.0 Security (Barrett's L1, L2)
- Livelihood, basic needs, stability
- Sense of belonging

2.0 Self-Centered Achievement (Barrett's L3, L4)
- Recognition, status and esteem
- Participation, stake in the results

3.0 Self-Actualized Mastery (Barrett's L5, L6, L7)
- Personal growth, development and fulfillment
- Purpose and profit, principles and performance, meaning and money
- Align personal passion and purpose with professional vision
- Help others to self-actualize
- Focus on making a difference
- Servant leadership
- Unconditional contribution
- Deep desire for selfless service and universal well-being

The state of the economy plays a major role in our individual and collective lives. Many of our decisions, actions, lifestyle choices, and organizational policies are guided by both micro- and macro-economic conditions. Appropriate compensation and fair economic distribution are critical ingredients for a thriving business organization, society, and nation. Motivating and inspiring employees, stakeholders and citizens of a country to perform and produce to their fullest potential are tied to the perceived fairness of individual

Figure C.5: Capitalism and democracy have evolved in the last 200-plus years.

compensation and collective economic distribution. The perceived fairness in turn is linked to hierarchy of human needs and the state of human consciousness.

1.0: Basic Human Needs

This era—from approximately 1900 through the 1950s—is characterized by a focus on basic needs of existence: food, air, water, security, stability, law and order. General aspirations were relatively simple—livelihood and security were the primary drivers for people and economies. This does not mean that people were happier. Economic opportunities and possibilities were limited. It also does not mean that they were less self-centered. Within the economic landscape of the time (livelihood and security) they were equally (if not more) self-centered than we are now.

During this time, people were relatively less evolved socially and therefore not as tolerant of diversity and minorities as we are now. This was an early stage of relatively slow growth with a gradual increase of prosperity, but wealth was concentrated with a few. It was not a fair and democratic process. Leadership style and governance were top-down and hierarchical in both public and private sector industries and organizations. Private business institutions in the United States and other Western countries predominantly followed an autocratic leadership style and a top-down hierarchical organizational structure. The command-and-control management practices and processes went against the grain of higher states of human nature. This was a legacy of the Second Industrial Revolution in the early 1900s.

The United States and Western Europe pioneered the convergence of economic capitalism and political democracy. Economy was generally characterized by protectionism. Many nations were autocratic and followed a socialistic model which stifled creativity, innovation, and did not adequately reward and incentivize hard work. Collective consciousness was focused on basic survival needs, hence society accepted such relatively unjust, dictatorial, and deceptive practices.

2.0: Consumerism and Materialism–Luxury and Status Needs

This era, from the 1960s to the present, has been characterized by unprecedented growth and prosperity. Aspirations are sky high—growth, status, and achievement have been the primary drivers for people and economies. Wealth is pursued with unprecedented zeal and enthusiasm in search of constant and relentless growth. Wealth is distributed among a larger population with many joining the middle class and affording greater material comforts.

This has also given hope and increased aspirations for many people around the globe, who tend to be much more open, broadminded, and accepting of diversity and minorities than in previous eras. Pursuit of wealth and material comforts is a common bond among the world's population. Leadership and governance are relatively more transparent and democratic. Business organizations are less hierarchical, share more information, and provide opportunities for all to have a stake in the organization. There have also been high profile scandals and business collapses, but this doesn't mean that there has been a sweeping degradation of values and ethics. On the other hand, we are demanding more transparency and accountability than in earlier eras. Democracy is on the rise. More countries pursue democracy or become democratic, and existing democracies are finding ways to become more inclusive and efficient, notwithstanding some recent setbacks which are actually disruptive corrections.

The free-market economy, driven by liberalization and globalization, has created a period of great innovation and improvement in productivity. However, the growth-at-any-cost mantra has caused stress and a loss of balance in business and in life. This period has also been characterized by record-high debt levels and cycles of false economies based on financial reengineering, which became progressively worse after a series of bubbles and crashes. Consumerism as the primary growth engine is proving to be unsustainable.

The 2.0 model is running out of steam as we are collectively moving towards higher ideals of caring, sharing, personal growth, and fulfillment. We are witnessing popular uprisings against excessive greed, crony capitalism, and exorbitant compensation for a few. We are also concerned about the depletion of natural resources, ecological balance, and quality of life. We are discovering that acquiring more and bigger "things" is not giving us lasting fulfillment. We have been economically liberated, not fulfilled by it—but liberation is essential for fulfillment to begin. We still have work to do in reducing inequality by introducing compassion, care, and consciousness in capitalism—this is the 3.0 model.

3.0: From Liberation to Fulfillment

We are on the verge of a kinder, gentler era with a shift from consumerism to contentment. We are migrating our focus from the single-minded pursuit of material luxuries. We are recognizing on a larger scale that people are not motivated by money alone and that acquiring and consuming more are not the keys to happiness; rather, we seek personal growth and fulfillment.

With improved economic prosperity and individual freedom, a significant percentage of the world's population have been gradually moving to the self-actualized state. They spend a generous amount of time and money on personal growth and fulfillment. There is a genuine and deep desire to serve and contribute to universal well-being.

Many people are deeply concerned about global issues that undermine peace and well-being and are actively engaged in helping resolve them. Examples include: energy crisis, quality and cost-effective healthcare; extremism and terrorism; HIV/AIDS; employment insecurity; social inequity; environmental degradation; and ecological imbalance. People from all walks of life are actively participating through financial contribution and voluntary efforts towards alleviating these serious challenges.

I call this shift in consciousness a spiritual awakening, a genuine desire to do good and contribute towards personal and universal wellbeing. This awakening is also changing our lifestyle and our buying patterns, which have an impact on the economy, our relationships, and our lifestyle practices. It also has an impact on the kind of organizational environment and leadership practices that are necessary to inspire people to give their best and be engaged, productive, and innovative. While it is not always necessary to experience awakening after material and emotional needs are met, it certainly helps that there has been a steady growth in economic prosperity, the current global economic challenges notwithstanding. This situation is enabling us to revisit our economic and business valuation models, our sense of priorities, and the keys to purposeful and meaningful life.

This shift was predicted by some of the greatest thinkers of the twentieth century. Einstein lamented more than 50 years ago, "It has become appallingly obvious that our technology has exceeded our consciousness." Jonas Salk talked about the impending shift from "Epoch A" (survival and competition) to "Epoch B" (collaboration and meaning).

Thriving in Diversity

While 1.0 was about tolerating diversity and 2.0 is managing diversity, the 3.0 era will be characterized by being comfortable with and thriving in it! This is also the key to resolving global conflicts based on religion, culture, ethnicity, and national barriers. These differences have been plaguing us for centuries with no apparent solution until now. Recognizing universal connectedness and common human aspirations for professional excellence and personal fulfillment comes with spiritual growth and a rise in consciousness.

We are better positioned now than ever before to overcome superficial barriers. We have a remarkable opportunity to ring in an era of deeper understanding that is in tune with higher states of human nature. This socioeconomic shift is rarely smooth and typically goes through a chaotic process of disruption as is evident by the developments in the United Kingdom, the United States, and several other western democracies.

The new economy will be driven by solutions to resolve global challenges and conflicts. The focus will be to create economies with services and goods that provide sustainable benefits to humankind. We will seriously examine what is valuable to the world and build economic systems that reward people and companies for creating that value. Moving away from consumerism will not result in a drop in economic flow, as some fear, but will be a shift. For example, instead of buying an extra-fancy vehicle that you can't afford and do not need, you may decide to hire a wellness coach and change your lifestyle. You are still spending money, just differently. It may be on more expensive organic food, a new hybrid or electric car to do your part for the environment, or on a wellness retreat to get recharged.

The global socioeconomic challenges provide us with an opportunity and a wake-up call. Business leaders and organizations can lead the way in revitalizing the economy, instilling confidence, and becoming role models for engendering socioeconomic prosperity. Businesses can further enhance productivity, engagement, and innovation by incorporating processes that allow higher states of human motivations to flourish. Liberalization, globalization, and free markets will thrive after some course correction. We can then turn this around and start a new cycle of growth and prosperity, but we will be also pursuing *meaningful* and *purposeful* growth.

An Era of Transparency and Authenticity

As we evolve, so should the socioeconomic models; our current models do not inspire people who are operating in or moving to 3.0. Capitalism and democracy were the twin engines that propelled remarkable growth of prosperity and peace. However human capital innovation has not kept growth with technological innovations. Most business leaders focus on external motivation and struggle to inspire people to greater performance.

Human capital innovation will elevate capitalism and democracy to their highest natural capability, resulting in a more inclusive, humanistic, and conscious approach to growing economy and resolving differences. The new breed of best and brightest leaders treat business as a playground to fulfill deepest yearnings, express their gifts, and realize their highest potential. They evaluate greatness holistically—financial, emotional, social, natural, physical, spiritual, ecological.

Leadership Evolution: Autocratic > Democratic >
Authentic / Enlightened

States of Human Motivation and Inspiration

You can excel in education and your profession with academic degrees, experience, and hard work. You can make a lot of money and rise up the ranks of organizations without overcoming your deficiencies. *However, you cannot lead a fulfilling, meaningful, and purposeful life without overcoming these deficiency needs.* Step back and think about this: You may have money, but you could lack meaning. You may make a profit, but you may not have a purpose: you may be selfishly and passionately driven and have not adequately developed the ability to collaborate and demonstrate care and compassion.

When individuals with unfulfilled deficiency needs lead teams and organizations, the result is poor alignment, low engagement and high stress. If those organizations grow their revenue and are profit-able, it is in spite of these deficiencies. Such leaders motivate them-selves and their people by focusing on the lower states—fear, anxiety, and greed for more. They are unable to tap into the full potential of their people and unlock the whole value of the organization.

You cannot move to higher stages of consciousness unless you learn how to master and release these fears and anxieties. You will feel stuck, burdened, and anchored to these lower states. The fourth state, or level of consciousness, is to learn to overcome these fears and transform to higher states. The next three levels involve your need to find meaning and purpose and activate that purpose by making a difference in the world, becoming a servant leader and leading a life of service and contribution. These needs inspire much higher levels of commitment, engagement, and creativity.

When you are operating at higher levels of consciousness as you lead teams and organizations, you experience stronger alignment, higher engagement, and a caring high-trust and low-stress envi-ronment. If you become this kind of leader, you will inspire others by appealing to the higher states of awareness and consciousness, thereby building a purposeful and profitable organization. In such organizations the basic functions of any business—communication, decision-making, negotiations, strategy development and execution, performance evaluation, compensation, incentives and rewards—will be conducted a lot more effectively, yielding much higher levels of performance as detailed in subsequent chapters.

When you operate from higher states of consciousness, commu-nication is more authentic and transparent. You are more decisive and engage in empowered and effective decisions. You hold yourselves and others more accountable. You engage in win-win negotiations; you proactively resolve conflicts and differences of opinion by over-coming the need to be right and by focusing on the right solution.

You also develop compelling strategies by tapping into the col-lective intelligence, and you excel in execution by including everyone early on and getting their buy-in. You evaluate performance more objectively and provide fair compensation by balancing individual and team performance—thereby inspiring everyone to give their very best toward a common team and organizational goal.

I use a much simpler three-level consciousness model when I work with business leaders and leadership teams. Level 1.0 refers to the deficiency needs of safety, security, survival, and belonging. Level 2.0 is focused on the need for self-esteem, characterized by self-centered achievement. Level 3.0 is about mastery.

I call the all-encompassing level of higher states of consciousness *self-actualized mastery*. This includes the following: uncovering your authentic self, understanding and aligning your ego with your essence; unlocking your passion and purpose by uncovering your values; defining a vision for the future you want to create, operationalizing your purpose to make a difference in the world, becoming a servant leader and leading a life of service and contribution in pursuit of your passion, purpose, and vision. Each level has a corresponding leadership model that is most appropriate to lead and motivate people to engage, align and perform, as I discuss in the next chapter.

Most leaders and organizations struggle to match theory with practice and convert good intention to impactful action. When the leader and leadership team are operating at a lower state with unmet deficiency needs, how can they expect their actions—and therefore the organization's processes—to match the lofty vision and stated core values?

Most successful leaders have the right intentions and intend to create a high trust, authentic organization with a noble vision and shared values, but they have not achieved a state of personal and organizational mastery to be able to convert their intention to impactful action. They do not deliberately try to create high stress, low trust, and poor engagement. That is the unintended outcome when personal and organizational mastery practices are not understood.

In most organizational surveys, CEOs and senior executives invariably rate leadership alignment and employee engagement much higher than the average rating. On the other hand, all of them have a high degree of professional mastery in their functional area of expertise. So how do we tackle this situation and convert intent-to-impact? Clarity of intent and consistency of action is key.

Many of the financially successful organizations and their leaders tend to be achievement-driven and operate at 2.0; however, a rapidly increasing number of leaders and organizations are motivated to pursue the 3.0 model. In this book I present a step-by-step approach for the CEOs, leadership teams, and their organizations to envision, embody, and empower a consistent 3.0 model and approach. With examples of pioneering CEOs who have been recognized for their cutting-edge practices, I present a high-trust/high-performance (HTP) operating system that transforms successful leaders and organizations to greatness. We will tackle and connect noble purpose, vision, and values to day-to-day operations.

We will discuss ways to overcome the apathy that is commonplace when the lofty vision statement and values are unfurled and plastered everywhere without being demonstrated and valued. We will reveal practices of CEOs and their teams that will enable them to embody the behavior connected with the vision. We will describe ways to conduct business operations and processes consistent with core values and operating principles and infuse mastery in the DNA of the organization. We will learn skills to engage in authentic communication, empowered and effective decisions, win-win negotiations, proactive conflict resolution, compelling strategy execution, objective performance evaluation, fair compensation, and inspire everyone to give their very best towards a common goal.

When leaders operate at lower states of consciousness, the ideals of noble purpose, servant leadership, making a difference and contribution, and building purposeful high-trust organizations remain a pipe dream. Results-driven leaders who pride themselves in being action-oriented are stuck and unable to get to the next level. The practices and approaches that got them to 2.0 do not get them to the next level of success. I have personally witnessed and helped others overcome the frustration, loneliness, and overwhelming sense of inadequacy that many successful leaders experience. They want to make a difference and feel purposeful. Financial success, power, and status fail to address this deep-rooted sense of unworthiness. This book and these practices are the answer to these questions, concerns, and challenges—I call them golden opportunities!

Self-Actualized Work and Servant Leadership

Howard Schultz, who was until recently Executive Chairman and CEO of Starbucks, penned an insightful article in *The New York Times* declaring that America deserves servant leaders. He is right. Not only do we deserve servant leaders, we need them. We should start with business leaders. Since business organizations and business leaders are ideally positioned with powerful socioeconomic influence, we should lead the way. Let us practice what we preach and implement what we want from our political and social leaders.

Because businesses are practically driven and are not burdened by special interests and bureaucratic pressures of governance, it is relatively less complicated to be inclusive of diverse perspectives and to engage the professional workforce in critical decisions. However, this is a skill that does not come naturally to business leaders who have traditionally exercised their authority based on position and power. Many drive performance with a carrot-and-stick approach to motivation. We can no longer afford to operate this way. We have to learn to inspire, and that's exactly what the most effective among us are doing!

Work can and should be fun, fulfilling, and flow in a joyful state. It can also be a place for us to pursue our highest potential and deepest yearnings. We have all had fleeting moments of such an experience. Leadership in this state feels like a sacred responsibility and stewardship, which invigorates us to create an environment where everyone can give their best and bring their whole self to work. However, for a vast majority of people, work is characterized by low trust, poor engagement, high stress, and a lack of meaning and purpose. If you are the CEO or a senior executive, it is emotionally draining and lonely to be in such an environment. When you begin to recognize that you influence or impact the quality of life and livelihood of hundreds and thousands of people, leadership feels more like a burden and less like a sacred responsibility.

For a few among us, being fulfilled and in flow is a natural and consistent state of being and a way of life at work. The secret I discovered is that for these leaders their work and business is a platform for their highest fulfilment, what we might think of as self-actualization, and some might even call *enlightenment*. While operating at this level, these CEOs and leaders are building wildly successful, purposeful, and profitable organizations. The leadership teams are aligned, cohesive, and push each other to get even better. The organizations are engaged, innovative, exceptionally profitable and sustainable, and operate in a high trust environment.

For business leaders in particular, the opportunity and scope is immense. We now have the significant possibility of living a meaningful and conscious life while building purposeful business organizations that reflect those same principles. Moreover, the best and brightest leaders today are already onboard. For the very first time in human history, we collectively are at a place where we have all the necessary resources to address every socioeconomic problem of finance, health, education, well-being—you name it. Only an inclusive consciousness is missing—and business can set an example. This is the greatest time in recorded human history for business organizations to be run in accordance with the higher states of human nature.

How Do We Accomplish This?

It is obvious that the unique challenges we are facing today require us to think and act differently than we have traditionally. (See Figure C.6.) We have to integrate two basic aspects of human nature:

- **Self-Interest:** We are driven by self-interest and have a fundamental desire for autonomy and a self-centered drive to grow and achieve.
- **Altruistic Connection:** We are social beings who yearn for connection and we are also altruistically driven to serve, to contribute, and to make a difference.

We can no longer afford to separate these two basic aspects of human nature and assume that it is self-interest alone that drives

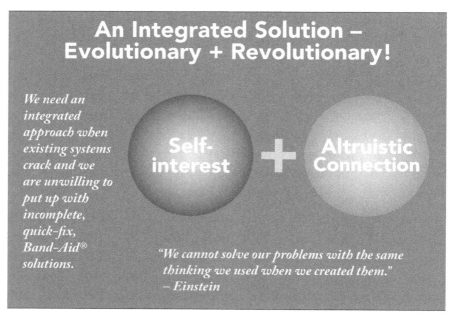

An Integrated Solution – Evolutionary + Revolutionary!

We need an integrated approach when existing systems crack and we are unwilling to put up with incomplete, quick-fix, Band-Aid® solutions.

Self-interest **+** Altruistic Connection

"We cannot solve our problems with the same thinking we used when we created them."
– Einstein

Figure C.6: Today's unique challenges require us to integrate two basic aspects of human nature.

business performance. We have to nurture an environment so that both aspects have an opportunity to flourish and serve self, team, and the organization. While we have seen glimpses of joyful and fulfilling self-actualized work, it continues to be a challenge for many leaders and organizations to make this a consistent reality.

In our desire and anxious quest to capture that magic and make this a lasting state and a regular way of life, we are going about it the wrong way. I don't mean morally, ethically, or legally wrong. We are just being ineffective by taking a piecemeal and compartmentalized approach. To quote Einstein again, "We cannot solve our problems with the same thinking we used when we created them." We need an evolutionary and revolutionary model that will help us to intentionally and systematically create a fulfilling, high performance culture. This model is focused on three key aspects:

1. **Personal Transformation:** Effectiveness begins with personal transformation at the top where leaders will walk the talk and

practice skills of personal mastery. An organization can only be as effective, evolved, and enlightened as its CEO and his or her team.

2. **Organizational Transformation:** Leaders will learn and practice organizational mastery skills so they can lead by example in the organizational transformation process.

3. **Systemic Shift—High-Trust and High-Performance Operating System:** A systemic shift requires us to clearly describe how the fundamental business operations will be performed, which is exactly what this operating system does.

Personal Transformation

Personal transformation is based on a shift in your mindset. As a leader, your actions and behavior impacts many people. An organization can only be as effective, evolved, and enlightened as its CEO and his or her team. Leadership behavior has a direct and disproportionate impact on profitability and the bottom-line.[vi] You have to live and lead consciously. The old way of separating personal and professional life, sacrificing emotional, social and spiritual development for the sake of unbalanced business growth is no longer viable and sustainable. You have to take this deeply personal journey of conscious authentic leadership.

All successful leaders and professionals spend years studying, learning, and practicing their craft, be it technology, marketing, operations, finance, or sales. This means you are actively pursuing professional mastery. To establish a self-actualized work environment of high trust and high performance, you must actively engage in two other dimensions: personal mastery and organizational mastery.

Since leadership effectiveness in organizations is determined by employee engagement and productivity, it is critical to understand what inspires those qualities, which are closely tied to individual fulfillment. Until recently, most leaders and organizations relied heavily on pure intellectual ability, often measured by a worker's intelligence quotient (IQ) to solve business challenges. More recently, management consultants and self-help teachers alike are looking at emotional intelligence (EQ). While they now appreciate the role of emotional and social development, they still do not have a good understanding of how visceral and self-mastery skills help in enhancing leadership effectiveness and organizational execution.

Now many leaders are striving for high IQ, EQ, and a deeper self-awareness and understanding of "human dimension." These folks are not only passionate, driven, analytical, and accountable; they also possess additional qualities of mastery and team collaboration, and the ability to simultaneously exhibit characteristics such as empathy, humility, generosity, compassion, care, and unconditional love. These leaders are not only well trained and experienced in business strategy, execution, and operations, but are adept at connecting on a deeper level and inspiring teams and organizations to superior performance. They integrate best practices in business with personal mastery.

Achieving Personal Mastery

Personal mastery is about staying on purpose and being inspired no matter what the external circumstances are. In this state, you are naturally present, aware, and awake. You are genuinely optimistic and enthusiastic in the midst of challenges and obstacles. You see facts and reality the way they are. You are aware of the beliefs and values that drive your thoughts, emotions, and actions. As a leader, it is not enough to have great intentions; you have to be conscious of the impact of your actions. You manage and master your emotions and stay conscious of how you are "showing up." It is this level of mastery that makes an authentic leader automatically more inclusive, fair, objective, and purposeful while being laser-focused on right action and effectiveness, thereby ensuring the best possible outcome. Personal mastery is the profound personal and inner work that all leaders and their teams have to undertake to achieve the greatness that they are capable of. There are no exceptions and shortcuts that I know of!

This new breed of authentic leadership creates an environment for everyone to express their natural gifts and pursue their highest aspirations and deepest yearnings to be the best they can be. They treat business as a playground to realize their highest human potential and create conditions for everyone to show up as a whole person, so they can utilize their intellect, heart, and spirit in pursuit of professional excellence and personal fulfillment. One of the business leaders I have the privilege of partnering with famously declared to his leadership team, "I am a good and successful leader, but to be a great leader, I need to become a greater person, spouse, friend and father." This business leader, with a track record of building profitable organizations, treats profit as a by product of building an aligned and mutually accountable team and an engaged and inspired organization.

Organizational Mastery and Transformation

While it all begins with self-awareness and personal transformation, nobody can do it alone. You need collaborative and mutually accountable leadership teams to transform an organization and to align its purpose with the business model and operations. Consider that recent Ernst and Young Oxford University study where only 37 percent of leaders said that their business model and operations are well-aligned with their purpose. What this means is that some of the most important aspects of business operations such as communication, decision-making, strategic planning and execution, performance evaluation, compensation, incentives and rewards will have to be conducted in a much more inclusive, objective, and conscious manner, and in alignment with the stated vision and values. To accomplish this requires an organizational shift simultaneously from top-down and bottom-up. You know all too well the obstacles involved in a systemic shift: A system is resistant to change and will always thwart your best efforts unless you make a sustained and targeted effort. This is the domain of organizational mastery.

Organizational mastery is the ability to inspire everyone in the organization to give their very best toward a common vision and goal. This is a requirement to build aligned leadership teams and a fully engaged organization. You know this is easier said than done. You have to create an environment in which both fundamental drives for self-interest and unconditional contribution have an opportunity to flourish, converge, and serve the organization.

Great leaders have no illusions about their personal abilities and charisma to mobilize large groups of people toward a common goal. They understand that only a noble vision truly inspires people from within to give their very best. They are therefore able to align people's self-interest with the team's shared vision and the greater good. This was the secret behind great transformational social leaders such as Mahatma Gandhi, Abraham Lincoln, Nelson Mandela, and Martin Luther King, Jr. They had an in-depth understanding and mastery of human nature. They understood that it was their vision that galvanized the people, not them alone. People follow a mission or a noble purpose, they don't follow leaders.

To be authentic and inspirational, leaders require the ability to get buy-in by connecting, empathizing, and influencing as opposed to commanding, controlling, and directing. This is the domain of organizational mastery and a skillset that does not come naturally to most business professionals and leaders. It can, however, be learned.

The High-Trust and High-Performance Operating System

Clearly, the processes and operating system of most business organizations today are wired for short-term and the single-minded pursuit of performance, profit, and professional excellence. This approach has brought us much progress and success so far. However, it is no longer sufficient to give us the highest levels of sustainable performance and excellence. In this "either/or" model, leaders measure lagging indicators (such as revenue growth and profitability), but do not know how to track leading indicators (such as engagement, alignment, and productivity) and pro-actively influence leading indicators before it is too late.

The best and brightest business leaders today acknowledge the gap between purposeful vision and daily operations. While there is intent, there is no platform and roadmap to integrate trust, purpose, and fulfillment in the context of a business organization.

The solution is to create a fundamental shift, with a new operating system and structure that is most appropriate for our current needs. This new system is geared to inspire with an "and" approach. This blueprint is designed to achieve breakthrough results by bridging the purpose and business operations gap and by proactively resolving personal, interpersonal and systemic breakdowns. Driving performance and building trust is a habit, a discipline, and a process.

The seven practices covered in this book will start you on your way toward a high-trust and high-performance operating system for your organization. When you diligently and consistently execute them, you can expect the following outcomes:

- Discipline and focus on the most important goals
- Authentic communication
- Empowering and accountable decisions
- Energizing and effective meetings
- Proactive and constructive conflict resolution
- Dynamic and inclusive strategy planning and execution
- Objective performance evaluation
- A system of fair and inspiring recognition, rewards, and compensation

The Bottom Line

Here's the bottom line for all of this: Business leadership has evolved from an authoritarian top-down model to a process-driven hierarchical model and is now evolving to a conscious and inclusive servant leadership approach. While leadership in general is a reflection of our collective consciousness, servant leadership is possible only when you align your personal needs, drives, and requirements toward a larger common vision.

As a business leader, you wield enormous power and authority, so you have to exercise the responsibility that comes along with it carefully and thoughtfully. You have to become a steward of this movement while shifting toward a more conscious way of conducting your business and leading your life. You have to lead and operate your business in tune with higher growth needs and aspirations. You have to infuse and bake core values and operating principles into the DNA of your organization. This is a journey!

It is a mastery journey that requires relentless focus, uncommon discipline, and an enormous appetite for consistent practice. It is not for everyone. As Michelangelo famously said, "If people knew how hard I worked to get my mastery, it wouldn't seem so wonderful at all."

When you take this journey, you practice what thought leaders have termed natural, inclusive, enlightened (or conscious) capitalism within your business organization. You strive to become the change you wish to see. You achieve your most audacious dreams, and you help usher in the new era—elevating the collective will and consciousness to create facilitators, ambassadors, torchbearers, and trailblazers. You become a role model for anyone looking to become an exceptional leader, while building aligned teams and engaged employees—the Holy Grail of all organizations!

i World Bank

ii www.visualizingeconomics.com; Angus Maddison, University of Groningren; **www.prb.org; www.worldbank.org**

iii Human Security report project. *Human Security Report 2009/2010: The Causes of Peace and The Shrinking Costs of War.* New York: Oxford University press, 2011

iv Forbes: **http://www.forbes.com/sites/ccap/2012/02/16/the-male-female-ratio-in-college/**

v Diamandis, Peter H., and Steven Kotler. *"Good-bye, Linear Thinking...Hello, Exponential." Bold: How to Go Big, Achieve Success, and Impact the World.*

vi In Maslow's hierarchy of human needs, the lower stages are deficiency needs which are driven by the dictates of the ego. The need to survive, belong, be accepted and loved, be recognized, rewarded and respected and the need for self-centered growth and achievement are ego needs. As long as we are operating in this space, we are driven by ego and we drive or motivate others by appealing to their deficiency needs of the ego. However, we cannot fully overcome the deficiency needs by feeding into them. For example: There are people who are never satisfied with the amount of money they earn. Such folks remain subconsciously focused at the survival level even though they may have overcome the deficiency need for acceptance and respect. Same is true with self-centered growth. After achieving a certain level of advancement and success, no amount of power, recognition, fame is sufficient to make us feel respected unless we take personal responsibility and accountability for our self-esteem. To be able to overcome the deficiency needs, we have to learn to manage and master our ego and emotions and release subconscious fears and anxieties. This is a necessary step to operate at higher levels of growth needs in the hierarchy.

Taking the CEO Mastery Journey

Ash Patel is a quintessential American success story. He was the founding president of Premier Commercial Bank (PCB) based in Anaheim, California, and now is president and CEO of Commercial Bank of California (CBC), a company with $1 billion in assets headquartered in Irvine with eight branches in Southern California. Ash started his banking career as a teller in Bank of America thirty years ago and rose to become one of the outstanding CEOs in the industry. Under his leadership, PCB grew steadily by deftly navigating the storms of the great recession and severe economic turmoil. In the process, PCB was recognized as one of the most successful community banks in the country with thirty-five consecutive quarters of profitability.

Creating a Transformative Company

My journey with Ash began in October 2010 at a business conference in Southern California, organized by the world's largest network of entrepreneurs. I was a lead presenter and had been working relentlessly to integrate state of the art skills in personal and organizational mastery with superior business practices. My goal was to deliver exceptional results in professional excellence and personal fulfillment. I was happy to note that my message of mastery and purpose to enhance business performance resonated with the hard-nosed, bottom-line-oriented executives and entrepreneurs in attendance.

After my session, Ash asked me to make the same presentation to his leadership team at the bank. He told them that he needed to develop additional skills to lead a $1 billion transformative bank. Professionally and personally, he wanted to make the shift from a successful leader to a great leader, from a good person, spouse, parent, and friend to being great in all of those areas. He decided to enroll in the CEO Mastery program that I had developed—and seeing his enthusiasm and commitment to doing so, his executive team was inspired to join him voluntarily.

What followed was, and continues to be, one of the most rewarding experiences in both lives and professional careers. By focusing on purpose and principles, we enhanced financial performance. The bank's record-breaking streak of profitable quarters continued in one of the most turbulent times in history for financial institutions. We even took it a step further and dared for the first time to be among the top 1 percent of performers in the industry. Ash was nominated for the Ernst and Young Entrepreneur of the Year award. In 2010, he led his bank to become the number-one Small Business Administration (SBA) lender in the country and got an invite to the White House. PCB funded $58 million in new SBA loans that year and recorded the highest percentage growth year over year since inception. How did they achieve this?

Ash and I embarked on an invigorating and exhilarating journey where we partnered and I became a de facto member of the leadership team. I took on the roles of leadership trainer, hands-on coach, trusted advisor, and chief cultural officer. We committed to living the philosophy that a company is only as conscious as its leadership. Professional excellence, personal fulfillment, purpose, profit, principles, and performance reinforced each other.

Ash and I engaged in intense training sessions focused on intentionally defining and living our values and culture. We connected our vision and values to daily operations and personal behavior. The executive team studied cutting-edge practices and fine-tuned their skills to:

- Communicate authentically
- Constructively identify and resolve conflicts
- Conduct empowering and energizing meetings
- Make effective and accountable decisions

Ash actively participated in these sessions. He was, in fact, the most diligent and devoted student. He led by example with a disarming vulnerability and inspiring transparency. The entire leadership team got deeply engaged resulting in a dramatic rise in trust, alignment, and commitment. We took the stakeholder-centric approach to heart and determined to make the organization a vehicle to help its employees, customers, investors and all of its stakeholders to realize their dreams. We galvanized to make PCB a role model and "best for" the industry where:

- employees are inspired and grateful for the opportunity to serve
- customers are delighted to do business
- investors are proud to be a part
- analysts recognize and admire accomplishments
- peers respect and try to emulate our success
- community is appreciative

The self-belief, mutual trust, and loyalty that this program engendered in the leadership team would soon come in handy. PCB was acquired by a larger bank providing a lucrative exit to the investors and at the same time cutting short the breathtaking journey we were on. We were able to skillfully navigate the uncertainty and stress associated with the acquisition. Many executives reported that enhanced relationships and the ability to cope with difficult situations in personal life were additional benefits of the program.

When Ash left PCB after the acquisition, each and every key stakeholder, in a remarkable display of solidarity, wanted to become a part of his new venture. Customers, team members, employees, and even new investors urged Ash to continue at another bank with the same exemplary zeal, noble vision, and uplifting values. We accomplished so much at PCB in a nine-month span that we figured we could achieve even more remarkable results with a supportive board and investors at a new bank that shared our vision and missionary zeal.

Ash became a highly sought-after CEO-in-waiting in the banking industry. We evaluated many offers to either run existing banks or start a new one. We settled on Commercial Bank of California (CBC) as the vehicle to continue our unfinished journey. We decided that we would have the freedom and support from the new board to build a people-centric transformative bank focused on human capital innovation.

Unique Requirements of Leadership Today

Why is a CEO's job so exhilarating, energizing, and rewarding but also daunting? It is exhilarating because a CEO has the unique opportunity to build a great, high-performance, and purposeful organization. It is daunting because he or she cannot do it alone but requires engaged employees, an aligned leadership team, and supportive investors and/or owners. Stakeholders must be aligned, balanced, and inspired. A CEO is like a conductor who must ensure all the musicians are playing in harmony.

Each of these stakeholders has different motivations—shareholders and owners are focused on growth and return; the leadership team wants to feel that they have responsibility, authority, and an active strategic role; employees want to be treated fairly and provided with the tools and resources to excel, grow, and express their gifts. Each sees the company from their own perspective. The CEO is expected to see the whole picture and connect with all these constituents, meeting them where they are and inspiring them to see the big picture, as well.

Let us take the case of employees. The first order of business is to ensure that their basic requirements are met and that they have ample opportunities for professional growth and development. It helps for everyone to have a financial stake in the company such as profit sharing, stock options, and stock participation plans. These are good motivators but still are not enough to inspire them to give their very best. This requires working together toward a larger common purpose with shared values and core beliefs in a high-trust environment. The key words are *common, shared,* and *trust!* How do you develop that?

Most successful CEOs have the functional expertise, intellectual capacity, and dedicated work ethic. That is professional mastery. That's what got them here, but it is simply not enough to inspire everyone to give their best to build a purposeful and profitable organization.

What is needed is a deeper understanding of human motivations and emotions and the ability to connect with employees at a visceral level, individually and collectively. It begins with self and the ability and capacity to go within. This is the domain of personal and organizational mastery which I discuss in detail in this book.

Major Problems and Challenges for Today's CEOs

Most CEOs looking to take their companies to the next level in today's hyper-competitive environment face similar problems. Perhaps these challenges reflect your own situation:

- You are struggling to operationalize the grand vision and core values, and execution can be much better. Revenue growth has plateaued and sustainable profitability seems very difficult to achieve.

- You are lonely, stressed, and emotionally drained. You are very busy and working extremely hard, but you are not sure if what you are doing will make any difference in the long run. You need mental and psychological space to reflect and be creative. You are struggling to inspire and lead a life that feels purposeful. Your job feels like more of a burden than a sacred responsibility.

- Your leadership team is not cohesive or fully aligned, and is hurting the performance of the organization. Not enough people in the team can see the big picture. Everyone is focused in their silo (area of responsibility) and unable or unwilling to collaborate towards the common goal. How do you build a world-class team and manage the egos of leaders? You seem to find leaders who are bright and creative but have big egos, or those that are better team players but lack creativity and fire. What does it take to have both?

- Employees are not fully engaged and are not inspired to give their very best. They are quick to point out problems without offering solutions. They do not speak up and suggest solutions in meetings.

- You know there is more to life. Work is not bad, you make a good living, but something is missing. There isn't enough personal time, and there is no spark in your family life. You do not deeply connect with your children and the relationship with your spouse is flat. Besides professional and financial achievement, you are seeking personal happiness and fulfillment.

Following Audacious Dreams

At the same time, you have your own goals for yourself and your organization:

- You want to build a high-trust, highly purposeful, and profitable organization that excels in execution. You want work to be not just intellectually stimulating, but also emotionally fulfilling and spiritually uplifting.
- You are inspired and feel purposeful. You are pursuing professional excellence and personal fulfillment. You believe in stewardship and practice servant leadership to build an organization where employees feel cared for and find work meaningful.
- You want to lead an organization where everyone is having fun and feels like they are owners. Everyone acts like this is "our" company, are all owners and individually bring different skills and expertise to make us successful.
- You are inspired by a vision to create an environment where work becomes a playground to pursue all of our highest potentials and deepest yearnings. The leadership team is fully aligned and holds each other accountable. Employees are fully engaged and bring their unique gifts to work every day.
- You care about the world and your role in it. You are frustrated by social divide and polarization. You want to contribute and make a difference. You are concerned about your legacy and what you will pass on to the next generation.

In spite of right and noble intentions, here are some typical mistakes made by the leaders, leadership teams, and their organizations:

- Underestimating the effect of CEO behavior, words, and actions on the bottom line, leadership alignment, and employee engagement. Not fully committing to personal positive behavior change.

- Doing more of what made them successful. Assume that professional competence, strong intellect, and a solid work ethic are enough to build a high-trust and high-performing organization. Not working actively on creating a caring and purposeful environment that helps unleash personal gifts, deep yearnings, and fulfill highest potential.

- Failing to track and measure leadership alignment and employee engagement as diligently as financial performance and customer satisfaction.

- Using old systems and structures that are no longer effective. For example: Using reward/punishment approach to motivation, encouraging stress and tension as a necessity for high performance, conducting top-down performance evaluations, and engaging in hierarchical decision-making.

- Not connecting noble vision and lofty values to daily actions. Not allowing mistakes and second-guessing the decisions of competent professionals. Slow to trust and quick to reprimand or withdraw authority.

- Not actively engaging in and taking charge of conflict resolution, personnel challenges, miscommunication, and misunderstandings. Trying to fix others before fixing themselves.

- Not proactively seeking feedback on leadership performance, or practicing reverse accountability. Ignoring how employees and stakeholders feel about leadership performance, fairness, autonomy, and satisfaction at work. Ignoring misunderstandings, passive conflicts, and hurt feelings. Does not create an environment and opportunity to vent concerns and frustrations that lurk under the surface. Takes criticism personally.

- Trying to come up with all the answers and solve the problems without encouraging debate and tapping into collective IQ.

- Forcing quick decisions—not getting buy-in by engaging everyone and providing airtime for diverse opinions and perspectives.

- Not fully committing to developing the culture of the organization. Seeking immediate financial return and getting impatient with the process. Falling back to old habits and sending mixed messages to the organization.

- Leading compartmentalized lives—utilizing primarily intellect at work and saving emotion for family, and deeper spiritual pursuit for weekends or retirement. Taking an "either/or" approach instead of the inclusive "and."

- Not investing the time required to create an environment of employee ownership and buy-in. Not involving the organization in developing core beliefs, shared values, common vision, and strategic priorities. No seeking employee input and feedback on profit sharing, employee ownership, compensation structure, and the gap between the highest and average compensation.

- Conducting wellness programs in isolation without connecting them to direct business activities and performance. Ignoring emotional mastery in performing day-to-day business functions, communication, decisions, negotiations, and strategy execution.

- Failing to align and balance the interests of all stakeholders: Employees, customers, suppliers, investors, and community.

Building an Enlightened Organization

Any business today is capable of leading the way in its marketplace by relying on the key principle of right action. Doing so will support the essentials of enlightened leadership and a powerful integration of work and life!

One narrative we hear is that business is about selfishness and greed and elevates a few at the expense of many. Therefore, we should apply regulatory controls to limit growth and concentration of power. The other narrative is that we are fine the way we are, and there is nothing wrong with the way we are managing our business and economy. Hence, we should continue with our short-term shareholder-centric, unbridled capitalistic model, and all will be fine. When we look at it objectively, both narratives are only partially right. Proponents of each narrative need to be willing to reach out and be open to the other perspective.

The truth or the solution is always somewhere in the middle—the middle way—or as I call it, the inclusive "and"—as opposed to the exclusive "either/or" approach.

The inclusive "somewhere in the middle" approach tends to be at work in many areas of life—in the broader human struggle between right and left, strategy and tactics, planning and action, purpose and profit, principles and performance, short-term and long-term, inward and outward. It's yin and yang. The answer is simple but not easy. You often have to transcend and include what at first appears to be opposing concepts in order to find a balance that leads to success. That's where the pathway to greatness, excellence, and fulfillment lies.

In a way, everyone has the same struggle—as individuals and as leaders of business, political, or social organizations. Since we are all part of the same ecosystem, instead of blaming each other we should go inward and get our houses in order. *You have to be the change you wish to see.* You cannot be a part of the solution unless you embrace the problem and acknowledge your role in creating it—whatever "it" may be.

In life and organizational leadership, how did we contribute to "the problem"?

- We follow a system of punishment and reward that is more in tune with the "fight or flight" state of human nature.
- By focusing on intellectual stimulation we ignore the heart, emotion, and spirit. We fail to appeal to the whole person and tap into the full potential of each individual.
- We set grand visons and espouse noble values but fail to operationalize them in daily activities and bake them in the DNA of organizations.
- While we rightfully focus on profits and financial wealth creation, we ignore emotional, social, natural, and spiritual health and fulfillment. We do not do much to improve what

our stakeholders have been asking us for: transparency, authenticity, inclusiveness, and a higher purpose and meaning to work.

At a recent World Economic Forum in Davos, Switzerland, global leaders recognized that businesses serve a higher purpose beyond profit. I call it an *evolved conscious leadership*, and that's the key to leadership mastery.

A conscious, enlightened business organization is one that I call 3.0—self-actualized. For example, a transformative organization in 1.0 state offers a steady and stable environment with lifetime, or at least long-time, employment. In a 3.0 state, the benchmark is higher—a high-trust and high-performance environment with purposeful growth. The table below details the key organizational characteristics of a 1.0, 2.0, and 3.0 organization, including the predominant leadership approach at the top.

Key Organizational Characteristics	1.0 Security L1-L2 Socialized	2.0 Self-Centered L3-L4 Self-Authoring	3.0 Self-Actualized L5-L7 Self-Transforming
What is a Transformative Organization?	Steady and stable, lifetime employment	Growth-oriented, high performance	Purposeful growth, high-trust, high performance
Leadership Approach	Autocratic, bureaucratic	Hierarchical, directive rules and processes	Authentic, facilitative, empowered teams, principles
Work Hours Expectation	9 to 5	24x7 electronic leash	Integrated, owner mindset
Execution	Average	Good but stressful. Tends to be chaotic and disorganized	Excellent. Smooth and prioritized in a flow state
Operational Roadmap	What's that?	No time, why bother?	Clear, detailed, buy-in from top to bottom
Executive Communication	Restricted, need to know, politically correct	More open, direct, blunt	Transparent, direct, constructive, empathetic

Decision-Making	Top-down	Hierarchical with input and feedback	Empowered and accountable
Strategy Planning	Centralized, annual	Hierarchical, periodic	Empowered teams, real-time, dynamic
Performance Evaluation	Boss knows best. Annual	360 feedback from multiple people. Frequent (2 to 4 times a year)	Peers and empowered teams Real-time
Compensation	Top secret, arbitrary	Confidential, large gap	Transparent, fair gap
Rewards & Incentives	Small, team performance	Large, individual performance	Integrated: individual, team & organization performance
Hiring and Retention Criteria	Conform, follow orders & direction	Driven, independent, high IQ, medium EQ	Open, collaborative, caring, high EQ
Org Teamwork	Parent-Child	Big brother, me first, bottom line-driven	Peer, team first, mission and purpose driven
Drive and Motivation	Fear, survival, belonging	Self-centered growth, achievement, recognition	Meaning, purpose, make a difference

From Success to Greatness

When you learn how to achieve professional excellence and personal fulfillment, everything in your life and business will change. You may no longer be satisfied with mere success since as you will be inspired to pursue greatness. So, what's the difference between a successful leader and a great leader?

A successful leader

- achieves very good financial results
- leads by demonstrating intellect, knowledge and passion. Motivates by the carrot-and-stick approach with a primary focus on

the deficiency needs of security, belonging, and self-centered achievement

- pursues success by focusing on short-term professional goals and drives leadership team and organization to deliver.

A great leader

- achieves exceptional financial results that are consistent and sustainable;
- leads by demonstrating intellect, empathy and care. Inspires by appealing to the growth needs of purpose, making a difference and serves and nurtures an environment for everyone to unleash their full creative potential;
- pursues purpose by integrating personal and professional goals and stretches leadership team and organization to consistently attain peak performance.

You can pursue greatness and lead a purposeful life by aligning your personal and professional goals. Many leaders compartmentalize their lives and behave differently in different environments. They tend to be more formal, rigid, and less personable professionally. We don't have to be as black and white; we can comfortably be ourselves in all situations. Rather than categorizing our identities, we can show up fully at work, home, and everywhere else all the time. This makes us more natural and authentic and deepens our connections with our people. You will inspire your leadership team and the rest of the organization to give their best.

Develop a business that consistently delivers superior and sustainable financial results. By focusing on execution and engaging your employees, you will operationalize and infuse excellence in business processes, increase productivity, and unlock the value of the organization. You can significantly enhance your ability and that of your team to communicate, negotiate, make decisions, resolve conflicts, and implement strategies. This leads to millions of dollars in revenue growth and profitability that is consistent and sustainable.

Build a leadership team that is aligned, collaborative, and mutually accountable. Team members trust and push each other to achieve a common goal and pursue a common purpose. They engage in open and honest conversations—bringing to the surface and then resolving passive conflicts. Everyone takes responsibility for their actions to uncover and solve personal, team, and business challenges. By converting their good intentions to impactful actions, they consistently deliver.

Gain emotional mastery and effectively deal with complex human challenges and conflicts. Leadership action has an extraordinary impact on the morale and productivity of the leadership team and the organization. By focusing on the source of behavior, you master human nature and learn practical skills to enhance emotional intelligence and resolve complex human challenges. This leads to improved engagement, productivity, and innovation.

Great leaders identify their core beliefs and values and uncover their life's passion and purpose. They align and integrate these with the business mission and core operating principles. This step is critical to leading a purposeful life and building a purposeful organization.

Great leaders do not compartmentalize their lives. Instead, they engage fully at work, home, and everywhere else. This makes them more natural, authentic, and trusting, and helps them connect with everyone at a deeper level. They lead with their heart, with a clear set of values and beliefs. They combine cognitive and rational skills with well-developed emotional intelligence and mastery. They take the time for self-care and wellness. They regularly recharge and rejuvenate the whole self, i.e., physical, mental, emotional, and spiritual.

The Key Principles for Effective Leadership and CEO Mastery Journey

How do you reach these goals? When you combine professional mastery with personal and organizational mastery, you can build a great organization with aligned teams and engaged employees. To do that, you need to develop the intellectual, physical, emotional, and spiritual capacity to deeply connect with and inspire all your stakeholders so they will bring their whole selves to work every day. Only then will you enter the domain of personal and organizational mastery. This is the CEO Mastery Journey.

- Personal mastery is the ability to stay positive, present, and grateful independent of external circumstances.
- Organizational mastery is the ability to inspire everyone to give their heart, mind, and soul to pursue a common purpose.

Success = Professional Mastery

A successful leader achieves very good financial results. He motivates by the carrot-and-stick approach with a primary focus on self-centered achievement.

Greatness = Professional + Personal + Organizational Mastery

A great leader achieves exceptional financial results that are sustainable. She inspires by appealing to the innate drive for purpose, to make a difference and to be of service.

The journey begins with understanding the key principles and all aspects of personal and organizational mastery. These include trust, inspiration and purpose; right action, emotional intelligence (EQ), and spiritual intelligence (SQ).

Trust

We always talk about business being a team sport, and trust is critical for a team to function at top performance. Most teams have not engaged in the process of exploring vulnerability in order to build trust. Trust is when you're able to hold each other accountable and push each other toward a common mission, paying attention to the results. That's when you connect deep trust and high performance.

Right Action

Another key principle for enlightened leadership is right action. This idea evolved from Dharma, a 5,000-year-old life principle originally enunciated in the *Vedas*, the most ancient and sacred texts of India. Despite its age, Dharma remains universal and timeless in application. Dharma means being true to oneself, treading one's own authentic path of thought, speech, and action. It's the path we each must travel for material, emotional, and spiritual fulfillment. On a broader scale, Dharma signifies moral uprightness, righteousness, behavior that upholds life and growth, and that is what right action is all about.

Intellectual Intelligence (IQ)

Everyone is familiar with intellectual intelligence, the conventional measure of the quickness and facility of your mind and understanding. In business, it also tends to be applied to how much you know about your industry and its processes, and how well you are able to come up with compelling strategies for success. Conventional leadership depends a lot on IQ, but so much more is needed to truly succeed in today's world.

Emotional Intelligence (EQ)

Emotional intelligence (EQ) includes such characteristics as accurate self-assessment, optimism, honesty, empathy, adaptability, self-confidence, transparency, and interpersonal skills such as influencing and shaping others, conflict management, teamwork, and collaboration.

Spiritual Intelligence (SQ)

To be spiritual is to seek actively. Being spiritual has no required connection with religion, nor does it imply being soft on non-performance, two common misconceptions. Spiritual intelligence (SQ) takes us deeper into self-awareness, self-inquiry, gratitude, compassion, understanding of the ego and connecting our deepest innate desire, and yearning in service of universal well-being. As our SQ increases, we develop the ability to see the big picture for what it is without the "personal spin", yet with the intellectual capacity to hold multiple perspectives. SQ is about taking right action and making the hard decisions in an inclusive and an objective, non-biased manner. It is the ability to consistently tap into the innermost yearning for excellence, fairness, purpose, and mastery that is the common heritage of all human beings.

Combining IQ, EQ, and SQ

To unleash your full potential, IQ, EQ, and SQ have to be equally developed. However, the reality is that in business and professional settings, you do not get much training in developing your emotional and spiritual intelligence. The few programs that are available don't generally connect them back to the realities of business.

By becoming mindful, self-aware, and spiritually intelligent, you can accelerate the shift of collective consciousness and become a role model for the change you want to see. You can facilitate the rise of democracy, capitalism, and human innovation to its most natural and fullest potential. You can also dramatically impact personal leadership, team collaboration, and organizational effectiveness. You can do this by being your authentic self, showing up fully with intellect, heart, and spirit.

The 7 Practices: A Preview

Integrating and nourishing IQ, EQ, and SQ to achieve personal and professional mastery requires personal, organizational, and systemic transformation. Following are the seven practices that are critical to making this shift and taking the CEO Mastery Journey—all of which are detailed in the following chapters of this book. Practices 1 and 2 cover personal mastery, which is the key to living an inspired and self-actualized life. This is necessary, but not sufficient to inspire others to give their very best. That is the domain of organizational mastery, which is addressed in Practices 3 through 7.

- **Practice 1—Master Human Motivations:** Businesses have been slow to adopt peak performance principles and practices. The science of human motivation and inspiration have not been well integrated into basic business functions to experience an impact on the bottom line. Wellness programs such as meditation are treated as stress-reduction exercises, but the more direct business benefits of personal and organizational effectiveness have not yet been fully embraced and implemented.

- **Practice 2—Lead with Self-Mastery:** This practice details the personal transformation from a successful 2.0 to a conscious 3.0

leader. Success as we define it here is a 2.0 mindset; greatness is a 3.0 mindset. While we all have the capacity to be great and have greatness within, we are all not focused on showing up and behaving consistently in that manner. When you take the time to know yourself thoroughly, you will have a good grasp not only of yourself, but of human motivations and emotions in general. You are better equipped to connect with and inspire people to higher levels of productivity and performance. We've heard the saying, "Everybody wants change but no one wants to change." The most effective way to bring about change is to change oneself, especially if you are a leader.

- **Practice 3—Inspire with a Noble Purpose:** People don't follow leaders. They follow the purpose and values that their leaders represent. You have to inspire, not command, your people to give their best. A higher level of motivation is achieved by appealing to each person's personal desire for greater fulfillment. An inspiring noble purpose that galvanizes everyone into action is crucial. This practice delves into the most effective method to inspire your people: by touching their hearts and spirits with care, inclusion, fairness, meritocracy, and most of all, purpose.

- **Practice 4—Assess Current Reality:** It has been said that you don't see things the way they are, but you see them as *you* are, conditioned by your unique filters and perspectives. It requires a high degree of personal mastery to rise above this conditioning. Unless you are operating at a conscious 3.0 state, where you have the natural ability to see the things the way they are, it is very difficult not to have a personal filter attached to your perception. So, taking the time and establishing the process to understand reality is critical. Unless there is an open, transparent environment where everyone can speak their mind, it's very hard to accurately understand the state of affairs. Of course, this still requires you to have the courage to take advantage of the environment and be vulnerable.

- **Practice 5—Bridge the Intent-to-Impact Gap:** Once you have identified the current reality, that is the gap between noble intent and practical reality, between aspiration and ability, you have to bridge that gap to make the necessary impact. Simply knowing your gap does not magically solve your problems. Action does, with the appropriate process and roadmap. Mastery is the ability to consistently convert our noble intent-to-impactful actions. Unless you proactively manage your awareness, these blocks or hindrances rear their ugly heads without warning at the most inappropriate times. You must hold yourself and your team accountable to take consistent action that produces results.

- **Practice 6—Engage in Action Leadership:** Business is a contact sport, and the leader is playing the captain. A CEO leads with several key attributes of personal and organizational mastery. Action leadership is first demonstrating and then training, followed by demanding of others the organizational mastery skills: authentic communication, proactive conflict resolution, effective decision-making, energizing and empowering meetings, conscious budgeting and goal setting, and inclusive, dynamic strategy planning.

- **Practice 7—Bake Mastery into Your Organizational DNA:** It is wonderful to have a noble purpose, grand vision, and core values. However, they alone are not sufficient to build a great organization or propel a successful leader to greatness. Vision and values have to be directly connected to critical business functions, operational processes, and daily interactions. Now you can make mastery a way of life in your organization.

Together, personal and organizational mastery constitute the high trust and high performance (HTP) operating system (OS).

What Makes Great Leaders?

I start many of my leadership presentations by asking the audience "What descriptors come to mind when you think of the characteristics of great leaders?" The answers include many of the following: authenticity, integrity, courage, a clear mission, vision, inspiring, humble, a great teacher and mentor, presence, open-mindedness and open-heartedness, passion, compassion, persistence, patience, values, commitment to serving others, forgiveness, generosity, centeredness, kindness, loving, calmness, and caring.

Are these characteristics evident in your business environment? If not, why not? What is stopping leaders from demonstrating these characteristics at work? Doesn't this behavior enhance engagement, innovation, collaboration, alignment, and improve the bottom line? Why is it that so many professionals don't freely demonstrate these qualities at work?

Business Evolution

As stated in this book's "Claiming the Next Level of Leadership" section, the nature of work has shifted significantly since the Industrial Revolution. Business environment, business culture, and business leadership follow socioeconomic evolution as explained in Figure D.1.

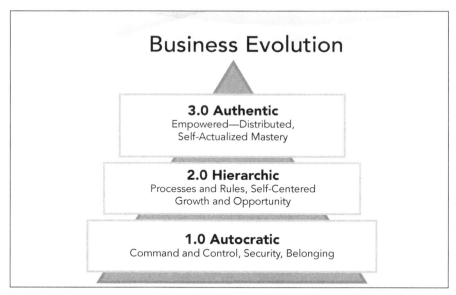

Figure D.1: Business evolution can be seen in three stages.

1.0 Top-Down Command and Control: Motivate primarily by power, authority, fear (stick)

- Advantages: Organization is stable, provides security, safety, and comfort to employees. It is organized, there is order, making it easier to scale and build large world wide organizations.

- Disadvantages: Inflexible, poor innovation and creativity. No incentive for individual professional and personal growth.

2.0 Hierarchical—Rules, Processes, Management by Objectives: Motivate primarily by self-centered achievement, greed (carrot)

- Advantages: Innovation, meritocracy, accountability resulting in unprecedented growth and prosperity.

- Disadvantages: Blindly pursuing growth results in high stress, burnout, lack of meaning and fulfillment. People are afraid to show up fully and be themselves. There is posturing at work— exaggerate strengths and hide weaknesses. This results in poor employee engagement, lack of teamwork and executive alignment, and of course, poor productivity.

As business people, we need to overcome the barriers in 2.0. Too many professionals are going about it the wrong way by pursuing two extreme and only partially correct solutions.

Position #1

- Hierarchy is bad. Power concentrated with a few at the top is the root cause of the problem. Everyone's viewpoint is equally important and should carry equal weight.

  This perspective leads to many of the problems we currently face, such as: slow and poor decision making, analysis paralysis, and consensus trap. We end up empowering incompetence without holding them accountable. We do not promote and reward individual excellence. By demonstrating hyper-sensitivity to power, authority, and hierarchy we end up sacrificing effectiveness big time and operate on the verge of chaos.

- Workplace environment should be meaningful and purposeful.

  This perspective has led to many positive developments such as a value-driven culture at work, an inspiring noble purpose besides just making a profit, shift from a shareholder to a stakeholder model, and inclusive conscious leadership.

Position #2

We have a capitalistic system that works just fine, let us double down and do more of the same. Stress is an unavoidable by product and may even be necessary for high performance. If we can only stop complaining and remove restrictions that impede growth, market forces will be fair to everyone and will solve all the challenges. This perspective led to remarkable growth and several advantages along with some serious challenges mentioned in 2.0 above. Bright, successful executives such as Ash feel stuck. They know what the problem is, and they are eager for a solution that works.

The solution to this situation is the 3.0 model which takes the best of what each approach has to offer and lets go of the disadvantages. Actually practicing this is easier said than done because it requires operating at a higher level of emotional development. When you operate at that level, the practices not only become obvious, implementing them consistently will become second nature to you. This is what it takes for successful leaders to transform themselves, their teams, and their organizations to greatness. This is the journey Ash and his executive team is taking.

Leadership Evolution: Autocratic> Hierarchic> Authentic

Human beings, including employees of business organizations, are holistic creations. They have the material, emotional, and spiritual needs and drivers indicated in the Maslow's hierarchy (see "Claiming the Next Level in Leadership"). After basic needs are met, emotional and spiritual requirements naturally kick in to a larger degree. These spiritual drivers come from the march toward the self-actualized state and are not related to religion. Employee engagement, execution, productivity, and business performance are connected to satisfying all the needs. The highest level of performance can be inspired by leaders and organizations.

Figure D.2 illustrates the evolution from the early autocratic model to the democratic model of the information age to the enlightened leadership that is now required.

Leadership Evolution

- Autocratic 1.0: Material & Analytical Dimension: IQ
  - Utilizes fear, control, and monetary rewards

- Democratic 2.0: And Emotional Dimension: IQ + EQ
  - Motivates: Fair, open, inclusive

- Enlightened 3.0: And Spiritual Dimension: IQ + EQ + SQ
  - Inspired: Tough love, service, self-mastery

Figure D.2: IQ: Intelligence Quotient; EQ: Emotional Quotient; SQ: Spiritual Quotient

A New Leadership Model for Today

Leaders are always striving to get the best performance from their respective organizations, employing the leadership style and skill that they are most comfortable with. The leadership model illustrated in Figure D.2 will help you to explore the effectiveness of different leadership styles. The categories in the model are not meant to be treated as separate and distinct. Most of us do not follow one style all the time (we may, in fact, practice a little of each) but have a predominant style which we believe in and demonstrate.

The exceptional and enlightened leader believes in unlocking his or her full potential by utilizing analytical, emotional, and spiritual skills. He or she takes democracy to its highest degree, respects and recognizes creative talent in everyone, and empowers them to produce their best. Tough love and benevolent dictatorship is practiced when necessary. He or she inspires by appealing to the deepest and innermost human yearning. Service, not personal ambition, is the prime motive behind this leadership position. The 3.0 leader becomes

an inspirational role model by pursuing self-mastery and a noble purpose for the organization.

As shown in Figure D.3, the conscious or enlightened leadership
at this 3.0 level inspires the highest level of performance and effectiveness from self, team, and organization. It transcends and includes
the traditional motivational practices based on security, fear, intimidation (1.0), recognition, achievement, self-centered ambition, and
greed (2.0), and inspires execution by appealing to the deep human
drive for excellence, mastery and meaning, and the yearning to satisfy
the whole being—intellect, heart, and spirit.

CEO Mastery Journey	1.0	2.0	3.0
Leadership	Autocratic Fear-Based Compliance Least Effective	Hierachic Rules and Processes Reasonably Effective	Authentic/ Enlightened Empowered Most Effective
Organization	Poor perfor-mance, Low Trust	High Performance Average Trust	Exceptional Performance High Trust

Figure D.3: Level 3 leadership will elevate your organization to one
with high trust and high performance.

The shift to enlightened leadership is a reflection of the times in
which we live. We are on the verge of a kinder, gentler era with a shift
from consumerism to contentment. We are moving our focus from
pursuing wealth alone to personal growth and fulfillment. Fear (1.0),
greed (2.0), and intellectual challenge are good but not great motivators. Providing an environment where pursuit of excellence and mastery and contribution to universal well-being are deemed critical. A
place where we can nurture our intellect, heart, and soul is the new
requirement.

Enlightened organizations are seeking to fix the disconnect between authentic living and economic success by integrating purpose and values with extraordinary performance. Spiritual intelligence is the required skill to inspire people in the self-actualized state. In 3.0, we want growth and progress without compromise. "IQ + EQ + SQ" is the new mantra, especially for the leadership team.

It is important to note that 3.0 transcends, but also includes 1.0 and 2.0, meaning enlightened leadership includes elements of dictatorial and democratic leadership. For example, as mentioned before: Toughness without care breeds rigid conformance and mediocre compliance, and care without toughness could lead to apathy. Neither of them is as effective as the tough love of enlightened leadership. This is what I remind Ash and other leaders who are committed to making the shift, and to help them get over the fear of letting go. Their understandable concern is that in doing so, they will become tolerant of poor performance and incompetence. They just need to be reminded of what they already know. It will make you more assertive and more effective, while at the same time coming across as more caring and considerate.

A Case Study

Antonio is the CEO of a medium-size company. He is a brilliant man, works extremely hard, and knows his business and market. Knowledge, intellect, and hard work have been his mantra for success so far. When we met, he identified three problems that he was facing: 1) He was unable to grow the company at the same pace that he had been growing for the past 10 years; 2) his leadership team was not collaborating as well as he had hoped; and 3) he was feeling stressed and burned out. "The good news" I told him is that all three of those issues are connected. He had relied heavily on his personal knowledge and skill. He did not empower his team and hold them accountable.

At times, Antonio did not see the simmering conflicts in his team. At other times, he ignored his team by making decisions himself. He had been working long hours to find solutions and did not devote much time to taking care of himself. I met his leadership team members individually and quickly discovered that they were a collection of extremely bright and hardworking individuals who did not fully trust each other. They were not used to finding collaborative solutions.

We embarked on a training program to resolve conflicts by having difficult conversations, authentic communication to build trust, and making rapid decisions with accountability. We had them role play real-life situations, coached them individually, and facilitated meetings to apply these techniques on the job. Antonio summed up the success of the initiative by saying, "I now realize how important emotional mastery and wisdom is to be an effective leader, coach, and an inspiring team player."

Working toward Leadership 3.0

A noble purpose inspires employees to give their best and all the stakeholders to engage. Living by core values enhances personal effectiveness and team collaboration. Establishing processes and monitoring adherence to stated values and purpose improves performance. If implementing these were easy, everyone would do it. Execution is what separates the best and brightest leaders and organizations from the rest.

Life and leadership are inextricably linked, and one cannot hope to achieve true and extraordinary business success without a fulfilling life. The beauty of this situation is that while we are pursuing the inner purpose of life—meaning and contentment—the outer purpose of stellar business performance is fulfilled. Isn't that what life is all about? Can there be a better and more fulfilling purpose for a business leader, and in fact, for all human beings?

The shift from 2.0 to 3.0 leadership is in alignment with the shift required in the organizational environment from an "either/or" to an "and" approach. This is the shift from success to greatness. In this regard, the western female leaders and eastern male leaders have an inherent advantage. Let me explain why.

The Eastern Male and the Western Female Edge for 3.0 Leadership

A common question I hear is, "Do women make better leaders or do men have an advantage?" I believe that's the wrong question. Every leader, every human being for that matter, has both masculine and feminine characteristics. Effective leadership requires cultivating and demonstrating a balance of masculine and feminine characteristics depending on the situation and context. It doesn't matter whether it is a man or woman. It matters how conscious and inclusive the leader is, and that comes from demonstrating traits that are both feminine and masculine. It requires you to develop the ability to implement the best of both.

In essence, 3.0 Leadership involves incorporating what has been traditionally defined as "feminine" characteristics such as collaboration, inclusiveness, and empowerment. In comparison, 2.0 leadership traits of individual drive, personal ambition, and accountability have been traditionally defined as "masculine." As a result, we are seeing women and men who are more collaborative and technically skilled, many who may have been considered not tough enough in the past. The result is that 3.0 leadership levels the playing field for men and women.

The Dalai Lama famously said that the world will be saved by western women. I believe he meant a balance of masculine and feminine characteristics that are present in modern women—such as Indra Nooyi of Pepsico, Mary Barra of General Motors, Ginny Rometty of IBM, Phoebe Novakovic of General Dynamics, Marillyn Hewson of Lockheed Martin, Safra Catz of Oracle, Sheryl Sandberg of Facebook, and Meg Whitman of HP.

A decade-long study conducted by McKinsey and Company, a global management consulting firm, has concluded that companies with more women in upper management are likely to be more profitable. This is because women are more likely to practice five of the nine management behaviors that McKinsey thinks are critical to a company's success. These behaviors include people development, defining expectations and rewarding achievement, promoting respect and ethical behavior, presenting a compelling vision and inspiring optimism about it, and encouraging people to participate in decisions.

One McKinsey survey found that 72 percent of companies think there is a connection between leadership diversity and success. At the same time, only 28 percent of them said gender diversity was a top priority. Recent research also finds that women occupy only 25 percent of management positions globally.

There are exceptions within the business community. The two largest banks in India are headed by women CEOs. The Indian banking sector is well represented by women with a total of nine CEOs, including the India heads of JP Morgan India, and Bank of America Merrill Lynch.

Conscious CEOs and leaders such as Tony Hsieh of Zappos, Howard Schultz of Starbucks, Jeff Weiner of LinkedIn, Charlie Kim of Next Jump, Bob Chapman of Barry Wehmiller, John Mackey of Whole Foods and Ray Dalio of Bridgewater Associates represent this code of masculine and feminine balance, with a strong emphasis on transparency and the courage to be vulnerable and authentic.

I would also include the fast growing list of Indian-origin CEOs such as Satya Nadella of Microsoft, Sundar Pichai of Google, Ajit Jain of Berkshire Hathaway, Shantanu Narayen of Adobe, Rajiv Suri of Nokia, Ajay Banga of Mastercard, Anshu Jain of Deutche Bank, Arun Sarin of Vodafone, and most recently, Vasanth Narasimhan of Novartis among this new breed of CEOs. They prove one of the key tenets of a 3.0 Leader: It is easy to be autocratic and "tough," but modern organizations need tougher CEOs with soft (i.e., harder and tougher) skills who master emotions and have the audacity to demonstrate them! Many of the Indian-born CEOs—both women and men—had the benefit of growing up in an ancient civilization that values diversity and inspires knowledge, wisdom, and inclusiveness. Two of the phrases I heard most often growing up in India were *vasudhaiva kutumbakam*—the world is one family—and *sarve jana sukhinobhavantu*—may everyone be happy. Diversity of thought is especially encouraged and accepted. It is common for people in the same family to have different belief systems and religious affiliations. I am an example of that. We have to demonstrate a lot more compassion and inclusion of different perspectives in our socioeconomic institutions. This will help in significantly improving employee engagement, and will address the challenges of inequality, excessive greed and cronyism, and heal a polarized society.

World-Class CEO Mastery Coaching

As a CEO, you directly impact the lives of many people, both personally and professionally. You are closely connected to the employees, investors, customers, suppliers, and all the stakeholders of your organization, including the communities you are a part of. You probably haven't thought about the enormous sphere of influence you wield. Every action is closely scrutinized, motives are speculated, and your perspective and approach is fodder for debate. A CEO's job can be deeply satisfying and fulfilling. At the same time, it could be stressful and debilitating. It could alternately or simultaneously be exhilarating and deflating, exciting and nerve-wracking, intellectually stimulating and emotionally draining. Above all, it is a lonely place to be because very few have been there, and no one person in your immediate circle can truly relate to your experience.

To tap into the collective intelligence and unleash the full potential of your organization, it is not enough to be professionally knowledgeable and competent. Behind every great CEO is a world-class professional partner, trusted advisor, friend, and coach you can count on; a professional who understands you, your life, and your business. This someone is competent, trustworthy, and maintains confidentiality, is humble and does not judge, is secure and not intimidated, and stretches your growth based on deep understanding of human nature and human potential. A true partner like this takes on multiple roles as needed, and understands, guides, and provides specific answers and instructions.

The key role of a coach is discussed through the practices in this book with more specific detail in the bridge Intent-to-Impact—Accountability Partnership Practice.

Back to Ash Patel: Transforming the Next Company

At Premier Commercial Bank, Ash Patel and I were able to nurture a highly profitable and growing business that has garnered great acclaim. Following our "Good to Great Program," we were well on our way to creating a unique and exceptional bank before PCB was acquired by another bank and the program was discontinued. Our next challenge was turning around Commercial Bank of California (CBC).

Without mincing any words, CBC was a distressed bank in dire need of a turnaround. It was formed in 2001, around the same time Ash co-founded PCB, but the two companies had experienced entirely different trajectories. PCB built a reputation for being one of the best community banks in the country and had a solid exit for its investors. CBC, on the other hand, had stagnated, had not been profitable, and was under the threat of being shut down due to strategic and cultural missteps. To say morale was low is an understatement; a colleague sarcastically likened the energy in the organization to a morgue.

Most CEOs, leadership gurus, and change agents would neither recommend nor embark on culture transformation for an organization that is in trouble and has been bleeding red ink for years. They joke that when the ship is sinking, the only purpose is to keep it afloat, meaning the primary focus should be on cutting costs and removing inefficiencies. They do not invest the time and money in building a unique and purposeful culture. Ash made a bold move and went against the grain. He declared that profit is a by-product of pursuing a noble purpose; he asserted that he would unlock value in the bank without sacrificing *our* values. He professed that he doesn't have to make a false choice between people and profit, meaning and money, principles and performance.

Ash was vindicated. Customers and visitors noticed the difference in energy and excitement almost immediately. The lead indicators of employee engagement and leadership alignment showed marked improvement. Revenue growth and profitability naturally followed. He achieved sustained growth in new loans, deposits, and net income. Asset quality improved substantially, garnering monthly recurring core earnings.

Exactly two years later, CBC became the proud recipient of the coveted 5-Star Rating for reliability and excellence from Bauer Financial, the highly respected independent rating agency for banks. A bank that had not been profitable for years doubled profits every year immediately in 2014, 2015, 2016, and 2017. The bank is on track to continue the remarkable and purposeful growth on its way to joining the top 10 percent of performers. The dramatic turnaround from the brink to breakthrough performance was complete. This was a team effort that required contribution from all of the stakeholders. How did it achieve these remarkable results?

Having been on the receiving end of PCB's acquisition, Ash and the leadership team already experienced how not to force and enforce change. Ash was clear; we did not want to do that to the folks at CBC. We reached out and laid out the vision and game plan. The board of directors was impressed but dealing with apathetic executives and employees was a different ballgame. It was tougher than anticipated to excite and inspire them. They had forgotten what it was like to succeed and win. A few had become closed off and cynical. They said that they heard the empty words before in this bank and in many others throughout their careers—of vision, people, trust and values—only to be disappointed with no follow-up action. We were however, undeterred in our mission.

Just like at PCB earlier, we started regular human capital training sessions with Ash and the leadership team. It took a while for some of the old guard and also the newer executives to warm up. We persisted and made gradual, incremental progress. We identified three categories of people:

1. A small group of excited and enthusiastic change agents who were all in. We provided the environment for them to excel.

2. Another small cynical, closed group who were actively disengaged. We helped them make a safe exit or stay if willing to collaborate.

3. A larger group of skeptical and open folks who gradually became believers. We equipped them with knowledge and tools to contribute and shine.

We had several open discussions and focused group meetings where doubts, dissent, and differences were aired. Ash again set an example with his disarming forthrightness and vulnerability. He candidly expressed his disappointment about being misrepresented without clarification, and for assumptions being made about him and our intent. In rare moments of self-doubt, he wondered if our "soft, people first" approach was working. We resolved to persist and stay the course. Several employees and executives were thrilled with the new transparency and authenticity and stepped up to actively participate.

We involved everyone that was interested to develop our vision, values, and core operating principles and got buy-in. We called it our "purposeful journey to a billion"—to build a billion-dollar transformative bank.

We formed two cross-functional teams—Culture Council and Excellence in Execution—to intensify practical implementation and to connect our core values to daily operations. These teams of highly committed professionals engaged in deep authentic conversations to resolve complex challenges, tricky conflicts, and numerous misunderstandings. Most of the issues were unintended and typical of business environments comprised of driven, goal-oriented professionals with different perspectives. These forums created the opportunity to air out differences and focus on problem solving rather than finger pointing. The morale and productivity gains that came from these exercises proved to be invaluable.

We ascertained that excellence in execution or peak performance is a habit, a discipline, and a process. We took a systematic approach to infusing our values in the DNA of CBC and proactively resolved personal, interpersonal, and systemic breakdowns. We diligently and consistently learned specific skills and cutting-edge practices to achieve these outcomes:

- Discipline and focus on the most important goals
- Authentic communication
- Empowering and accountable decisions
- Energizing and effective meetings
- Proactive and constructive conflict resolution
- Dynamic and inclusive strategy planning and execution
- Objective performance evaluation, and
- A system of fair and inspiring recognition, rewards and compensation.

We used tools and processes to track all three dimensions of performance. We achieved steady sustained growth in new loans, deposits, and net income. Asset quality improved substantially, garnering monthly recurring core earnings that the bank had not experienced in over five years. Regulators commented on the remarkable culture shift. This was a team effort that required contribution from all of the stakeholders.

While still in the thick of turning around CBC, we acquired another bank. Having tasted success, Ash and the growth-oriented board could not pass up an opportunity that came knocking. Los Angeles-based National Bank of California (NBCal) needed capital infusion and a fresh start to reinvigorate their troubled bank, which was under consent order. Some in the executive team were rightfully concerned that turning around two banks almost simultaneously would be a bit too much even for us to take on. Because of the confidence they had in Ash and his team's ability, the CBC board decided that this was a rare opportunity; and we would take a calculated risk and go for it.

It turned out to be a risk worth taking. We achieved record breaking growth of 400 percent in three years and increased total asset size more than four times to $850 million. We doubled net earnings four years in a row with total assets almost at $1 billion, an extraordinary feat. We set the necessary foundation and are now poised to become a 3.0 transformative organization that Ash and I so passionately want.

Each transformation project has its own unique challenges. This thirty-three-year-old bank with a proud history and strong track record had been hit hard with the turmoil in the banking industry. Integrating the entrepreneurial, hard-driving style of CBC with an old school professional—and a bit more laid back—approach of the executive team at NBCal required deft handling. We were sensitive to the culture issues and were committed to lead with humility, respect, and inclusiveness. Our rallying theme for the new integrated culture was to incorporate the best of both: to leverage key strengths and improve efficiencies.

Of course, we had the expected roadblocks and hiccups associated with different operating styles and personalities. These were further aggravated by the uncertainty of regulatory approval and the new structure of the combined entity going forward. Two key events served as turning points in the alignment and collaboration between the two banks and our respective executive teams:

1. **Company-wide Visioning Process:** We invited and engaged everyone in the bank to provide their input in determining our why—purpose, vision, values and core operating principles. The manner in which we involved everyone and deeply listened to their input made all the difference.

2. **Strategic Offsite:** We held an offsite for the teams to understand and connect with each other. Executives shared their values and beliefs with personal stories that were authentic and heartfelt. This allowed everyone to openly express their concerns and misgivings and established trust to inclusively develop winning strategies. The most significant and profound insight we all recognized was that "we have a common thread and a noble purpose to build a great bank by treating each other with respect and inspiring each other to be the best we can be." For many executives this was an unexpressed and unfulfilled dream. The by-product of this right action will be excellent products and services, exceptional customer care, and outstanding profitability. Everyone felt that we established a strong foundation to create that unique billion-dollar bank by

combining the best of both organizations. We confirmed that we were all bound by a burning passion to take this purposeful journey and resolved to consistently engage in right action.

Once the tide turned, we seized the opportunity to accelerate the momentum, teach best practices, and infuse excellence into the DNA of the bank. We invited the most passionate and obviously enthusiastic executives committed to change and opened it up for anyone else interested to join. We called this group the Culture Council—the members of this group were the culture ambassadors, change agents, and role models. This team agreed to go through a systematic, structured, and methodical training to build and track a high-trust and high-performance environment similar to PCB and CBC. The focus of this training was to

- Learn cutting-edge practices that can be applied immediately to improve personal and professional effectiveness in business and in life;
- Review, customize, and implement disciplines followed by exceptional teams and outstanding organizations to avoid the plight of traditional bottom line-driven companies that suffer from low trust, poor engagement, and high stress;
- Complete pragmatic short modules on key topics such as conflict resolution and win-win negotiation, and leadership effectiveness: shifting from motivation to inspiration, authentic communication, and deep listening;
- Role-play, practice, and resolve real life business and organizational challenges to gain maximum impact.

Members of the Culture Council learn, demonstrate, and later teach how to conduct our business in line with the stated vision and shared values. In addition, we coach and mentor leaders that are willing to push the envelope and accelerate their pursuit of personal and organizational mastery.

Now hope has translated to concrete results. Morale is up, the leadership team is more aligned, and engagement is on the rise. By focusing on culture and human capital innovation, along with revenue enhancement and expense management, we accomplished a dramatic turnaround.

Our chairman of the board, Paul Folino, is a former CEO and a seasoned corporate executive who has been a part of numerous mergers, acquisitions, and transformation projects. He said to Ash, "I have seen many successful turnarounds, but never have I witnessed two companies being turned around simultaneously." A transformation of this complexity and magnitude had not happened in the history of banking.

One of the keys to success is to recognize that the unique challenges we are facing today will require us to think and act differently than we have traditionally. We work hard to integrate two basic aspects of human nature:

- **Self-Interest:** We are driven by self-interest and have a fundamental desire for autonomy and a self-centered drive to grow and achieve.

- **Altruistic Connection:** We are social beings who yearn for connection, and we are also altruistically driven to serve, to contribute, and to make a difference.

We can no longer afford to separate these two vital aspects of human nature and assume that it is self-interest alone that drives business performance. We have to nurture an environment so that both needs have an opportunity to flourish and serve self, team, and the organization. It is natural and expected for each stakeholder to focus first on their self-interest and primary goal:

- Employees crave respect, recognition, autonomy, fairness, and an opportunity to grow and unleash their full creative potential.
- Managers and leaders seek to be involved and engaged in setting the direction, key strategies, goals, and prioritizing implementation steps.
- Customers need and want product and service offerings that make their business and life more productive.
- Investors pursue solid returns and consistency.
- Communities wish for a responsible and involved bank.

Fulfilling the Promise ... Achieving the Dream

With Ash and the bank we achieved exceptional results and laid the foundation for the next phase. There is work to be done in our march to becoming a 3.0 transformative organization, a unique bank the likes of which no one has ever seen. A couple of concerns we are addressing now:

We set high expectations for the board without explaining to them what's involved. To use a football metaphor, we took a 2-14 team and achieved a 11-5 record too soon, without taking the time to establish a solid foundation. This set an unrealistic expectation for a 14-2 season and Super Bowl championship. Consequently, the executive team did not take the time necessary to master 3.0 skills and practices, but that is changing day by day.

Ash himself is now ready to shift from a hard-driving entrepreneurial leader to a visionary and empathetic facilitator who will mentor and coach and nurture. One key trigger was an article he had read about Microsoft's remarkable turnaround (with an eye-popping $250 billion in market value gains in less than four years), engineered by new CEO Satya Nadella. As the article explained, that came about by emphasizing collaboration and what Nadella calls a "learn-it-all" culture versus the company's historical "know-it-all" attitude.

Once Ash had fully absorbed the import of this approach, he held a momentous "breakthrough" executive meeting. We started the meeting with two inspirational videos—one of Apple's iconic "Think Different" ads, and a powerful TED talk on having a meaning in life. Ash then explained that his actions often had not matched his words— that he had been following a "command and control" approach, and going forward intended to truly empower and inspire by actions.

"I want to learn the art of coaching and mentoring and become a 3.0 leader," he said, promising that he would be "present" and respect everyone's viewpoint and time. He shared his vision of creating a bank where we help one another become the best version of ourselves. Grown men and women got emotional, some had tears and everyone was inspired.

Two weeks later, Ash followed up with the following email to everyone in the bank:

To all,

We hear you ...

We received your responses to the most recent survey question: "How authentically do you feel we live our cultural values?" And also the one before that: "What's your favorite cultural value of our organization?"

Your responses are clear and consistent: That senior management including the CEO does not practice the cultural values, there is negative tension in the company, there is no work-life balance, etc.

The successes we achieved from 2013 to 2017 are all due to the hard work and dedication of our staff. We doubled profits and achieved double digit growth every year. While we should all be very proud of this achievement, I realize that it has come at a personal cost to everyone in our bank.

We are committed to transitioning to a purposeful and passionate company. We need your help! Let us all work together too: So we make a commitment, and we will need ALL your help to assist us in transitioning our bank to the following:

- Move from a command and control to an inspire and empower bank
- Move from a "know it all" to a "learn it all" bank
- Understand "why" we exist and define the "purpose" of our bank
- Practice and demonstrate more "empathy"

We are a team, and we want to learn from our mistakes, starting with me. Please "help me" become the leader you all want me to become so I can practice what I preach. This applies to the leadership team as well.

In 2018, we will introduce more work-life balance, allow more time for personal growth, and provide opportunities to pursue your passion and ultimately create a purposeful bank.

Thank you, from a learning President/CEO

Following is a sampling of the immediate responses:

"What a heartfelt, sincere and passionate email. So inspiring. Thank you for your humility and grace. You have taught all of us something in this and inspired us to improve ourselves. I was very touched by this message. Extremely so. As for you as a leader—I have seen a change in you that has inspired me to further improve myself."

"Awesome message, Ash. Very well thought out. There is a sincerity in your words and I know our staff can say and feel the same. Thank you for helping me to be a better me each day. Well said and thank you for hearing. It's why so many people love you."

As I told Ash, "When you know what you want and take the right action, the world will conspire to make it happen for you."

It is our job to create a high-trust and high-performance environment so that individual self-interest, along with the yearning to contribute and make a difference converge in service of the larger shared vision and values. A CEO is a steward of this sacred responsibility. This responsibility is a blessing when there is leadership alignment and employee engagement. The same responsibility can feel like a burden when there isn't the collaboration and mutual accountability.

Ash is determined to pursue this path of stewardship, and he is self-aware enough to understand the gap he needs to bridge to fulfill this lofty role. As his partner and trusted hands-on advisor, I offer the necessary tools and practices to make this journey productive, effective, and fulfilling. This is a journey that you can follow as well.

PART II: Practical Steps to CEO Mastery

Practice 1: Master Human Motivations

"The greatest ability in business is to get along with others and influence their actions." — John Hancock

How badly do you want to pursue greatness? You can achieve financial success with deep functional expertise, a solid work ethic, strong intellect, and good strategic skills. These traditional capabilities are necessary, but are not sufficient to unlock the full value of your organization or to excel in today's hyper-competitive environment of higher expectations. Achieving these require a deep understanding of human emotions, along with a high emotional quotient (EQ) and mastery of human motivations and potential—a high spiritual quotient (SQ). These self-actualized skills are critical to bringing out the best of everyone in your organization.

Business organizations are made up of people who have intellect, emotion, and spirit. As a society, we have traditionally focused on intellect at the expense of emotion and spirit at work. Businesses have been slow to adopt peak performance principles and practices. The science of human motivation and inspiration have not been well integrated with business functions in a way to impact the bottom line. Wellness programs such as meditation are treated as stress-reduction exercises, but the more direct business benefits of personal and organizational effectiveness have not been grasped and implemented.

Can we afford to ignore aspects of our being and continue that way? Since it is critical for people to work well together, we need to understand the elements of what it takes for us to be collaborative. What do we respond to? How can we connect well and inspire each other to give our very best? How can we create an environment that allows us to nurture our innate capabilities and unlock the unique greatness that we are capable of, in service of the organizational vision?

Ultimately, a mindset based on mastery of human emotions and motivations is necessary to thrive in the challenging environment of business. This mindset is the key to building trust and overcoming some of the hardest challenges involving people.

This practice works on how your personal state of awareness can affect individual, team, and organizational performance. It is based on a practical model that incorporates and expands on the hierarchy of human motivations, clarifying why business organizations should pay attention to mastering human nature and nurturing human potential.

A New Level of Inspiration

Ed owns a fairly large private enterprise. When I asked him about his personal vision for life, he told me that he wants to make a significant difference in the world by creating decent jobs in a caring work environment for thousands of people. What was most fascinating about his response was when he said that he wanted to do that while remaining anonymous. I asked him why, and he said he didn't want ego to get in the way of achieving great stuff. He went on to explain that business people and politicians are all about attention, ego, and power. They're not really making a difference when they are focused on themselves, he said.

I had an issue with that blanket statement because I do not think it is valid or accurate to generalize about a whole group of people in a profession or an ethnicity. However, I fully understood the part about ego getting in the way at a certain level.

Ed also believed that to make money and be really successful in business, you have to be manipulative and driven by self-interest. I actually get that sentiment from a lot of business people. They feel stuck. They want to be successful, they want to make money, and they want to grow the business, but they feel like the only way to do that is by pursuing a path of self-centered achievement where a large, dominant ego is critical for achievement in a dog-eat-dog world.

"I understand where you're coming from," I told him, "but you don't have to approach leadership success in that way." Especially now in the last few years, and going forward, there is a tremendous opportunity to achieve success as a self-actualized business leader and direct an operation like that. Mastering human motivations begins with belief that you can do that.

Another leader, Tim, runs a fast-growing, private consulting firm. When we first met, he was going through a lot of stress, coupled with his belief that to be successful in business, you have to sell your soul. He was really struggling, having a midlife crisis, fighting depression, and taking medication. Meeting every week for two years, I talked with Tim about forgiveness and gratitude and how that would help in being more present and more assertive with his partners and more successful in the way he led his business organization.

Eventually, he experienced a remarkable turnaround. After a lot of one-on-one work and guided introspection, Tim began to better understand human nature, and that, you don't need to sell your soul to be successful. You can be a good, self-actualized human being and inspire people through purpose and understanding.

Here's the core secret of achieving organizational success through mastering human nature: There's a difference between simply motivating and *inspiring*. You have to understand what makes people tick; what inspires them. That ability to inspire others begins within yourself. This approach has worked with Ed, Tim, Ash Patel, and many others with whom I've worked, allowing them to positively evolve the culture in their organizations.

What Makes Inspirational Leadership?

I start many of my leadership presentations by asking the audience, "What comes to mind when you think of the characteristics of great leaders?" The answers often include someone who:

- Is authentic
- Has integrity
- Has courage

- Has a clear mission
- Has vision; is inspiring
- Is humble
- Is a great teacher and mentor
- Has presence
- Is open-minded and open-hearted
- Is passionate, compassionate, persistent, patient, and values-driven
- Is committed to serving others, and
- Is forgiving, generous, centered, kind, loving, calm, and caring

Are these characteristics evident in your business environment? If not, why not? What is stopping leaders from demonstrating these characteristics at work? Doesn't this behavior enhance engagement, innovation, collaboration, and alignment, and thus improve the bottom line? Why is it that so many professionals don't freely demonstrate these qualities at work?

Purpose and Passion: Three Key Questions

Business execution, leadership effectiveness, and pursuit of a purposeful life are compatible. But the steps required to reach that integrative, highest level of conscious leadership have remained elusive: They require a deep inner exploration of mastery. You first start with being inspired, but that is not enough. You also have to inspire the organization by providing inspirational leadership. Consider the following:

- Why are qualities and characteristics associated with inspirational leadership not widely and regularly demonstrated at work?
- How can you show up fully—intellectually, emotionally, and spiritually—at work like you do in your personal, social, and spiritual life?
- How can you live life to the fullest, as defined by being present and alive with high energy and enthusiasm during your waking hours?

Aren't these the questions we all have? Isn't this our common journey? In working with multiple organizations and people from all backgrounds, I discovered that we all have the same innate yearning; we may simply be at different stages in this journey in our desire and capacity to give expression to that drive.

Can you truly be purposeful without mastering your emotions and yourself? Peter Senge, author of *The Fifth Discipline*, defines personal mastery as "continually learning how to see current reality more clearly." I like to up the ante and define it as the ability to translate noble intentions to consistent and impactful actions both by oneself and through the organization. Leadership is therefore a journey of mastery.

At a higher 3.0 state of awakening, we are fully focused on the present. We no longer look back or forward. We don't lament the past or fear the future.

Decoding the Black Box of Conscious Leadership

Bestselling author Jim Collins, in his book, *Good to Great*, discusses the highest level of conscious, or enlightened, leadership. He beautifully describes the characteristics of leaders at that level but admits he had no specific steps to suggest how to get there. He said somewhat facetiously that there are three possible ways: Change your genes by changing your parents, religious conversion, or near-death experience. I was not willing to leave it at that and looked everywhere for answers on practical how-to steps to become a more conscious leader.

The task seemed endless and daunting. It certainly helped that I carried many of the Type-A characteristics—the good, bad, and the ugly—of a typical modern professional. Fortunately, I knew from a young age that these predominantly masculine characteristics had to be balanced with the nurturing, inclusive feminine traits for me to be more effective.

I researched some of the best and seminal works in business execution, strategy, leadership, and organizational effectiveness. My quest to find answers to these questions took me on an intense journey of inner and outer exploration for more than 20 years. These answers are also the key to decoding the black box of conscious leadership. My exploration surfaced four major themes:

1. The two sets of questions which reflect two critical aspects of our whole life cannot be artificially separated. The pursuits of business and life have to be integrated.

2. We are on the cusp of a socioeconomic transformation which makes this integration now possible, unlike in the past.

3. We have to overcome some deeply entrenched personal and systemic obstacles to make this integration and transformation happen. For example: A personal obstacle is the inability to accept and address our limitations without feeling limited and insecure. A systemic obstacle is our use of outdated systems and structures that are based on a self-centered, carrot-and-stick approach to motivating growth and performance.

4. Some of the best and brightest business leaders and organizations are making this transformation. The practices that lead them to greatness combine advanced human potential and mastery techniques with superior business practices and cutting-edge work in neural science.

Mastery and Inspired Action

Mastery is a mindset or a state of being. It is the ability to demonstrate some of the toughest things, such as being truly transparent and authentic, detaching from wanting to be right, and accepting criticism and praise evenly. Our mindset determines our thoughts, and the nature of our thoughts determine where we are in our personal evolution or development. Mastery is converting your greatest and deepest intentions to consistent and impactful actions. Our mindset evolution can be described in three levels:

1.0 Mindset of Survival and Security: The primary concern, fear, or anxiety is about comfortable living and security. These fears are mostly unconscious. This state is characterized by a denial and unconsciousness of fears and anxieties.

2.0 Mindset of Self-Centered Achievement: The predominant concern in this state is about money, power, success, status, recognition and achievement. There is some awareness, sporadically we "know" and admit to our fears.

3.0 Mindset of Self-Actualized Mastery: This is a "know"-fear zone. We are fully aware of and easily accept our fears, concerns, and anxieties. For the most part, we operate without any fears or anxieties. We give full expression to our highest dreams, deepest yearnings, and are driven to contribute, to serve, and to make a difference. Purpose and meaning is important in our career and in anything we undertake.

Until you start operating in a predominantly 3.0 state, the talk of meaning, purpose, values and making a difference is just that. There may be intent but that has not been translated to consistent action and practical impact. When you are operating in 3.0, everything changes—the way you show up personally and the way you lead the organization. The way you communicate, make decisions, conduct meetings, develop and execute strategies, evaluate people and performance, compensate, reward and incentivize.

Our intrinsic beliefs and values fuel our conscious and subconscious thoughts that in turn drive our behaviors and actions. Many of our actions are automatic responses to situations. Sometimes the responses don't come out the way we intended them to or are not received the way they were supposed to be. We are unpleasantly surprised by the unintended consequences. Wouldn't it be nice to have more control over our behavior and consciously continue or change our behavior? Of course it would, and yet as we all know, behavior change is one of the most difficult aspects of human life.

No wonder many professionals and leaders in business organizations act as if behavior change is not possible. We can't blame them either, because that seems like the practical thing to do. It doesn't have to be that way. As human beings we have enormous innate capacity for change and transformation. The trick is to unleash that latent capacity. This is critical to achieve exceptional teamwork and organizational greatness. Besides, how can we pursue and achieve organizational transformation without personal change? By understanding and intervening at the source of our behavior, we significantly enhance the likelihood of change in our behavior and actions.

This requires a deeper understanding of human nature. For example: How can you be courageous in your actions? Courage is not absence of fear but knowing your blocks and fears. What is personal change and growth? It is the ability to address your limitations without feeling limited. This is the essence of wisdom and personal mastery. Since the goal of understanding the states of being and mindsets is to be in a state of inspired action and to achieve exceptional results, we are naming them appropriately.

A sign of progress in mastery is positive behavior change. The best, fastest, and most effective way to change behavior is to work at the source of behavior, e.g., the mindset. Your being and mindset drive behavior.

Living in a state of inspired action, independent of external circumstances, is what human beings have aspired to since the dawn of creation. Is there anything more important than this characteristic for a business leader, CEO, or a corporate executive who is constantly pulled in different directions by various constituents of the business, and is frequently faced with "right versus right" choices?

The following mindsets and the respective outcomes are the pillars of mastery and the key to living a self-actualized and inspired life.

- **Accountability**–Outcome: Inspired in right action

- **Humility**–Outcome: Pursuing the right solution over the need to "be right"

- **Presence**–Outcome: Exhibiting freedom in action, detached from outcome

- **Gratitude**–Outcome: Always giving your very best

- **Courage** – Outcome: Remaining truly transparent, authentic, and vulnerable
- **Self-Esteem** – Outcome: Exhibiting composed equanimity in criticism and praise
- **Integrative** – Outcome: Being completely inclusive, fair, and objective

Mindset: (Innate) Accountability. Outcome: Inspired in Right Action

Accountability is the state or ability to take personal accountability for every situation that life or business presents to us. We do not want to play victim and blame external circumstances for our less than satisfactory condition or poor performance. We take unconditional responsibility for our situation, however terrible it may be. We refuse to blame external people or events, as some of the statements below demonstrate.

- **Q.** Why are you below budget? **A.** Because our customers are crazy and easily switch loyalties.
- **Q.** Why is your income steadily going down for the past two years? **A.** Because of economic conditions, the market is awful, competition is cut throat, and the policies of this government are only making it worse.
- **Q.** Why is your organization not among the elite performers? **A.** They just got lucky, they are not very honest. Trust me. We work harder than they do.
- **Q.** Why is employee engagement so low? **A.** It is no big deal, it has always been that way and there is nothing we can do to change that. It is because of the greedy businessmen or those rich guys on Wall Street.
- **Q.** Why are we so anxious and worried in our country? **A.** It is because of the selfish politicians. They don't get anything done and are ruining our country. The world is a terrible place and people are becoming more violent and intolerant. What can I do? We can't tackle a messy system.

The list goes on. The point is that some of those statements may be true and factual, but a mindset that does not invoke our innate accountability is always looking to play victim and give excuses. Fred Kofman explained mental models in his book, *Conscious Business*. When we play victim, we are saying, "Don't blame me, I am innocent." As Fred says, "Playing victim is like a feel-good drug, we want to be perceived as innocent, being absolved of blame. However, it also makes us powerless, that's the price we pay."

Why do we avoid taking ownership and not engage in right action? At lower states of operation, we choose short-term pleasure over long-term gain, move toward comfort away from pain, and use the least amount of energy we can. We avoid taking ownership by denying the problem exists, saying we can do nothing about it, and blaming the problem on someone else.

Personal mastery is about taking charge, taking action, and becoming a warrior dealing with the circumstances instead of becoming a victim of circumstances. This means being an active player in the game of life instead of being a spectator watching and critiquing, not involved in the change we want to see. Below are some examples of the warrior mindset.

- Viktor Frankl found a way to stay amazingly positive and feel purposeful as an inmate in the dreaded Auschwitz concentration camp during World War II. His sense of personal accountability was so phenomenal that, in spite of being daily subjected to horrific and inhumane conditions, he refused to be stripped of his self-esteem. He made an unbelievable observation in those conditions—he said that he found there were good Nazis and bad prisoners.
- Nelson Mandela and Mahatma Gandhi's remarkable and peaceful fights for freedom are well documented.
- Allan Mulally engineered a dramatic turnaround of Ford Motor Company by inspiring his executives to speak the truth about business conditions and take personal accountability to fix the situation.

- Steve Jobs did not waste time playing victim when he got ousted from the company he co-founded. Instead he got busy building new businesses and came back stronger and rejuvenated the Apple computer.

You may be a warrior in your intent, but how often are you a warrior in your actions? When you are operating from this state, you tackle complex issues and serious challenges with self-confidence and self-assurance knowing fully well that the outcome is not guaranteed. When you are grateful for what you have, you accept your limitations without feeling limited and accept the limitations of others. By accepting who you are, you will loosen and release the grip of judgment that gets in the way of giving your best. Suffering and forgiveness, anger and gratitude, fear and passion cannot co-exist.

Below are examples of how a person with a player or warrior mindset might respond to challenging questions.

- **Q.** Why are you not being a team player? **A.** It is difficult to be a team player in this environment. I will try harder and set an example.

- **Q.** Why are you so stressed? **A.** I am allowing the stress of the environment to get to me. I need to develop a stronger inner core.

- **Q.** Why were you late with the report? **A.** I didn't realize until much later that I was not given enough information.

- **Q.** Why did we lose the client? **A.** It was a combination of unreasonable expectations from the client and our inability to offer compelling alternatives.

Even though we do not have direct control over the circumstances and outcomes, we can still derive immense power by doing our part—responding immediately and softening the blow. We can learn from this situation and do our best in preventing the same problem from occurring again. This is an innate accountability mindset where we are inspired to perform right action under all circumstances.

Humility: Overcoming the Need to Be Right

To be truly and consistently humble in thought, speech, and action is one of the most difficult things to do. If we showed up in this state, we wouldn't have the perennial conflicts and unresolved differences of opinion at a micro level in a business organization and at a macro level in our country. One of the hot topics and areas of concern today is the divided nation we have become and the inability of Congress to come up with right solutions to pressing challenges such as health care and economic prosperity, with a comfortable standard of living for all. What is the root cause? It is certainly not the lack of will, intellectual horsepower, or work ethic.

What is missing, and therefore the root cause, is to overcome the need to be right. A right solution cannot be achieved if you believe your approach is right and the other one does not have any merit. Instead, the approach to take is, "Your perspective does not match mine, but both may be equally valid, reasonable, and rational. Neither of us has a lock on truth—maybe there are multiple partial truths. Let's discuss further and determine what makes sense."

Humility comes from the wisdom to derive your self-esteem from finding the right solution and not from being right.

Some hard-driving personalities tend to brush off opinions of people who display a lot of emotion. However, as Pascal said, "The heart has its reasons of which reason knows nothing." You may notice that these people do not even have the patience, respect, or humility to listen to and acknowledge others' perspectives. How on earth can the right solution be arrived at? This is not because people intend to disrespect or ridicule; their poor attitude comes from not having developed emotionally.

In a business organization, achieving humility is not as challenging or complex as it is in politics; however, it is still a major underlying issue that gets in the way of engagement, productivity, and effective decision-making. There are several crucial areas that can make or break an organization:

- Do we focus on revenue growth or profitability?
- Do we cut expenses or invest in resources?
- Do we hire more sales people or pay the exceptional producers more?
- Which products or services do we prioritize?

I have been in numerous executive meetings and planning sessions where just respecting a different perspective without agreeing goes a long way toward making exceptional decisions, rapidly implementing them, and building enormous trust.

The quality of the output and decisions in such sessions boils down to one aspect: humility and the ability to arrive at a right solution. The best leaders and leadership teams give air time to all reasonable, and even out-of-the-box crazy opinions, by demonstrating and establishing an environment of humility. This has two significant benefits. First, having tapped into the collective intelligence of the group, you make the best possible decision. Second, the chances of successful implementation are much higher because everyone feels heard, and reasonable folks get on board even if their opinion or decision was not the final one.

Being humble requires us to operate in 3.0 state. In other states, the intention may be there but noble intent to practical impact are missing. In typical hierarchical organizations, the boss wields a lot of inherent power and authority. Leaders tend to have a dominating, hard-driving personality anyway. In order to have an open and honest conversation, I encourage and conduct role-play sessions for the boss to demonstrate "humility" and his or her subordinate to exhibit "courage."

We all have perspectives and opinions about almost everything that matters to us. These are the mental models that shape our thoughts and actions and are based on our nature, background, and experience. For example, I grew up in a diverse multi-religious, multiethnic environment with strong women role models. As a result, inclusion, objectivity, and thriving in diversity come naturally to me. However, I was also overly sensitive and critical of authoritarian leadership and have now overcome that hypersensitivity and judgment. This enabled me to recognize that effective leadership includes tough love and artfully balancing directive and facilitative leadership as the situation demands.

Jean Piaget proved in his famous cognitive development experiment (involving a wooden block with a green side and a red side) that typical five-year-olds cannot recognize and appreciate a side that they or, can't see, although someone else does. This is funny with children but is disastrous when we have five-year-olds with thirty, forty, and fifty or more years of experience in leadership positions.

It is dangerous when we treat our opinions as facts. Consider these real-life examples:

- Aariz, the CEO of a media company, has an open door policy. Loren, a longtime customer service employee walks into his office and informs him about a customer complaint directed against two departments. Aariz is furious and fires off an email to both departments directing them to get to the bottom of the issue and resolve it immediately. Allan and Linda, the recipients of the email, feel unfairly attacked without being given the benefit of their perspectives. A thorough due diligence is conducted, and it is discovered that this customer has a track record of being difficult. There was also a lost opportunity for the company to proactively defuse the situation. However, the damage had been done. The CEO and his two senior executives could have demonstrated more humility in finding the right solution instead of reacting. Aariz could have politely discussed the situation with Alan and Linda before passing judgment about their incompetence. Allan and Linda could have not taken the inquiry from Aariz personally and understood his intent behind the passion. They judged him and could have been humbler.

- Sofia, a senior executive at a financial institution, complained that her older colleague, John, doesn't take her seriously and never listens to her ideas. She added, "I have faced this situation all my life." I know both of them well and can categorically say that while John has other issues to deal with, not listening to and disrespecting a younger woman's ideas is not one of his challenges. In this case, Sofia made an incorrect assumption based on her past experience. She did not test her assumption— instead of being curious, she was certain and did not demonstrate humility.

Following are examples of a hubris versus a humility mindset.

- You make no sense. / I don't understand what you are saying.
- Define goals unilaterally. / Define goals collaboratively.
- Manipulate information. / Be transparent with information.
- Use external motivation. / Utilize intrinsic inspiration.
- Suppress feelings. / Work with and integrate feelings.

Hubris	Humility
Says, "You make no sense."	Says, "I don't understand what you're saying."
Defines goals unilaterally	Defines goals collaboratively
Manipulates information	Is transparent with information
Uses external motivation	Utilizes inspiration
Suppresses feelings	Works with and integrates feelings

Humility comes from the wisdom to derive your self-esteem from finding the right solution and not from being right.

Courage: Being Truly Transparent, Authentic, and Vulnerable

Courage is synonymous with leadership. It is a minimum require-ment for effective leadership and for unlocking your greatness poten-tial. Dealing with difficult situations and tough challenges is a normal day's work for a leader. Adversity, the way it is commonly described, is a constant companion for a leader.

Great and effective leaders thrive under adversity. It brings out the best in them. Outstanding examples of courage: Mahatma Gandhi and Nelson Mandela for freedom, Abe Lincoln for abolition of slavery, and Martin Luther King, Jr., for civil rights. These noble souls demonstrated that great leaders are willing to stake their reputations and even their lives on what they believe in. They were fighting for the fundamental beliefs, principles, and values more than the outcome itself. In doing so, they went against the grain of conventional wisdom and faced constant opposition, criticism, and cynicism. They needed courage to overcome such powerful negative forces. They were willing to perish, as many do, in the process.

To build a 3.0 high-trust and high-performance organization, you will need to go against the grain of conventional business wisdom. Following are some of the beliefs and drivers of a typical 2.0 leader:

- The primary purpose of business is to make a profit.
- Self-interest, fear, and survival instinct drive performance.
- Stress is an unavoidable by-product, and even necessary, to get work done.
- Shareholder return is top priority. Our primary obligation is to shareholders, we don't have to go out of our way to please other stakeholders.
- Large profits and strong returns take care of all other stakeholders—employees, customers, suppliers, and community.
- Culture is primarily about feeling good. It is okay to invest time, money and effort only as long as it does not come in the way of performance.
- Operating at higher states of awakening is good for personal development but it is not directly connected to running a profitable business.

Asserting our truth and perspective in the face of entrenched beliefs takes an enormous amount of courage. This becomes even more daunting when we have been repeatedly reprimanded in poorly run, autocratic, and political companies where covering up your weaknesses and amplifying strengths is modus operandi for survival. We cannot be like the huge circus elephant that is tied with a rope to a small pole—it does not breakaway because it tried many times before as a youngster and now believes that he can never be free.

Success is achieved by focusing on our strengths, but greatness requires us to overcome our biggest weakness.

In the situation earlier involving Aariz the CEO, his key executives, Linda and Allan had an opportunity to step up and express to him how they felt about his approach. They could have courageously and constructively shared that they would have felt a lot better, and the process would have been much more productive, if Aariz had asked for their input before assuming the worst regarding the customer complaint. When another incident cropped up among the three of them, I took the opportunity to push the envelope.

Aariz, Linda, and Allan are all part of a growing organization. They all have many things in common. They are highly skilled in their professional craft and have enormous stamina for working long and hard. However, they do not have the experience of leading a $1 billion organization. They are entrepreneurial and hands-on but not yet adept in organizing, delegating, empowering, and holding people accountable. Aariz gets frustrated with Allan and Linda but does not have a solution for them and even makes his own similar mistakes.

The more upset we are about someone's mistake, the higher the chances are that we will commit the same or similar mistake.

Aariz is rightly concerned that Allan and Linda are not getting the most out of their people. They are doing most of the critical work themselves, not training and not delegating and, in some cases, tolerating missed deadlines and commitments. Aariz's solution is for them to spend time with their respective teams in order to understand each employee's job description and why they feel so overwhelmed. Both Allan and Linda confided to me that Aariz's action made them defensive, undermined their authority, and sent mixed message to their employees. I suggested the following process to deal with the micromanagement challenge from Aariz:

1. Acknowledge the problem and commit to doing better.

2. Appreciate the intent behind Aariz's suggestion, and let him know that his approach makes the situation worse because it
   a. makes me defensive
   b. undermines my authority, and
   c. sends mixed message to my troops.

3. Commit to presenting a solution to Aariz for his review and approval by a reasonable date.

Their immediate reaction was, "He won't go for it, we already tried that." My reaction was, "Did you really? How did you that? How were you feeling inside? How are you feeling now as you think about that situation? Is there fear or anger or judgment? How can you expect to deliver a powerful and authentic message when you are not fully free from fear and judgment? There are no guarantees that you will achieve the desired outcome when you do so. However, the chances of realizing that outcome will be much higher, and more importantly, you will be content in the feeling that you have truly given it your best shot." They were now fully on board.

We then had several practice sessions where I alternately took their and Ariz's position in this mock conversation to help them with the delivery. I also had them practice with each other until they got comfortable. The results were remarkable. Allan and Linda became more self-assured and confident. They inspired the team to step up and perform at a higher level. Ariz was pleasantly surprised and very appreciative of the shift. We shared this case study with the other senior executives, many of whom were visibly excited and committed to follow their lead.

There is a school of thought (I would say it's old school) that a leader's job is to not let them see him or her sweat. This approach does not work if you want to be a 3.0 leader and build a 3.0 organization. In such an environment, you cannot fool people. They can see through the façade and view you as disingenuous and untrustworthy. If you are anxious or worried about a serious challenge, you are much better off saying, "I am concerned but I am confident that we will find a solution." It requires courage to be transparent, authentic, and vulnerable. Courage is not absence of fear or worry; it is the ability to accept, own, and express your fears, worries, and blocks. None of us are perfect; greatness and being a 3.0 leader is not absence of limitations, but accepting and acknowledging our limitations without feeling limited. Ash (see "Taking the CEO Mastery Journey") is really good with this. He leads by example, owns up to his personal challenges, and inspires his people to do the same.

Courage and humility go hand-in-hand. They reinforce each other to instill self-confidence. Courage without humility is hubris or arrogance and humility without courage is weak and ineffective.

Integrative: Nurturing Fairness and Meritocracy

Growing up in India, I was fascinated by the oft encountered phrase *Vasudhaiva Kutumbakam*, which means "the world is one family." It sounds wonderful, but how many of us can truly rise above our narrow, superficial identifications and see the truth that we are all similar underneath and come from the same source. Sociologists and developmental psychologists have identified different levels of consciousness to which we evolve: ego or self-centric, ethnocentric, and world-centric and beyond. (Read Ken Wilber's *Integral Theory* for a comprehensive description of stages of personal development and consciousness.) A borderless world, global trading, and world peace are good intentions but are pithy, toothless statements unless we have risen to a higher level of awakening.

In any organization, especially a business organization, people are excited, engaged, and give their best when they are treated fairly, evaluated objectively, and rewarded appropriately by nurturing and instilling meritocracy. In such an environment, we are not bogged down by personal relationships, connections, obligations, and attachments. These factors are hard to overcome. The famously hard driving poster boy of the shareholder-return mantra, Jack Welch, was nicknamed "neutron Jack" for his ability to quickly terminate poor performers. He, however, felt that he was not fast enough and allowed his personal feelings to come in the way.

I am not suggesting that you should not have feelings and emotions of compassion and empathy. There is an abundance of that in 3.0 leaders; however, they are directed toward building an exceptionally purposeful and profitable organization. I remind the CEOs and leaders I advise to stay loyal to the mission and be objective with people. Some executives who excelled before may not be operating at the same level now. You have to directly, constructively, and objectively evaluate them and encourage them to course correct and excel.

Completely involving and engaging everyone in key decisions and processes does wonders in enhancing performance and establishing an owner mindset in your employees. Imagine the power when every employee feels and acts like they own the company. This is the Holy Grail; everyone is in charge of shaping the collective destiny of the organization.

This is my advice to directive leaders who are used to giving instructions and having all the answers. You don't have to, and won't lose your edge and you don't become passive by tapping into the collective intelligence and facilitating the best solution. As the situation demands, you can facilitate or direct and take strategy execution and performance to the next level. What got you here alone won't get you there—Ash (see "Taking the CEO Mastery Journey") is making this shift in journey from a successful banker to building an extraordinary and transformative high-trust and high-performance bank.

Presence: Focusing on "Now" without Distractions

"If you are depressed, you are living in the past. If you are anxious, you are living in the future. If you are at peace, you are living in the present."—Lao Tzu

The mindset or state of being present is the ability to be fully immersed in the present moment, focused on the process now, and unburdened by the expectation of a particular outcome. This does not mean you are not interested in setting goals and achieving exceptional results. It simply means that you are not distracted by these lofty goals. You set audacious goals and become attached to action detached from results. There is freedom and power in such an action.

Business organizations such as Decurion Corporation, Next Jump Inc., Bridgewater Associates, Barry-Wehmiller, AES (Applied Energy Services), Morning Star, Sun Hydraulics, Valve, and many others are adopting this peak performance principle to achieve exceptional results. Some of these cutting-edge companies go so far as to not set quarterly goals and are focused instead on execution. Why cap growth by setting goals that limit us? They believe intrinsic inspiration delivers better results than external motivators. It's like the great Zen archer who suddenly started losing. His master reminded him that he was thinking too much of winning, and to only focus on doing his best. Meeting or even exceeding a goal does not tell us if we gave our best! Giving our best may not result in winning or meeting unreasonably high expectations either!

When you are present, you achieve what I call *real-time success*. Your values are in alignment with your behavior and you live in integrity. Real-time success is immediate, unconditional, and guaranteed. You have control over your actions alone and not the result. Doesn't it make sense to focus on the now and present? Carl Ripken Jr., the hall of fame baseball player, showed up to work every day and gave his best. In doing so, he achieved real-time success and traditional success, received several external accolades such as the highest number of consecutive games ever played, was a 19-time All Star, and was twice the American League Most Valuable Player (MVP).

When your actions become an expression of your deepest values and your highest self, you achieve a level of presence and freedom that is untied to particular outcomes. You act for the sake of expressing your highest purpose, for the sake of the highest good. You are not tempted by short-term gain, but you have an unshakeable commitment to excellence and long-term greatness. You have the outlook of a winner and maintain your dignity and the self-satisfaction of giving your best. You are no longer encumbered by a desire to please others or have the scarcity mentality of "winner takes all."

A presence mindset also helps you overcome the modern "when/ then" malaise, which basically says: I refuse to live fully, be myself and have fun...until evening, weekend, next year, after my child's graduation, after my retirement, after I own that house, car ... I will celebrate after I reach that goal and be miserable in the meantime because it is worth the sacrifice ... you get the point!

Being present requires us to let go of the past and be confident of the future. The ability to be in the moment and not be burdened by the thoughts of past and future is difficult and inspiring. We all have a past with our share of joys, disappointments and traumas, and we all have a future that is hopeful, scary, uncertain and ambiguous.

As I have noted, the things that are most important to us in our practical lives are good health, loving relationships, financial stability, and a satisfactory career. It is unlikely that all of these are in harmony all the time. If you are lucky, you may experience harmony for a short time; even then, there would be someone you love dearly who is facing a crisis in one or more of these areas.

Many of the fears and concerns we have about the future may never come to pass. "My life has been full of terrible misfortunes most of which never happened," wrote the sixteenth century philosopher Michel de Montaigne. Similarly, Mark Twain once lamented, "I've had a lot of worries in my life, most of which never happened."

You can be confident of the future if it is positive and certain. But that is unrealistic; no one can guarantee a positive and certain future. So, how can you be confident of your future without knowing what it holds? This is possible only if you are detached from the outcome. When you take that stance, you overcome fear, anxiety, and worry. This state of joyful existence is independent of external circumstances, as many great souls have proven time and again in the history of human existence.

It is foolish to expect and hope for a life free of difficulties. Great leaders and master CEOs develop the ability to be unaffected and detached from crises. Even the most catastrophic events imaginable, including death, do not sway a person in this state. Imagine the power and effectiveness of such a CEO.

It is not the absence of difficulties, but the ability to accept, embrace, and navigate complex challenges that makes a person resilient and joyful.

Intellectual knowledge, while useful, will not rid you of your conscious and subconscious negative thoughts regarding the past and future. Scientists say that humans have 60,000 thoughts per day, and about 80 percent of them are mundane and repetitive. Brooding over past disappointments will not resolve the issues you need to tackle now. Your future challenges will not be solved by fear and worry. The best you can do is fully accept and comprehend each problem at hand and work toward resolving it with full attention and presence, not by fear and worry. We all have this innate natural capacity.

However, this innate state is clouded by layers of ignorance and ego, which make you pursue material rewards in the hope of achieving peace of mind and contentment. Peeling off these layers of ignorance can be accomplished by what I call *technologies of consciousness.* Some of these are self-inquiry, prayer, yoga, meditation, running, walking, martial arts, basking in the glory of nature, and giving—as well as receiving and experiencing—unconditional love.

Gratitude: Always Give Your Very Best

Gratitude, they say, is the mother of all virtues. To give your best and show up fully, you have to be always in an innate state of gratitude. If you are not, you can be easily affected by external circumstances. It is relatively easy to be grateful when things are going your way. In fact, the typical "unconscious" mindset is that you will be grateful when things are aligned the way you want them to be. This is a recipe or an excuse to never be grateful. You can't unleash your greatness this way. A conscious, peak-performance mindset requires that you stay grateful no matter what life or business throws at you.

The primary focus areas for most people are health, finances, career, and relationships. It is extremely rare, if not impossible, for human beings to be in an excellent state in all of those four areas simultaneously. Even if some of us are lucky enough to experience well-being in all of them for a while, someone near and dear to us maybe going through a crisis or trauma that we have to help them deal with. Your external circumstances are not going to be perfect; they are always fluctuating and going through ups and downs. You cannot tie your mindset to them because if you do, you will rise and fall with them.

Can we be in gratitude if one or more of these areas in our life are suffering? Even more challenging, can we be grateful when we are having a crisis in one or more of these areas? We have to, in order to be in peak performance and to operate in a state of self-actualized mastery. All of us have the innate capacity to be untouched by external circumstances and be in state of fulfilled equanimity at all times. We can always find a way to be grateful even under the direst of circumstances. Only then can we truly give our best.

When I was down and out, bedridden for months (see "From Brink to Breakthrough"), I learned the hard way that gratitude was my only hope for a full recovery. I did a good job of not playing victim and fully accepting the circumstance I was in. This state allowed me to cope with the physical and emotional pain. But being grateful, wow! it was very difficult, I didn't think it was possible but I eventually did have the pleasure of that experience. That's when magical outcomes became possible.

I gradually appreciated the opportunity to reflect and course correct. I was, at times, ecstatic about developing the newfound ability to completely accept my condition and release the tension and disappointment I was holding on to. It was really up to me alone to let go—it had nothing to with the external other person or event. The magic of full recovery and emotional mastery happened only after I started feeling grateful for the opportunity to go through the experience. This led to getting all the answers to my questions on life, leadership, purpose, excellence, and greatness.

Every week there is a new challenge or a new opportunity to improve your customer experience or employee engagement or financial performance. If a CEO and executive team do not have the ability to be grateful for the opportunity to build an exceptional organization, they can easily feel overwhelmed and wonder if they can ever experience the euphoric feeling of building an exceptional and transformative organization. Gratitude is the foundational state or mindset that allows us to show up with presence, accountability, humility, an integrative mindset, self-esteem, and courage.

A hard driving top-down leader owns all the problems, gets overwhelmed and emotionally drained. A transformative leader inspires his or her team to own the challenges, removes the obstacles, and is emotionally charged.

Forgiveness: Freeing Yourself from Burden

To forgive does not mean that you approve of or condone the actions of the perpetrator. You are simply refusing to be weighed down by that burden and want to give yourself permission to look ahead and live your life fully. If you are having a hard time forgiving, watch out for an internal dynamic at play. You are probably being too hard on yourself and expecting perfection. Instead, accept not being perfect and pursue excellence. By giving yourself space and time for not being perfect and not expecting to live up to your ego-imposed standards, you will dissolve the unconsciousness that stops forgiveness. You will loosen and release the grip of judgment that comes in the way of forgiveness. Gratitude spurs us to inspired action by transcending complex challenges and pushing us beyond mere success to unleash our greatness. Hence, it is the mother of all virtues.

Intelligence: The Key to Mastery

To master human motivations, you have to understand and enhance your intelligence in many areas. There are three critical ones—IQ, EQ (emotional intelligence) and SQ (Spiritual intelligence). Professionals typically have a well-developed intellect and IQ which help in logical analysis and problem solving. A leader needs a high EQ to be successful, and a high SQ to unfold his or her greatness, in addition to a solid intellect.

Using Emotional Intelligence (EQ)

Business organizations have been slow to adopt personal mastery and enlightened principles. Perhaps one of the reasons is an overreliance on intellect to solve business problems, and a genuine concern (even belief) that emotions get in the way of objectivity, resulting in poor decisions and tolerance for sub-par performance. In reality, there is a difference between being emotional and emotional maturity. When we say, "He is being emotional," we imply that he is not being rational or objective. But in its truest sense, we all have emotions. The real issue is this: Are we emotionally mature enough to not be influenced by personal connection and attachment in making sound business decisions?

In early stages of emotional development, people have difficulty separating personal relationship from professional assessment. The solution is not to cut off emotion and rely solely on intellect. As we mature emotionally and grow in wisdom, we become less resistant to demonstrating empathy, compassion, and care while simultaneously demanding excellence and accountability. We treat each person and situation objectively. This is emotional maturity, a sign of a high emotional intelligence (EQ).

Spiritual Intelligence (SQ) and Why It Matters for You

Since there are many misconceptions, misunderstandings, and a lack of clarity about spirituality, let's begin by stating what spirituality from my perspective is not. Spirituality is not religion; it is religion-neutral. You don't have to be religious to be spiritual. Religion can be helpful in spiritual development, but we have to be free from dogma and fanaticism to be truly spiritual. Spirituality unifies people of diverse backgrounds; religion, on the other hand, does not have a great track record of unifying people. Neither is spirituality supposed to be esoteric, mysterious, or based on a faith or belief system. Spirituality does not mean being soft, passive, or not living fully. It certainly does not mean being tolerant of poor behavior or performance.

A spiritual person is someone 1) whose speech, thoughts, and actions match; 2) who pursues excellence in any endeavor; 3) who can connect with and relate to a diverse group of people or constituents; 4) who pursues wisdom, well-being, and wealth; and 5) who performs actions beneficial to self, society, and planet. These are outcomes of being a sincere and humble seeker. This person is comfortable acknowledging what he/she doesn't know and actively seeks to learn.

Why is that seeking important? Why does it matter to you? There are two primary reasons:

- Seeking is natural. We know intuitively that it is this dimension that drives our intellect, emotion, thoughts, behaviors, and actions. When we give expression to our natural drive to learn and to grow, it makes our life fulfilling and meaningful.
- The quality of objectivity and inclusiveness that is expected of business leaders to inspire high performance is an example of spiritual behavior. Spirituality is critical to improving executive alignment and employee engagement and to achieving exceptional business performance.

How does a person with superior spiritual intelligence show up? A person with high SQ demonstrates the ability to stay present in a state of equanimity and take a decisive right action independent of external events and circumstances. Equanimity is the ability to be calm and balanced, especially in changing and turbulent conditions. Right action is the capacity and competence to make a wise and effective decision that is objective, unbiased and inclusive of all perspectives.

Cindy Wigglesworth, who has done plenty of good work on SQ, defines it as "Acting with wisdom and compassion and with inner and outer calm no matter what the external circumstances are." Tony Schwartz defines being spiritual as "Doing more of what they do best and enjoy most, and by feeling connected to a higher purpose at work."

IQ versus EQ and SQ

A knowledge worker needs a good IQ. A solid EQ is very important to function collaboratively in teams, and especially in leading high-performance teams, departments, and organizations. A high SQ is critical to be an inspired and inspiring leader who is driven to build highly engaged, creative, and purposeful organizations. Some of the toughest, type A, shareholder- and profit-centric" leaders that I work with know that they can be faster and more decisive in making difficult calls. They are certainly not short on intellect or passion to succeed. The primary factor is the ability to be completely objective and detached from personal feelings. I remind them that your loyalty is first to the mission and then to the people. Operating at this level requires a high level of spiritual intelligence to take right action.

Organizational execution requires the ability to collaborate and to inspire people to perform. To truly collaborate and be inspiring requires us to connect, at a deeper visceral level, to the heart and spirit. Team building, motivating, and inspiring others certainly has an intellectual and material component, but the emotional and spiritual intelligence plays a very big and necessary part. A leader with high SQ inspires a higher performance.

Today's Leadership "Triple Play"

To be inspirational in this 3.0 era of authenticity, transparency, and heightened awareness, leaders are required to have high IQ+EQ+SQ unlike in the previous eras where it was okay to take a fragmented approach to leadership based on command and control, rules and processes, with limited access to information.

Many business leaders also feel that their financial success is being achieved at a personal cost—a lack of balance among physical, mental, emotional, social and spiritual well-being. Their mindset is that loss of balance is the price to pay for enhanced execution, whereas a high SQ leader has an integrative mindset, that is, to not separate personal and work life but to show up fully all the time. As I said to a CEO recently, "You have to view every interaction as an equal opportunity to give your best, as opposed to seeing them as good, bad, or a necessary evil." I further suggested that he should monitor his mindset to determine if the interaction is energizing, depleting, or neutral. When you operate at a high SQ, you are naturally energized, positive, and present.

We all want to be ourselves and we want to show up fully at work and play—that is being spiritual. It is completely aligned with execution, teamwork, business performance, and leadership effectiveness. Deep down none of us want to pretend to be someone else. We want to be consistently ourselves in different business and life situations. It is very stressful and ineffective to play different roles and to not show up fully.

While all of us are inherently spiritual, our SQ and spiritual development is different. This is true for IQ and EQ, too—we all have a capacity to be analytical and display our emotions, but the degree of intelligence and emotional maturity varies and can be improved with practice. As we develop and mature emotionally, we move into the domain of spiritual wisdom. As we grow spiritually, we enhance our emotional development which helps in further spiritual growth, mutually reinforcing each other. Let me explain.

EQ includes such characteristics as accurate self-assessment, optimism, honesty, empathy, adaptability, self-confidence, transparency, and interpersonal skills, such as influencing and developing others, conflict management, teamwork, and collaboration. SQ takes us deeper into self-awareness, self-inquiry, gratitude, compassion, understanding of the ego, and connecting our deepest innate desire and yearning in service of universal well-being. As our SQ increases, we develop the ability to see the big picture for what it is without a "personal spin", and also the intellectual capacity to hold multiple perspectives.

This means as SQ increases, so does our EQ and IQ. This has been my personal experience, and I invite you to observe this phenomenon in your own development like I have. To unleash your full potential, IQ, EQ, and SQ have to be equally developed. The reality, though, is that in business and professional settings, we do not get much training in developing our emotional and spiritual muscles and intelligence. The few programs that are available don't generally connect them back to the realities of business.

By becoming mindful, self-aware, and spiritually intelligent, you can accelerate the shift of collective consciousness and become a role model for the change you want to see. You will facilitate the rise of democracy, capitalism, and human innovation to its natural and fullest potential. You can also dramatically impact personal leadership, team collaboration, and organizational effectiveness. You do this by being your authentic self, showing up fully with intellect, heart, and spirit.

As we evolve, we transcend and include, which means enlightened leadership includes the motivational aspects of the earlier models. For example, toughness without love and care breeds rigid compliance, and care without toughness could lead to apathy. Neither of them is as effective as the tough love of enlightened leadership.

Measuring and Enhancing SQ

SQ is the best indicator of our ability to live an inspired life, achieve personal mastery, and provide inspirational leadership and organizational mastery in order to build an exceptional organization. So how do we know where you are and, more importantly, how can you improve your SQ?

Since SQ is about how you show up, your behaviors and actions give an accurate indication of your level of development. The best way to evaluate your personal development, leadership effectiveness, or SQ is to determine your behaviors and actions, not your intent or what you say. How do you do that?

1. Get input and feedback from people who know you best and interact with you in different environments. Talk to anywhere between 8 to 12 stakeholders—people who interact with you closely and also have a vested interest in your development.

2. Use a standard measurement tool that provides a rigorous analytical, unbiased, and objective result. Examples are: Richard Barrett's *Personal and Leadership Values Assessment* and Cindy Wigglesworth's *SQ21*. I find Barrett's assessment particularly useful since it builds on Maslow's hierarchy and comprehensively defines levels of human development.

The fastest and most effective way to build a purposeful and profitable organization is to have the CEO and the leadership team operating at higher levels of development, awareness, or consciousness. How can you enhance your spiritual intelligence? Having an accountability partner makes a big difference. An experienced master coach who has personally made the transition can accelerate development. How do you know you are making progress? You go back to your stakeholders for an evaluation.

This process digs into the root cause of your current behavior. Once you know and accept that, you can effect positive change in your behavior. I periodically meet with the leader and communicate regularly to ensure that he or she is making conscious effort in every interaction. This process guarantees progress. I have had the distinct pleasure and honor of facilitating this transformation for many courageous leaders who are willing to push the envelope and take charge of their life, leadership, and business!

I highly recommend the following steps to help with this process:

1. Self-inquiry: Why do you do what you do? What is the noble intent and root cause for your behavior and actions? Engage in this practice every day to hold yourself accountable to all your thoughts and actions

2. Meditation: Observe your mind's thoughts since you are what you think. When you dispassionately witness your negative thoughts without judgment, their negativity decreases. When you dispassionately witness your positive thoughts without self-righteous ego, the positivity increases.

3. Treat every interaction at work and in life as an opportunity to participate with high SQ: Course correct and keep learning and growing. When you are operating at a high SQ, personal and organizational mastery come naturally. However, you cannot expect that magical state to happen overnight. In the meantime, you have to mimic and force that enlightened behavior in how you show up (personal mastery) and how you inspire others to perform at a higher level (organizational mastery).

Developing spiritual intelligence is no different than improving your physical fitness. Identify the steps, establish a routine, and act on them consistently. Will you notice obvious changes in your physiology in one day or one week of training? Of course not, however, there are almost immediate unmistakable signs. You will feel internal calm that translates to noticeable external calm—you will listen better, laugh more, and feel lighter. You will have fewer emotional outbursts. You will be more expressive, more curious, and less judgmental. This is how you evaluate your progress and check with your stakeholders, the ones who are with you and your best, normal, and worst moments.

Real-World Mastery Practice 1

Lisa is a successful 2.0 leader. She is frustrated with her VP, Robert, who keeps missing deadlines and gives heavy workload and feeling overwhelmed as excuses. One of the problems is that Lisa is giving Robert deadlines or pressuring him to set an aggressive schedule. There is no clear buy-in from Robert, and there are no serious consequences except periodic outbursts of displeasure from Lisa. She thinks of Robert as a valuable team member but keeps sending mixed messages to "keep him honest." I suggested that she should get buy-in from Robert, and let him own the problem (not her). I also recommended the following three-step process:

1. Create a safe environment; make Robert feel like a valuable contributor and team member.

2. Ask him to set a deadline, but do not pressure him to overcommit. Negotiate a tighter deadline if necessary. Ensure he has the right priorities.

3. Ask him to proactively update you on the status and alert you with a recovery plan if there is a risk of missing the deadline.

You have to apply practical rigor and execution to qualities of human dimension. (See the sidebar on this page.) This is a crucial shift where many leadership teams and organizations seem to be stuck. The so-called hard business actions such as strategy development and implementation, decision, making, or negotiations are separated from the so-called soft wellness and personal development programs. Most often, these programs do not have any direct connection to day-to-day business activities.

Exceptional leadership teams and organizations integrate business and IQ skills with the emotional and visceral qualities of SQ, and deliver consistently. Many organizations and their high IQ leaders do a good job of articulating the importance of buy-in and collaboration, but it is the ones with emotional depth and spiritual wisdom that translate it to effective and consistent practice. They remove the obstacles that get in the way and establish the environment to inspire full engagement and commitment.

Real-World Mastery Practice 2

Howard is a CEO struggling with his two brilliant top executives, Claire and Charles. According to Howard, Claire and her department always seem overwhelmed and overworked, and Charles does not delegate and empower. His solution is to work with their respective teams and fix the problem for them. Claire and Charles acknowledge the problem but do not like Howard's heavy-handed approach. Besides, they believe that he suffers from the same problem of which he is accusing them. I suggested to Claire and Charles (and informed Howard) that they should follow this process:

1. Acknowledge the problem and agree that you can do better.

2. Acknowledge that Howard's suggestion is well-intended but does not solve the problem. In fact, it will make it worse.

a. Makes me defensive

b. Undermines my authority

c. Sends mixed message to my troops

3. Respond with, "I will come back to you with the most effective solution by ... Please don't rush me, I push myself hard enough."

Critical Point: How a message is communicated is extremely important. The ideal mindset is being assertive, humble, and confident without fear, anger, and judgment. They initially tell me that they have tried, but it does not work. When we dig deeper they acknowledge that their mindset was not right. The correct mindset does not guarantee the perfect outcome, but it certainly increases the odds and most importantly, it liberates the participants because they have done their best.

Building Blocks of Greatness

It is obvious how personal mastery and high SQ can be the keys to happiness and contentment in life. They will also lead to superior business performance and leadership effectiveness. With a high SQ, you will be able to perform the fundamentals such as communication, decision-making, performance evaluation, strategy, and execution much more effectively.

Mastering human emotions and motivations is a journey; you should not expect dramatic overnight improvement. Progress is guaranteed if you stay consistent with the steps identified for enhancing SQ. You can accelerate but cannot skip steps. Progress is not necessarily linear or gradual, sometimes it is dramatic and at other times it feels like you are stuck. You will ultimately come into your own. The key is to persist and be regular, relentless, and consistent in your practice. You will experience an increase in presence or any of the seven mindsets. You will develop the ability to recognize when you are not feeling present. You become more conscious of how your mindset is and how you are showing up.

Taking the Journey Together

Overall, the most effective way to master human motivation is by taking the journey together with the leadership team. How do you do that? As professionals and human beings, none of us are perfect. We all have strengths and weaknesses, at least one significant gift for genius, and a major block or blind spot that gets in the way of being the best we can be. This block is obvious to the people who regularly interact with other. What's the point in living in denial and pretending it doesn't exist? Besides, we want to get better. Why not share what is obvious? When I am working with leaders, I have them identify their most important improvement goal. I ask them to list actions they engage in that sabotage and get in the way of their improvement goal and prevent them from unleashing best.

I then ask them to dig deeper and self-inquire—why do you do what you do? Identify the noble reason for why we do silly things. The answer usually is: "I don't want to lose my sense of self-worth and do not want to be seen as being less valuable or ineffective." I challenge them to push the envelope and uncover the root cause. This ultimately leads to "I am not good enough, valuable enough, or effective enough." These are limiting beliefs and assumptions that hold all of us back. I know this because I have gone through this process myself to overcome many of my blocks, including the big one, being critically judgmental.

As a leader you have to be patient and appreciate the progress your people are making. You have to equip them with the right tools and inspire them to step up and get better. Allow them to come up with their own solutions. You should not provide the answers but set an example and share your own process. How did you shift from a hard driving and entrepreneurial 2.0 leader to a visionary and conscious 3.0 leader? For way too long, many of us have cut off our emotional and spiritual dimensions, inhibiting the full development of ourselves, our teams, and our business organizations. That division is not natural and is detrimental to execution and organizational performance. The key is to not separate the disparate portions of your life, but to master human nature and motivations—practice courage, accountability, gratitude, humility, self-esteem, inclusivity and objectivity, and presence—and integrate that human dimension with your business processes. Only then is a sustainable change possible for you and your organization.

Identifying weaknesses can be immensely cathartic and incredibly liberating. However, it is only 50 percent of the challenge at hand. The next step is to work continually on improving and building those emotional muscles to keep getting better while monitoring your progress and course correcting when needed. You will read more on how to do this in Practice 2, "Lead With Self-Mastery."

Practice 2: Lead with Self-Mastery

"Knowing others is intelligence; knowing yourself is true wisdom. Mastering others is strength; mastering yourself is true power." — Lao Tzu

"It is absurd that a man should rule others, who cannot rule himself." — Latin Proverb

Exceptional leadership is largely dependent on the ability to master human motivations, but it all starts with self. How can you master anything without mastering yourself? When you are self-aware, you are conscious of your behavior and the effect you have on others. You can then be intentional about your actions and favorably impact the outcome. Leaders who are adept at self-mastery have the confidence and discipline to actively work on surfacing the unconscious and subconscious beliefs that could be adversely affecting their behavior and leadership effectiveness.

Examples of behaviors that negatively affect leadership effectiveness are being judgmental and micromanaging. CEOs who are committed to greatness take a deeper dive into their psyche and begin to understand the presumed noble reason behind their counterproductive behavior. Ask yourself these questions:

- Why am I being critical and judgmental?
- Why do I micromanage?
- How can I pursue my noble purpose more effectively?
- Can I get there faster by being humbler and letting go?

I have worked with successful CEOs who have noble intentions but struggle with how they impact others. It is important to be aware of your intentions and actions, though that in itself is not sufficient. Self-awareness has to be followed by a willingness and commitment to change, and then taking the steps to actually change. The typical steps are:

1. **Self-Confidence:** Accept feedback and input from people who observe you and on whom you may impact in all situations, not just when you have your game face on. These are your stakeholders who care for your growth and well-being and get to see you when you are up, down, and neutral.

2. **Self-Discipline:** Develop actions for improvement and execute them consistently.

3. **Self-Transformation:** Consistent practice leads to change in behavior.

4. **Self-Actualization:** Eventually leads to operating in a state of mastery.

Personal Mastery: One of the Hardest Things a Human Can Do

Living in a state of inspired action, independent of external circumstances is what human beings have aspired to since the dawn of creation. Is there anything more important than this characteristic for a business leader, CEO, or a corporate executive who is constantly pulled in different directions by various constituents of the business and is faced with "right versus right" choices frequently? There are enough people to rely on to provide technical knowledge and professional expertise. How can he or she lead self, the leadership team, and the organization to extraordinary execution, effectiveness, and business performance? How can basic business functions be performed even more effectively? Personal mastery can be achieved by focusing on the following seven attributes, which have been described in detail in Practice 1, "Master Human Motivations and Emotions":

• **Presence:** Exhibit freedom in action, detached from outcome.

• **Accountability:** Be inspired in right action.

- **Humility:** Pursue the right solution over the need to "be right."
- **Integrative:** Be completely inclusive, fair, and objective.
- **Self-Esteem:** Show composed equanimity in criticism and praise.
- **Courage:** become truly transparent, authentic, and vulnerable.
- **Gratitude:** Always give your very best.

Most of us know that these characteristics are desirable, and they are natural and spontaneous when you are operating in a 3.0 state. You intellectually intend to act in these ways and often believe that you are doing so. But how do you know that you are truly demonstrating this behavior consistently in your daily interactions? Do you solicit honest feedback from those who know you intimately? An important consideration is the ability to accept your limitations without feeling limited. You need to have a high degree of self-awareness to identify your blind spots, self-esteem to receive both criticism and praise evenly, self-confidence to accept and admit the (intention to action) gap, and self-discipline to work on it relentlessly.

This is personal mastery, and this is what being spiritual is. It includes and goes beyond the domains of both IQ and EQ. These are qualities of being in higher states of consciousness. Mastery is often considered the key to happiness and contentment in life. What is now being understood and appreciated is that personal mastery can significantly impact performance and execution, as well as inspire innovation and the ability to effectively solve critical business challenges. Superior business performance and leadership effectiveness are directly connected to personal mastery.

After I finished my presentation on "How to Build Great Organizations" to the executive team of the bank he was leading, CEO Ash Patel stood in front of his team and said that he needed to develop additional skills to lead a $1 billion transformative bank. "I want to be a better father, spouse, sibling and friend—I believe I am good, but I want to be great." He knew intuitively that improving as a person would accelerate his growth from a successful business leader to a great inspirational leader.

An organization's inspirational or purposeful growth is capped by the CEO's personal development. The consciousness or spiritual intelligence (SQ) of the organization does not rise above that of its CEO in a hierarchical structure where power is concentrated at the top. IQ on the other hand certainly can—it is expected and desired to have professionals and individual contributors in a knowledge economy to have a high IQ, preferably higher than the boss. Ash understood the essence of great leadership and its direct connection to personal development, EQ, and SQ. He decided to enroll in the CEO mastery program that I had developed—his executive team was inspired by his enthusiasm and commitment and joined him voluntarily and the rest, as they say, is history!

An extensive Zenger Folkman study found that a leader's development is directly related to business performance and that extraordinary leaders double profitability. The one characteristic or pivotal competency that stands out is the ability to inspire and motivate others to higher performance. In our lexicon, motivating by appealing to the self-centered growth mindset is a 2.0 leader; inspiring others to give their very best is a 3.0 state of leadership. Being inspirational requires you to be a role model, to establish a clear vision and direction for your organization, to create an environment of risk-taking, innovation, and collaboration, in which the members of your team push each other to be the best version of themselves.

It is not just the small private organizations that directly reflect its leader's mindset or state of development. It is no accident that organizations such as Unilever, Starbucks, Whole Foods, Zappos, and Tata's demonstrate a culture that focuses on both profit and purpose, and inspires their employees to give their best. Why? Because their respective leaders during key growth periods—Paul Polman, Howard Schulz, John Mackey, Tony Hsieh, and Ratan Tata—have embodied those same principles and behaviors. Satya Nadella accomplished a stunning turnaround and extraordinary profitability for Microsoft in three short years with an "inspire and empower" culture. Bill Gates gave him the ultimate compliment when he said that Nadella's unique strength is his ability to give inspiring feedback to executives that needed to improve performance. This is a 3.0 mindset.

3.0 Vision with 2.0 Strategy and 1.0 Operations

Ajay is a very wealthy CEO of a financially successful organization that he founded over 20 years ago. He has a noble vision to make a difference in the lives of thousands of employees, customers, and partners he works with. However, his approach to fulfilling this vision is based on a win-lose style of negotiation, and behavior and an organizational culture where the primary motivators are survival and self-centered growth. He is sharp with a high IQ, but a relatively lower EQ. I told Ajay that he has no business complaining about the culture of self-centered behavior and high stress in his organization. The lofty vision and value statements in the company literature do not match the leadership behavior and the way his organization rewards, incentivizes, and compensates its employees.

I recently met a successful international businessman who moved into our neighborhood after obtaining a special immigrant visa to the United States for providing employment to local professionals. We connected immediately at a deeper level; he was intrigued and inspired by my work. He said, "You know, Sudhir, I am beginning to wonder if I set my goals high enough. I achieved everything I set out to do and I bet I could have done more." I knew what exactly he meant; he was self-aware enough to recognize that we cap our own growth. I see this all the time among the most successful business leaders I work with. Here are just a few examples:

- Kiran is one of the top CEOs in her industry and was recruited to turn around a chronically ailing organization. She took a lower salary than what she could have gotten, over-promised, and delivered results remarkably fast. The board of directors surprised her and significantly bumped up her compensation. She is in a position to build a legendary organization by asserting more freedom from the board and by inspiring her management team to stretch and push the envelope. She knows she can do it, but she hesitates. She is torn between being grateful to the board for giving her the opportunity, and assertively seeking more autonomy. She is also torn between driving the management team towards her goals for the company and inspiring them to set and execute lofty goals. My job is to keep nudging her to claim her greatness and unleash her full potential.

- Hector has the freedom to build the organization of his dreams—he has the money, the vision, and the smarts. He tells me, "Sudhir I am my worst enemy. I don't invest where I have to and accept mediocre performance from my executives." Hector has fully embraced his weakness; he has not run away from it or played victim by blaming external forces. Most importantly, he is actively working on overcoming his limitations by engaging in self-inquiry, meditation, group learning, and a 1:1 accountability partner.

- Steve is in his fifties. He is a master of his craft and one of the most respected senior professional executives in his industry. I asked him his highest goal that he wants to achieve in this lifetime. He said that he never thought about it, so I encouraged him to do so now. A year later, he has not taken the time to do it yet.

- Jamal is a self-made multimillionaire who built a business empire by aggressively negotiating and pursuing deals. He could be a conscious capitalist, an inclusive and collaborative owner like Warren Buffet, but he doesn't think so. He has not visualized or embraced that possibility. He craves respect and recognition, but his self-centered business approach makes it difficult to achieve these in a larger scale.

Obstacles to Overcome

We have to overcome some deeply entrenched personal and systemic obstacles and powerful opposing forces to make the transformation from a 2.0 to 3.0 organization, and business leadership transformation from hierarchic to self-actualized. What are those obstacles and opposing forces? The voices of fear, doubt, and inadequacy, sometimes masquerading as the voice of reason, implore us to hold back, stay the course, and resist change. They warn us not to be foolish and urge us to be practical. They like to keep us small, pseudo-safe and pseudo-secure in a familiar environment.

I call this pseudo-safe and pseudo-secure because safety and security is a state of mind, independent of external circumstances.

True freedom and security is experienced only when you embrace the uncertainty of future with self-confidence. Ironically, that's when you experience the intuitive or higher-self "knowing." No one knows the future, and nobody can guarantee an outcome. An enlightened person and a great leader is one who can be fully present and focused in the current activity that is aligned with a purpose, knowing that this does not guarantee the outcome he or she is seeking. Great leaders don't fight the doubters and naysayers within and without; they find a way to creatively and courageously work with them or around them as the situation demands.

It Begins with You

Your first job in transforming your organization is to engage in personal effort to operate in a 3.0 mindset. As noted in the introduction, a 2.0 leader pursues professional mastery, whereas a 3.0 leader adds two other dimensions of personal and organizational mastery. If you aspire to lead your organization to new heights, you need to understand where you are in that development cycle. This requires you to be clear about your aspirations. If your aspiration is to build a 3.0 authentic organization, then you have to start with transforming yourself.

What kind of business organization do you want to build? Do you see business as a place to fully express your gifts and genius? Is there place for emotional mastery, meaning, purpose, and spiritual intelligence in your business? How do you see the connection between your business and your life? Do you compartmentalize business and personal life, or is it one integrated continuum? When you take the time to know yourself thoroughly, you will have a good grasp not only of yourself, but of human nature and human motivations in general. As a result, you are better equipped to connect with, collaborate, motivate, and inspire people to higher levels of productivity and performance.

You'd be surprised how many of my clients initially miss that point. Typically, CEOs get excited and caught up by the needs of the job in terms of financial performance, and tend to delegate to others the development of the team and the rest of the organization. I have to remind them that they have to be part of the process—I cannot work with others on the leadership team without having the top person lead by example. It takes personal commitment and discipline to make a shift. Here's something that I tell everybody: If you cannot make that personal commitment to evolve at this time, then you are better off postponing your effort to build a great organization. It's a prerequisite. None of this is going to work unless you first make that change in yourself.

Know Thyself: Self-Awareness

In order to transform, you have to first know where you are. Who are you? What do you stand for? What is your vision and what is your world view? What is your purpose? What is your highest aspiration in life and in business? What are your gifts and strengths? What are your blocks and weaknesses? What is your level of development—how evolved and how conscious are you? How are your personal mastery and organizational mastery skills?

When you become self-aware, you realize that your opinions and perspectives are shaped by your unique circumstances. You will know how conscious you are and will come face-to-face with your level of development. This is not easy—it is tough to face your own failings, and tougher still to accept them. A 3.0 leader needs to have the ability to face his or her limitations without feeling limited. By closely examining your belief system and the values that shaped your perspective, you can be more conscious and deliberate about your behavior and the actions you take. Well begun is half-done. Self-awareness and acceptance are a good start. For example, "right action is more important than being right" is a concept that is easy to understand intellectually. However, consistently implementing it is a whole different ballgame and requires a deeper dive.

This is what great leaders pursue and ask themselves: Why do I sometimes derail and focus on being right? Why is being right so important? You may uncover some harsh facts such as: if you are not right, you don't feel good, you don't feel like you are adding value, and your confidence and self-esteem is tied to being right. This self-realization helps you to let go of the attachment to being right. Another reason you may uncover is that your emotions get in the way of following through on good intentions. To operate in a 3.0 mindset, you must uncover the emotional triggers that set you off. You can be more vigilant in future, and enlist the support of people around you who are affected by this behavior. In doing so, you are significantly improving your ability to walk the talk, enhance trust with your peers and subordinates, and inspire them to take similar action. I discuss this in more detail in Practice 5, "Bridge the Intent-to-Impact Gap." Great leaders work hard on mastering emotions.

When you courageously accept and own your weaknesses and blocks, you overcome 50 percent of the problem. When you unravel the root cause for the block and commit to specific solution steps, you unleash your greatness.

Having overcome the need to be right, you will actively seek and achieve win-win resolutions to complex active and passive conflicts. You will avoid the pitfalls of typical scenarios where people identify themselves with their position and unconsciously want to win. Great leaders recognize that when emotions take over, you end up causing serious, sometimes irreparable, damage to teamwork and relationships. You must work hard on mastering emotions.

Differences between a Successful 2.0 and Exceptional 3.0 Leader

Success as we define it here is a 2.0 mindset; greatness is a 3.0 mindset. While we all have the capacity to be great and have greatness within, we are all not focused on showing up and behaving consistently. A word of caution, it is not wise to connect short-term financial results with leadership skill. I don't mean to underestimate the leadership task, but one can cut expenses, improve efficiencies, and achieve short-term profitability. This can be a serious problem if short-term profitability is achieved at the expense of long-term sustainability and sacrificing the well-being of other important stakeholders. Most organizations evaluate its leader on short-term financial performance. This is a 2.0 organization with a 2.0 leader. A 3.0 organization, on the other hand, evaluates its leader on his or her ability to provide sustainable financial performance, develop an aligned and collaborative leadership team along with a high level of employee engagement, customer satisfaction, and win-win, high-trust partnerships. A 3.0 leader is pushed to demonstrate empathy, humility, and purposeful behavior, whereas a 2.0 leader can get away without it.

How is self-actualized 3.0 leadership similar and different from high-performance 2.0 leadership? Many of us can readily relate to characteristics that we believe high-performance business leaders demonstrate. Let's review how a conscious, enlightened 3.0 business leader, would compare in performing and demonstrating these typical traits.

- **Vision:** This is an essential trait for both high-performance and enlightened leaders, except in the case of an enlightened leader the vision tends to include the well-being of the larger community and planet.

- **Courage:** The basis for courage in the case of a high-performance leader could be fear or paranoia, whereas an enlightened leader displays courage from a state of fearlessness, self-confidence, and love.

- **Passion and Compassion:** While both leaders are passionate about what they do, compassion is not a requirement for a high-performance leader. An enlightened leader, on the other hand, combines his or her passion with compassion which inspires the stakeholders in the organization resulting in extraordinary performance and execution.

- **Execution:** High-performance leaders execute well. They are fast, have a sense of urgency, but tend to be restless and impatient. An enlightened leader executes exceedingly well. His or her effectiveness is based on a sense of serene flow.

- **Ability to Inspire:** A high-performance leader motivates with material and intellectual incentives with a focus on achieving financial results. An enlightened leader inspires by appealing to the innermost, deeper human yearning for material, emotional, and spiritual well-being, and achieves higher levels of engagement from the organization.

- **Excellence Culture:** A high-performance leader tends to judge and criticize setbacks and failure to promote a culture of excellence. An enlightened leader provides non-judgmental feedback, tough love, and encouragement to inspire mastery and excellence.

- **Decisiveness:** A high-performance leader utilizes well-developed analytical and cognitive skills in demonstrating decisiveness, while an enlightened leader is in a state of spontaneous right action by utilizing the full range of analytical, cognitive, emotional, and visceral skills.

- **Judgment:** Knowledge and experience are the basis for sound judgment. However, these alone are not sufficient in dealing with the complex issues leaders have to face. An enlightened leader derives the capacity for judgment by integrating knowledge and experience with wisdom and presence.

- **Discernment—Evaluation:** A high-performance leader evaluates functional performance and rewards results. An enlightened leader evaluates adherence to core values and performance and rewards right action and results.

- **Objectivity:** A high-performance leader is focused on bottom line and financial results but could be swayed by human attachments and relationships. An enlightened leader treats all with respect but is detached and isn't influenced by personal relationships and obligations. A sense of duty, righteousness, and responsibility are the primary motives.

- **Listening Skills:** A high-performance leader listens politely and intellectually with an open mind and possible internal static. An enlightened leader listens deeply and viscerally with empathy and an open mind and heart.

- **Drive:** Personal ambition, money, fame, and ego could be the primary motivators for a high-performance leader. An enlightened leader, however, is driven by a sense of duty, service, universal love, and humility that is characterized by a smaller ego and a pursuit of self-mastery and higher states of consciousness.

- **Teamwork and Alignment:** A high-performance leader is focused on, and could even force, strategic alignment. Passive conflicts are either ignored or go unrecognized and unresolved. An enlightened leader is focused on alignment of values that lead to collaborative development of a compelling strategy or rallying behind a strategy that may not have consensus. An enlightened leader facilitates difficult conversations to resolve passive conflicts and increase trust.

- **Personality:** A high-performance leader is typically in a hurry, rushed, impatient, stubborn, is very competitive, and engages in win-lose dealings. An enlightened leader presents a more balanced and well-paced flow approach, is strong willed, is striving to improve self, and engages in win-win interactions.

- **Basic Philosophy:** A high-performance leader believes wealth ensures well-being and opportunity for pursuit of wisdom, whereas an enlightened leader believes that wisdom drives well-being and provides "sufficient" wealth.

- **Leadership Style:** A high-performance leader is typically hierarchic and open, but tends to be closed and autocratic at times. An enlightened leader is open and empowering, and takes on a situational role of providing tough love when necessary.

- **Inclusiveness:** A high-performance leader is practically inclusive and manages diversity well to achieve strong results. An enlightened leader is naturally inclusive and collaborative; he or she fully embraces and thrives in diversity.

- **Universality:** A high-performance leader identifies with and could derive strength from a social, religious, ethnic, or political affiliation and could alienate those that do not share the same affiliation. An enlightened leader looks beyond affiliations and works to do the right thing and unite.

- **Wealth Distribution:** A high-performance leader is focused on generating shareholder value and is not overly concerned with compensation gaps in the organization. An enlightened leader believes that balancing and aligning the interests of all the stakeholders will ensure superior and sustainable shareholder value. He also believes that fair compensation and distribution of wealth is crucial to engaging and inspiring employees to give their best.

- **Diet and Exercise:** A high-performance leader's diet tends to be nutritious and lavish. Focus is on physical exercise to provide physical and emotional well-being. An enlightened leader's diet is simple, nutritious, and effective. Focus is on spiritual, emotional, and physical exercises to ensure overall well-being.

- **Health and Energy:** The high-performance leader's workaholic and imbalanced compartmentalized approach could strain health resulting in reliance on willpower, adrenaline rush, and addictive intoxicants, such as caffeine, for energy. An enlightened leader's integrated approach enhances wellness and being in a natural state of fulfillment provides high levels of energy and inspiration.

- **Leadership Development:** A high-performance leader relies more on intellectual knowledge, academic learning, and experience and less on self-awareness and mastery compared to an enlightened leader.

The following table compares these and some other characteristics of 2.0 and 3.0 leaders.

QUALITY	Successful HIGH-PERFORMANCE (2.0) LEADER	Self-actualized ENLIGHTENED (3.0) LEADER
Vision	Strong	Excellent. Includes larger community and planet.
Courage	Fear or paranoia could be the basis	Self-confidence, love, and fearlessness is the basis.
Passion	Excellent	Excellent

QUALITY	Successful HIGH-PERFORMANCE (2.0) LEADER	Self-actualized ENLIGHTENED (3.0) LEADER
Compassion	Not a key requirement	Excellent. Turbocharges inspiration and execution.
Judgment	Strong. Knowledge and experience is the basis.	Outstanding. Integrates knowledge and experience with wisdom and presence.
Decisiveness	Strong. Based on analytical and cognitive skills. Focused on quick decision.	Outstanding. Based on analytical, cognitive, emotional, and visceral skills. Focused on right decision and right action.
Excellence Culture	Tends to judge and criticize performance to promote excellence.	Provides non-judgmental feedback, encouragement, and tough love as needed to inspire a culture of excellence.
Discernment–Evaluation	Very good. Evaluates functional performance and rewards results.	Excellent. Evaluates adherence to core values and performance and rewards right action and results.
Focus	Strong. Utilizes past disappointment and fear of failure for motivation.	Excellent. Naturally present. Let's go of the past and future, is fully present and here now.
Flexibility	Good. Open to change but tends to be inflexible.	Excellent. Embraces change.
Execution	Fast, mostly effective, sense of urgency, restless, impatient.	Timely, highly effective, sense of serenity, flow and urgency.
Basic Philosophy	Wealth ensures well-being and pursuit of wisdom.	Wisdom drives well-being and provides sufficient wealth.
Lifestyle	Stressed, hurried	Balanced, well-paced flow
Personality	Type A, competitive (win-lose), impatient, stubborn and inflexible.	Flows. Slows down at times to get fast results, competitive (win-win), strong willed, patient, and flexible.

QUALITY	Successful HIGH-PERFORMANCE (2.0) LEADER	Self-actualized ENLIGHTENED (3.0) LEADER
Transparency	Very good. Complies with rules and regulations.	Excellent. Very naturally open. Integrity is independent of legal compliance.
Intellect/ Analytical Capability	Excellent	Excellent
Emotional Maturity	Good enough	Excellent
Spiritual Awakening	Not a requirement	Strong. Pursues Mastery
Self-Confidence– Courage	Tends to be arrogant and certain. Fear and paranoia could be the basis.	Tends to be humble and curious. Fearlessness is the basis.
Drive	Strong. Ambition, money, fame, and ego are primary motivators	Excellent. Service, duty, and universal love characterized by humility and less ego.
Ego	High ego. Self-esteem is tied to achievement and being right.	Low ego. Self-esteem comes from right action, contribution and being of service.
Energy/Stamina	High. Could be forced with will power, adrenalin rush, caffeine, alcohol.	Naturally high. Emotionally balanced and fulfilled.
Ability to Inspire	Good. Focuses on material and intellectual incentives.	Excellent. Focuses on material, emotional, and spiritual incentives.
Fairness	Good enough	Excellent. Universal wellbeing and connectedness is the basis.
Objectivity	Good. Focus is on financial results. Could be swayed by personal attachments and relationships.	Excellent. Believes in right action. Personally detached and stays focused on performance and core values. Respects all as people and differentiates on performance.

QUALITY	Successful HIGH-PERFORMANCE (2.0) LEADER	Self-actualized ENLIGHTENED (3.0) LEADER
Inclusiveness	Good. Competitive. Manages diversity.	Excellent. Collaborative. Embraces and thrives in diversity.
Patience	Good, but not sure if it is seen as a virtue.	Excellent. Is self-assured and has enormous patience.
Persistence	Good. Personality and system (short-term orientation) does not encourage it.	Excellent. Has natural and extraordinary capacity for persistence.
Diet	Lavish, tasty, and balanced.	Simple, nutritious, and effective.
Exercise	Excellent. Primarily physical, may be some mental and emotional aspects.	Excellent. Physical, emotional, mental, and spiritual.
Listening Skills	Good. Listens politely with an open mind and possible internal static.	Excellent. Listens deeply and viscerally with an open mind and an open heart.
People skills	Good enough, pragmatic.	Excellent, excels in understanding human nature.
Leadership Style	Typically hierarchic and open, but tends to be closed and autocratic at times.	Primarily open and empowering. Takes on a situational role of providing tough love when necessary.
Health	Stressed	Radiant
Work Ethic	Workaholic. Imbalanced. Compartmentalized.	Flows 24x7. Balanced. Integrated.

Thanks to a higher spiritual intelligence, an enlightened (3.0) leader demonstrates the same traits more effectively and more consistently, thus making a greater impact than a high-performance (2.0) leader.

Leadership

Leadership is not about position, rank, or authority. John Quincy Adams said, "If your actions inspire others to dream more, learn more, do more and become more, you are a leader." A person who solely depends on position or rank to exercise his or her authority is not a true leader. He cannot inspire others to give their best. He operates at the lower ego states and motivates by fear, intimidation, and the carrot-and-stick approach of reward and punishment. A true 3.0 leader consistently operates in the growth needs of human hierarchy and appeals to the higher states to inspire superior alignment, engagement, and performance.

Personal Effectiveness and Mastery

In a state motivated by fear, survival instincts, and the need to grow materially, you are managed by your ego and your emotions. This means that your effectiveness is limited. When you master your ego and emotions and release subconscious fears, you are on purpose. You are inspired to give your very best, and therefore are a lot more effective. Personal mastery is being in this state of inspiration consistently, where you align your personal passion with professional vision.

Organizational Effectiveness and Mastery

To enhance organizational effectiveness, you have to inspire others to give their best. It is not enough to be personally, although it is a necessary step. To inspire others requires us to connect with empathy, touch their heart and spirit, and build trust. You can do this only when you are authentic and vulnerable and are operating beyond the needs of the ego. When you operate beyond these base ego needs, you are organizationally effective. When you perform in this state consistently, you arrive at organizational mastery.

Mastery and Ego

A leader, especially an enlightened leader, needs high self-esteem, not a large ego. High self-esteem leads to a dignified, composed, and understated self-belief and self-confidence. A healthy self-esteem also leads to humility and the ability to accept praise and criticism evenly.

I'll give you an example: At the very beginning of a corporate workshop I was conducting, a high-strung VP challenged me with the statement "I think you're selling snake oil. This culture stuff is nonsense—success is all about meeting the numbers by driving hard, and you've sold the CEO a bill of goods." Rather than get defensive, I immediately thought to myself, "Wow, this is beautiful—a test of my self-esteem and confidence." It was an opportunity to "walk the talk" of my own coaching philosophy. I listened respectfully, shared examples and stories of success calmly, and invited him to participate with an open mind. I also challenged him and said that if he remained closed and cynical, it would turn out to be a self-fulfilling prophecy that it would not work for him. I noticed an immediate shift in him, a hint of anticipation and curiosity. I also noticed a sense of relief, inspiration, and admiration from the rest of the participants. This VP, like many other hard-charging, successful executives I have worked with, is now a raving fan. My favorite leaders are bright, successful skeptics with an open mind, heart, and spirit and a passion for learning and growth.

This is the essence of self-actualized state—not becoming overly excited with success or distraught with failure. Five thousand years ago, this was described as the Sthitaprajna state in Gita. For example, Ash Patel's biggest wish is to stay humble despite the increasing financial success and recognition he is achieving. I will let him know when I see early signs of slipping.

A large ego gets in the way of developing self-esteem and shows up as defensiveness, insecurity, and fear. Some people confuse bluster with true self-esteem—these types of professionals and executives don't survive in an organizational culture that nurtures and values mastery. How can a leader inspire trust when he or she has those emotions? A large ego will prevent you from assessing yourself accurately and will encourage you to ignore constructive and difficult feedback, or even respond with denial and anger. Obviously, none of these are good or productive.

Many thought leaders and action leaders (cutting-edge CEOs, corporate executives, and business leaders) agree that mastery and enlightened leadership principles help in enhancing execution and effectiveness. There is also consensus on the values, behaviors, and characteristics that represent enlightened leadership. However, the mechanics of what it takes and how to get there has largely remained a black box.

Mastering Ego: The Key to Personal and Organizational Mastery

Conquering your ego in favor of strong self-esteem represents the ultimate victory and is the master key to enlightened living and leadership. This is easier said than done, and many people go through life without achieving this victory over ego. Modern life and history is replete with examples of people who get into serious emotional, and even physical conflicts rather than admitting they made a mistake or were wrong. No wonder people would rather go to war than lose face. We go through life assuming ego is critical for survival, to conduct business, develop relationships, and to avoid being taken advantage of. The truth, however, may be that the success we achieve is despite the ego, not because of it. Many executives believe that ego is necessary for success and are afraid to let go for fear of being viewed as soft or a pushover. For example, when you negotiate a business deal, generally there are three possible outcomes:

1. **Lose–Lose:** A dysfunctional approach involving low self-esteem.

2. **Win–Lose:** Approaching it as a zero-sum game, with a large ego.

3. **Win–Win:** Low ego, high self-confidence and self-esteem.

Most people I deal with sincerely want to have win-win deals. However, because they are operating at a self-centered level—coming from a win-lose place, their communications and negotiations suffer. One of the parties may tell rather than ask, creating a win-lose conversation. For example, being critical of a proposed budget without first asking its author her rationale for what was presented. The solution is to get a grip on your own evolutionary state and ego. This requires self-inquiry and self-awareness. When you're working with a mutually accountable leadership team that takes this approach and are comfortable with challenging and understanding each others' assumptions without ego flaring up, then you're on the right path: what I call the "ego to essence journey."

Many successful leaders intend to engage in win-win negotiations but struggle because they have not risen above the level of self-centered achievement and overcome the needs of the ego. A good intent is not sufficient; mastery bridges the gap between intent and impact.

Two of the most popular questions I get from successful, results-oriented leaders are:

1. Don't we need ego to be effective leaders?

2. How do I manage the egos of my executives and build an exceptional world-class team?

These crucial questions express our ambivalence about the role of ego. We are basically saying, "Ego has helped me grow thus far and brought me and the organization a measure of financial success. At the same time, it seems to be getting in the way of further success, team alignment, and engagement." One of the fundamental requirements of businesses, organizations, people, and professionals is growth and expansion, isn't it? We grow and expand when we are effective. An organization is more effective when the leadership team is aligned and when the employees are engaged.

Ego

Ego is not separate from who we are, it is a part of us. Ego's role is to alert us and protect us from danger and from being taken advantage of. However, ego flares up even when the threat or danger is not real. It may just be our fear-based perception of a problem that triggers the ego. As innocent children, we did not need ego. Somewhere along the road, we developed our ego because we got hurt and felt taken advantage of. We decided to protect ourselves, we had our guard up, and we did not trust so easily or naively anymore. We do pay a price for this, though. Ego weakens the connection to our pure inner essence, and we lose the sense of joy, wonder and curiosity. This makes us less effective personally and gets in the way of developing healthy and trusting relationships and building collaborative teams.

In the hierarchy of personal development, the lower stages are deficiency needs which are driven by the dictates of the ego. The needs to survive, belong, be accepted and loved, be recognized, rewarded and respected, and the need for self-centered growth and achievement are ego needs. As long as we are operating in this space, we are driven by ego and we drive or motivate others by appealing to their deficiency needs of the ego.

We cannot fully overcome the deficiency needs by feeding into them. For example, there are people who are never satisfied with the amount of money they earn. Having not overcome the need for respect and recognition, such folks try unsuccessfully to compensate for that deficiency by pursuing and acquiring more wealth. Even after achieving a certain level of advancement and success, no amount of power, recognition and fame seem to be sufficient to make them feel respected and fulfilled. Fulfillment and respect come from inner work—when we take personal responsibility for developing our self-esteem.

To overcome the deficiency needs, we have to learn to manage and master our ego and emotions, and release the subconscious fears and anxieties. This is a necessary step toward operating at higher levels of growth needs in the hierarchy. When we are operating at these higher levels, our ego merges with our essential being and our essence. Some call this our soul, our spirit, our inner self, or higher self. In these elevated states of awareness or consciousness, we are no longer motivated by the basic needs of survival, belonging, and self-centered achievement or greed. We are inspired to unravel our purpose and passionately pursue that purpose by aligning it with our personal and professional life.

We seek professional excellence and personal fulfillment and discover that they mutually reinforce each other. We are no longer driven by the dictates of the ego. Our essence, or our higher self, is now in the driver's seat guiding us in our pursuit. The beliefs of the ego are merged and integrated with the values of the higher self. We are now inspired to unfold our full capability and we inspire our team and everyone around us to give their very best.

Assertiveness

Assertiveness is the intersection of high self-confidence, disarming humility, and healthy self-esteem which comes when we overcome the demands of the ego and align with the dictates of our essence, the higher self. How we respond to situations depends on our mindset and where we are in our development in the hierarchy of human needs. We cannot be truly and fully assertive till we overcome the deficiency needs of the ego in 1.0 and 2.0, and operate at a higher growth needs stage of our essence in 3.0.

1.0 Docile and Meek: Low self-confidence and self-esteem. We are overly sensitive and get hurt easily. This is a state of passivity with a tendency to implode internally. Passivity and inaction does not mean we are humble and we do not have ego. It is a myth to think that being in this state means humility and low ego.

2.0 Forceful and Aggressive: Medium confidence and self-esteem with a large ego, misplaced arrogance, and low level of humility. In this state, our ego is in charge and we get easily offended and insulted. We constantly get into conflicts and explode, resulting in damaged relationships and poor outcomes.

3.0 Serene and Assertive: A high level of self-confidence and self-esteem. We master our emotions and ego is in service of our essence and higher self. We are not easily triggered, we direct our destiny. We are naturally humble yet very clear. We own and take responsibility for our feelings, emotions, and happiness. We directly and constructively hold people accountable by reminding them of mutually agreed goals and principles.

An important point to remember is that when we are operating in 1.0 or 2.0 mindset, we do not clearly see the distinctions among Meek, Aggressive and Assertive behaviors. In fact, we mistakenly assume and argue that we are being assertive, humble and constructive even when we are not. We have to be careful not to critique, argue with, condemn, or judge a person in that state. Our best hope is to operate at 3.0 and lovingly and firmly hold our position.

Success and Greatness

To many in business, success is focused on material and intellectual dimensions. This means the company meets its financial targets of revenue growth and profitability and individuals are reasonably compensated while being offered work that is intellectually stimulating. However, an increasing number of employees and professionals are no longer satisfied with this narrow focus. They are seeking more. Gallup's employee engagement survey proves this point with the following average results for the past twenty-plus years: Engaged—32 percent; Disengaged—50 percent; Actively Disengaged—18 percent.

True success includes and goes beyond the material and intellectual dimensions. You are also seeking meaning and personal fulfillment from your work. The best and brightest organizations and leaders are therefore creating an environment where you can unleash your gifts and creative talents and pursue your dreams. Armed with this perspective, consider the following questions:

- **Don't I need ego to be a good leader?** If your definition of good is financial success and motivation by carrot-and-stick approach, ego has its role. If you want a higher level of success and achievement and want to inspire superior performance, ego will get in the way. You cannot afford to let ego be in the driver's seat—it has to be integrated in service of a higher purpose.

- **How do I manage the egos of my executives and build an exceptional world-class team?** If you learn how to manage and master your ego, managing the egos of the executives and the leadership team will follow naturally. You will engage the team in developing a common, noble purpose and shared core values. You will lead by example by operating at higher states, having overcome your ego needs. You will actively learn and teach ways to conduct your business operations in alignment with your values. As a result, your communication is authentic, decision-making is empowered and accountable, strategy planning is inclusive, and performance evaluation and compensation are fair and objective.

When you learn how to manage and master your ego and your emotions, you will no longer be satisfied with mere success. You will instead be inspired to pursue greatness!

Dealing with Adversity

Effectively overcoming adversity is another key skill for mastering human nature. When something seriously goes wrong (and it invariably does for all of us at some point), and when it appears like you have done everything right and nothing wrong, or when it seems clear that certain people, events, and the world has conspired against you, then you have a choice:

- **Do the obvious thing:** Get angry, upset, frustrated, disappointed, and either become paralyzed or hit back with vengeance.
- **Do what is extremely difficult:** Do not blame anyone or any event, fully accept and absorb the enormous physical and emotional pain. Then take right action to decisively resolve the crisis.

This is exactly what I shared with Ash to help him overcome the most challenging crisis of his career and achieve his greatest triumphs (see "Taking the CEO Mastery Journey"). It was the same for Tim in helping him overcome his midlife crisis (see Practice 1, "Master Human Motivation"). The new Tim is full of zest and pursuing his dreams with a passion that he did not demonstrate even during the best of times as a youngster.

When you choose the second option, something magical begins to happen. The stress and pain melts, giving way to an enormous sense of peace and lightness in the heart. You dig deep for the root cause, take the high ground, and choose a noble response. Doors begin to open and opportunities that you may not even have dreamed of appear right in front of you. Your anger and sorrow shift to appreciation and gratitude, the "tragic situation" becomes the catalyst for a life changing transformation. You feel invincible, yet humble; certain, yet detached; passionate, yet calm; and you flow through life acting on your deepest and truest yearnings and aspirations. Success and positive outcome seems imminent, but paradoxically, you do not care in this case since you have already tasted the greatest success. You are fully present now and you are doing the best you can!

One of the most critical and toughest requirements for a leader is the capacity to convert difficult situations to great opportunities and treat them as experiences for personal growth. There is a certain "unfairness" in leadership—you are expected to give your very best without complaining about the cards you are dealt, and at the same time be understanding of other people who may not live up to the same standards.

While you have to treat adversity as your ally to build the emotional and spiritual muscles, you can't push others too hard and too fast to do the same. Part of mastering human nature is the art of stretching people without breaking them in the process. It doesn't mean you have to accept or tolerate incompetence. Rather, you have to empathize with the emotional state of people you lead and help them overcome their fears, doubts, and uncertainty.

It is natural for a leader to feel anger, frustration, and disappointment at times. The stress and loneliness comes from the difficulty of sharing and expressing these emotions effectively. An exceptional 3.0 leader refines these emotions and converts them to compassion, assertiveness, resolve, and tough love. This cannot be faked; you have to genuinely feel it in your soul. You have to get comfortable and thrive in these circumstances.

Moving from Disappointment to Inspired Action

Adversity and complexity is the way of life for a leader. You can never be completely free from it, so stop wishing for it. The key is to learn the skill of being free in the midst of adversity and complexity. What does that look like? How quickly can you move from disappointment to taking inspired action? There are typically three stages most go through:

- **Stage I:** Disappointment, anger, frustration, despondency: Become paralyzed in a state of suspension, unable to take concrete action.

- **Stage II:** Worry, stress, (perhaps even look for revenge and redemption): Stress, fear, and worry drive us to take action.
- **Stage III:** Fully accept the current situation and take inspired action, free from the sadness of the past and worry about future. In this state, it's not fear or stress which motivates, "presence" inspires action.

Getting to Stage III in the shortest possible time is a function of SQ and is the hallmark of enlightened leadership. Consider the emotional dynamics that can help you to get to this state of inspired action and presence. It starts with full acceptance of the situation the way it actually is, not the way you may hope or fear. You are then able to shift to gratitude for what you have, and the opportunity to do even better. This leads to self-confidence in your ability to come out of the situation stronger than ever and become even more resilient. Finally, you get to a state of humility since you know self-confidence could result in arrogance and derail you. This brings you to a state of fully alert presence, ready to spring into inspired action.

For a leader who is constantly dealing with challenges related to personnel, customers, partners, suppliers, board, advisors, investors and analysts, is there anything more important than being in a state of inspired action all the time?

How Do You Become a Conscious, Self-Actualized 3.0 Leader?

While many thought leaders have accurately and eloquently described conscious behaviors and conscious leadership, none have provided a process for how to get there. This has long remained a black box. Jim Collins was not joking when he responded to the question on how to become a Level 5 Leader—he said one has to have the right parents (DNA) near-death experience or a religious conviction or conversion (see Practice 1, "Master Human Motivation"). This has been my quest—to dig deep and come up with a simple and effective "how-to" process.

We have all heard the saying, "Everybody wants change but no one wants to change." Leo Tolstoy was a bit more specific, "Everyone thinks of changing the world, but no one thinks of changing him-self." Recently, a well-known spiritual leader, Sadhguru Jaggi Vasudev, asked a group of Nobel laureates who had been working hard to make our world a better and more harmonious place, if they experience personal peace. Their honest and not surprising answer was, *no we don't*. I say this only to underscore the human challenge we all face in operating at a self-actualized level where peace of mind, being pres-ent, and positive thinking are natural, spontaneous, and consistent. The most effective way to bring about change is to change oneself, especially if you are a leader. Mahatma Gandhi was more direct, "Be the change you wish to see." This is the most effective way to lead and facilitate change.

Self-Awareness with Self-Discipline Leads to Transformation

Self-awareness is a critical part of the transformation process, but it is only the first step. A lot of people are self-aware, but that doesn't mean anything unless you can develop a game plan and a roadmap to demonstrate genuine positive change in behavior. Ash's journey in this regard is typical of all hard-charging successful business leaders. He identified the need to be a better listener, to encourage risk-tak-ing where it is okay to fail, and to empower people to take decisive actions. Being an open and transparent person by nature, he shared this freely with his leadership team. However, as is always the case, it took a while for a demonstrable and noticeable shift in his behavior. In the meantime, people were wondering if the desire to change was genuine and if change was even possible for a grown man who has been successful doing things a certain way. I would hear statements like, "A leopard cannot change its spots; the tiger cannot change its stripes."

One of the keys to greatness is to develop the discipline to do what we know we should do even if we don't want to do it.

Having been through this journey myself and having helped others do the same, I would remind Ash and his executives to be patient, to not lose trust in each other or the journey, and to celebrate progress and small improvements along the way. I would caution them that those statements are true for animals, but we are different. We are conscious beings with a capacity for reflection, discernment of what is right and wrong, and the ability to take right action. Change is difficult but not impossible. I have personally gone through the process to reduce and remove judgment and anger and become a much deeper listener. I say, "Old dogs can learn new tricks." The mind is a powerful tool—if you think change is impossible, possible, or difficult, you will do what it takes to be right.

Another leader with whom I worked, Larry, was very self-aware in private with me. He admitted to his bouts of temper and directive, dictatorial approach with his executives. His progress was noticeable, and his direct reports shared that with me. However, Larry did not have those conversations with his executives. He was not comfortable being vulnerable. As a result, his progress was limited and did not blossom further into trusting, deeper relationships with his team. Larry managed to survive in his role, because business continued to be good despite his poor personal development and poor morale. Market conditions were favorable and building a great culture was not a priority. It is not wise to connect short-term financial results with leadership skill, especially 3.0 characteristics.

To achieve self-awareness, start by identifying your personal passions and beliefs, and find those areas in which you have talent that is aligned with your professional vision. Once you have done that and stick to it, you have begun your journey toward personal shift.

People can be held back from making the shift because of concerns that they will have to correct the mistakes and do things twice, be taken advantage of and walked all over, lose the sense of who they truly are, or even be seen as ineffective and not adding value. Dramatic, positive shifts in their leadership effectiveness happen when they share these concerns with their subordinates, peers, boss, and close friends, and have those colleagues periodically evaluate their progress. When they do this, their leadership teams work much better together, and they inspire and coach their next-level managers to do the same. The ripple effects are felt throughout the organization.

Authenticity and Vulnerability

Authenticity is the key to personal self-actualization and to building a self-actualized organization. You cannot be authentic without being vulnerable. Most successful, hard driving, functionally bright, and knowledgeable leaders get to this place by driving, commanding, directing, and providing most of the answers. I ask these people to commit to being more connected with their teams by becoming deep, less-critical listeners who can be counted on to guide, coach, and mentor.

Great leaders recognize the power and effectiveness in being authentic. They know that people don't give their best and collaborate unless there is trust. We cannot inspire trust unless we are authentic. However, even the best among us are not free from moments of doubt and uncertainty. Being authentic means that you have to open up about the doubts you experience. This requires you to be vulnerable. How do great leaders deal with such a situation? They have the self-confidence to be vulnerable, and that's exactly what makes them authentic and trustworthy. Since they are not easily overwhelmed, they stay positive and work toward a solution from this place of confidence.

As part of their authenticity and vulnerability, great leaders are open to identifying their blind spots and have the self-esteem to accept the gap between their intention and behavior, self-confidence to admit their shortcomings, and the self-discipline to relentlessly work on inner development or self-leadership.

Commercial Bank of California CEO Ash Patel, whose leadership and organizational transformation I described at length in "Taking the CEO Mastery Journey," was self-aware enough to know that to become a great leader he needed to work on mastering his emotions. He stood in front of his entire leadership team and said he knows he is a good leader but has to learn skills to become a great leader. With that action he demonstrated the convergence of self-awareness, self-confidence, and vulnerability. As a result, he inspired his leadership team to likewise look within themselves and collaborate with each other a lot more effectively. Ash set an example, by diligently participating with the team in training sessions and relentlessly applying the principles in his personal and professional interactions.

Like many outstanding leaders aspiring to greatness, Ash consistently checked his blind spots with people around him who held the mirror and told him the truth. Many of us are on our best behavior with our superiors and even with our peers. Great leaders know that our subordinates bear the brunt of our weaknesses and poor behavior. By creating an open and transparent environment, they encourage them to speak up and benefit from their feedback. By engaging in this activity, Ash not only grew considerably as a leader but also engendered loyalty from the team.

When we come face-to-face with our intimate self, we notice feelings and thoughts that challenge us and seem to tell us: Who do you think you are? How dare you pursue greatness! These feelings and thoughts indicate 1) fear of rejection—people may ridicule, humiliate, reject, or worse, abandon us; 2) fear of owning our greatness—we feel inadequate, we may be given greater responsibility than we can handle, we could become a target of envy and of direct and indirect attacks.

One of the keys to Ash's remarkable transformation was his ability to accept the tough feedback from his team. For example: There was a perception that he was playing favorites, making it difficult to establish trust. By having candid conversations, the environment of trust immediately enhanced the level of engagement, productivity, and collaboration. Ash's transformation had a remarkable impact on his ability to lead.

Integrating Work, Life, Intellect, Emotion, and Spirit

Work-life balance is key to your self-mastery, and it's best not to view these two aspects as separate. Doing so implies that work is drudgery that takes you away from life. In the past, the boundaries of personal and professional life were clearer. You showed up at work, checked your feelings at the door, did your job from 9 to 5, and had evenings and weekends to give expression to the important aspects of life such as connection, emotion, fulfillment, and happiness. Work was a place to earn a paycheck. Work-life balance, as it was understood, is a relic of the Industrial Revolution where semi-robotic compliance was the requirement in a top-down management structure. It worked well, perhaps even beautifully, for that time.

It is no longer possible in professional jobs to set those work hours and establish clear boundaries. You are in a different time now. Your expectations from work have changed, and why not? You are working longer hours and the boundaries—of time and space—are getting blurred. It is a lot more difficult to separate personal and professional fulfillment. Since you do not have as much time away from work anymore it is only reasonable to seek contentment in an integrated manner. There is sufficient evidence that professional excellence and personal fulfillment mutually reinforce each other. Employee engagement surveys are telling you time and again that you are more engaged when you feel connected, cared for, recognized, and are given opportunities to excel and share your greatest gifts. In other words, you do not want just a paycheck and intellectual stimulation alone from work; you are seeking emotional and spiritual fulfillment too. In my experience, professional excellence and personal fulfillment, reinforce each other.

The leaders I work with have a passion to be loving spouses, caring parents, and dependable friends. They want to integrate all these characteristics at work while driving for professional success. I personally exercise my emotional and spiritual muscles a lot more in tricky personal situations with family and friends. This helps me in dealing with relatively less emotional scenarios at work. I don't mean to downplay the serious emotional turmoil and conflicts people go through at work. In fact, these issues are made worse by our inability to accept and deal with them. It gets even more dysfunctional when the expected culture is to pretend that all is well.

I know firsthand the price paid by individuals, leaders, teams, and organizations for not resolving emotionally charged issues. The point I am making here is that if you learn to dive 40 feet underwater, it is much easier when most of the time you are only required to be at 20 to 30 feet. The mastery you are after to pursue your own greatness is a package deal: personal, professional and organizational. CEOs and leaders cannot afford to artificially separate them.

Breaking Through with Self-Inquiry

Self-inquiry is one of the most powerful tools in a CEO's arsenal. It is the act of going within to discover the underlying reason behind our feelings and actions. It is a powerful exercise that helps us understand our unconscious or conditioned responses to people and incidents. By recognizing and understanding why we respond and react to certain situations the way we do, we can improve our response and make it more helpful and effective. We take responsibility for our actions. The trigger may be external, but the reason is always internal.

Suppose somebody's behavior triggered you to get angry or hurt. Did you feel justified to get angry and judge? Did your anger solve the problem or improve the relationship? Instead of blaming and judging them, you can get curious, asking yourself, "Why did I get angry? Why was I hurt?" Through self-inquiry you can discover the underlying reasons, some deep-rooted beliefs and values that were violated. You may recognize that you suffer from the same or similar problem you accuse others of. You may discover that the fear of not fulfilling your desires may be the true reason for your anger; that it was actually about you, and not the external other.

This humbling realization helps great leaders to reach out and solve complex, tricky issues by connecting with care and compassion. They assert their position with humility and listen to the other perspective with a curious mind and an open heart, thus engaging in a constructive dialog.

We all experience positive thoughts, neutral thoughts, and negative thoughts. Facing our negative thoughts could be difficult initially because we come face-to-face with our shadow side. We can no longer deny this "unpleasant" side of ours. In self-inquiry, we try to determine the root cause for why our thoughts are positive, neutral, or negative. Once you determine the underlying reason, you can influence your thoughts, and therefore, your subsequent actions.

When I am working with leaders, I help them identify their most important improvement goal. I begin by asking them to list actions of theirs that may sabotage their pursuit of the goal, thereby preventing them from unleashing their full potential. I then ask them to dig deeper and self-inquire, "Why do you do what you do?" You need to work continually on improving and building your emotional muscles while also monitoring your progress and changing course when needed. I have helped many other successful leaders make a similar shift and transformation. Following is a representative example of the work:

- Most successful hard-driving, functionally bright, and knowledgeable leaders got there by driving, commanding, directing, and providing most of the answers.
- The improvement goal I work with them on is: I am committed to being more connected with my team by becoming a deep listener, less critical, and an inspiring leader that can be counted on to guide, coach, and mentor.
- The key reasons that hold them back from making the shift are concerns that they will:
  - Lose sense of who they truly are. What got them here is by being hands-on and doing stuff themselves.
  - Be seen as ineffective and not adding value.
  - Be taken advantage of and walked all over.
  - Have to correct the mistakes of others who may not do it right.
- Dramatic shifts in their leadership effectiveness happen when they share this with their subordinates, peers, boss, close friends, and have them periodically evaluate their progress.
- Leadership teams work much better together, they inspire and coach their next level managers to do the same, and the ripple effects are felt throughout the organization.

The results are even more remarkable when leadership teams engage in this powerful exercise together. Your teammates will objectively evaluate your progress and feel comfortable to hold each other accountable when you give them permission. This significantly enhances trust, alignment, and team work. I developed this for Ash and other leaders I am working with. Asking yourself these kinds of questions, then getting past the roadblocks to becoming a more self-actualized leader will put you on the path that has been and is being taken by the likes of Steve Jobs, Satya Nadella, Ray Dalio of Bridgewater Associates, Charlie Kim of Next Jump, Jeff Weiner of LinkedIn, John Mackey of Whole Foods, and Bob Chapman of Barry-Wehmiller.

I suggested the following approach to a 2.0 CEO who was getting frustrated with his executives—he felt that they did not embody the vision and values the company stood for. However, the CEO had not clearly defined the vision, did not clarify how it was beneficial for them, and did not get their buy-in. Besides, he created two challenges: he did not prioritize actions—everything seemed equally important, and he did not assign accountability.

Here are several specific steps you can take to foster positive evolution in yourself as well as the members of your executive team:

1. Reiterate your vision and purpose with more clarity. Get their emotional involvement and buy-in by explaining what is in it for them.

2. Be direct in expressing your genuine concern and frustration with the leadership team not embodying the values. Give specific examples.

3. Take personal responsibility for the situation. Don't just blame them. Ask for their opinion and perspective.

4. Ask for solutions. Pause, encourage, and listen.

5. Prioritize and assign accountability along with timelines to complete strategies and tactics for addressing the issues.

As the CEO, you have a larger responsibility to grow and to evolve since your personal development is directly connected to the growth and culture of the organization. You have to dare to dream big, an audacious goal inspires but you need a roadmap and an action plan to make progress and deliver on the dream! If you want to build a high-trust, high-performance organization, you need to lead the charge by learning personal and organizational mastery skills to deliver on the dream!

Practice 3: Inspire With a Noble Purpose

"Never doubt that a small group of thoughtful, committed citizens can change the world, indeed it's the only thing that ever has." — Margaret Mead

To invoke top performance from those in your organizations, you need to inspire them. You and they need to be inspired by a cause that goes beyond you, by a purpose that is bigger than each of us individually. To be inspirational means to be purposeful. When you are and feel purposeful, you can be most effective as a leader because you will inspire others to give their best. When people give their best, they execute well, and business is all about execution. An inspirational leader, therefore, achieves breakthrough results in business execution, leadership effectiveness, and the pursuit of a purposeful life.

According to Gallup, only 40 percent of Americans feel purposeful. More importantly, 88 percent of employees feel that they are not cared for and do not find work to be meaningful. Fulfillment and meaning are connected to each person's career, so feeling purposeful at work is a necessary precondition to inspirational leadership. As a leader, the purpose of your business has to be aligned with the purpose of life. The primary purpose of life is the same for every human being: It is to be alive, to be awake, and to be fully present in the moment, in the now, independent of external circumstances. This leads to being at peace with who we are, and thus able to consistently experience happiness, joy, and fulfillment. This is what our highest self and deepest inner being craves. It is known by different names—soul, spirit, essence, higher self. However, understanding this concept is more important than what we call it.

Many people confuse their material and surface level desires with purpose. Personal and professional growth, achievement, recognition, and respect are desires of ego. These are important, necessary, and even unavoidable. However, they do not by themselves lead to fulfilling our primary purpose as humans. This recognition dawns for some only after achieving a great deal of material success, fame, and fortune. Most people are too busy chasing success in the hope of fulfilling the primary purpose but never get there. This pursuit of material and financial success is not to be confused with our primary purpose and our calling. At best, we can call this pursuit of material success a secondary purpose.

We all have natural gifts, talents, and passions that may not necessarily align with our professional experience. For a lucky few, there is alignment, and that significantly helps in the pursuit of their primary purpose. Progress in your primary purpose will be accelerated when you treat your career as something more than a means to make a living and gain intellectual satisfaction. Your career can be a vehicle to develop personal and organizational mastery and to make a difference by unconditionally serving and contributing to society, community, and the world.

Many of today's most dynamic organizations are driven by a strong sense of purpose that transcends simple sales goals. Apple Inc. doesn't just sell cool technology products—its aim is to "change the world." This resonates with its employees and drives them to push the envelope on innovation and productivity. Zappos sells shoes, clothes, and accessories, which might seem a little boring on its face, but the company has achieved great success largely because of its stated purpose to "deliver happiness." Corporate stalwart Johnson & Johnson doesn't just sell healthcare products; it stands for "caring for the world, one person at a time." Seventh Generation manufactures and sells relatively mundane cleaning, paper, and personal care products such as detergent, diapers, fabric softener, and dish soap but aspires to a much loftier purpose: To "inspire a consumer revolution that nurtures the health of the next seven generations." Apparel maker Patagonia says it exists to "build the best product, cause no unnecessary harm; use business to inspire; and implement solutions to the environmental crisis."

But an organization's purpose cannot simply be a string of pretty words. To inspire, it needs to come from the inside, be authentic and passionate, and resonate with human nature, beginning with your own. This requires self-exploration to find the passion and purpose that you will transmit to the organization.

Why Have a Noble Purpose in Business?

I asked the CEO and his executive team, "How is the level of trust in the team?" These were successful, upright professionals with an average of over 20 years of experience in the industry. They were almost annoyed by the question; I could read the body language. They said it was very good and high. I knew the team well enough to know that was not the case.

They were polite to each other. They had a tremendous work ethic and high personal integrity, but they did not confront professional disagreements directly. They would dance around issues and joke about it creating more confusion for each other and their respective teams. As the tension built up and escalated to active conflicts with team members, some of them would erupt and blurt it out bluntly. A familiar pattern with many teams, right?

I said the trust we are talking about here involves addressing professional challenges directly and constructively. Do you consistently do that? Do you call each other out and hold each other accountable if the behavior is not in alignment with your core values? Do you address issues directly and constructively? How do you address commitments that are not kept? I asked them to rate trust in the executive team on a scale of 1 to 5. They were clear and honest and rated themselves somewhere between 2 and 2.5. As I said before, these are successful, upright individuals who are experts in their respective functions. They have clearly set targets and goals toward which they are working. This is the opportunity almost every executive team has. Just imagine the success that is possible when trust and alignment moves up to 4 or 5.

You cannot build trust intellectually; you have to connect at a deeper level with emotion, heart, and spirit. The typical financial and market share goals and targets motivate us to do well to survive and achieve material success and intellectual stimulation. Do they move our heart and spirit to give our very best? Do we push our teammates, and do we give permission to our teammates to push us and hold us accountable to become the best version of ourselves? How do we do this—how can we get personal without losing our professional edge and risk missing our business goals and targets?

The other important issue is employee engagement, which, according to the Gallup poll, has been around 30 percent for the past twenty years, with about 20 percent actually disengaged at their place of work. In spite of all the remarkable progress in the workplace such as technology innovation, improved communication, reducing layers of bureaucratic hierarchy, higher wages, flexible hours, and wellness programs, we have not moved the needle on employee engagement. How can we get people passionate about their work and to show up with a missionary zeal where they feel purposeful and fulfilled? Is it possible to bring the level of commitment and conviction that we see in people involved in socioeconomic movements, such as freedom and democracy, humans on the moon, women's rights, and civil rights in a business environment?

Let's be clear: People don't follow leaders; they follow the purpose or vision, mission, and principles for which they stand.

These are two of the toughest challenges in any business environment—leadership alignment and employee engagement. When we crack the code on those, organizations will thrive by unlocking their full value, while helping their people to unleash their full potential. The answer is to inspire with a noble purpose that goes beyond profitability. Let's be clear: People don't follow leaders, they follow the purpose or vision, the mission, and principles. This was the secret great leaders such as Abraham Lincoln, Mahatma Gandhi, JFK, MLK, Helen Keller, and Rosa Parks knew.

In business organizations, leaders can achieve compliance and a certain level of engagement with rank, authority, and a reward-and-punishment approach to motivation. To inspire people to give their very best and achieve mutual accountability requires digging deeper. The answer is to develop a purpose where profitability is a by-product or a strategy to achieve the noble purpose. I will present a process that achieves this and instills an owner mindset in everyone, the Holy Grail of a business organization.

As former French President Charles De Gaulle once said, the graveyards are full of indispensable men. Business is a team sport; no one can do it alone. An organization cannot rise above the developmental level of its leader and the leadership team. You can certainly achieve a level of organizational success with professional skill and strong personal effort and a lot more success with the right product or service at the right time. Leadership success begins with self-awareness and self-leadership but also requires an aligned leadership team, engaged employees, and a noble purpose to fully unleash the organizational potential.

In business, no matter how persuasive you think you are, you can't simply make others do what you want. You can only help, guide, and facilitate people to do what they want. You have to inspire, not command your people to give their best. Nobody willingly follows a tyrant. Leading by fear, power, and authority only drives minimal compliance and produces mediocre results. Here, the focus is on lower levels of motivation. A higher level of motivation is achieved by appealing to each person's innate personal desire for greater fulfillment which leads to more growth, more success, and more achievement.

This practice delves into the most effective method to inspire your people—by touching their hearts and spirits with care, inclusion, fairness, meritocracy, and most of all, purpose. Great leaders mobilize the organization with a compelling cause, noble purpose, and a vision that galvanizes everyone to give their very best. A vision that addresses the fundamental human drives such as freedom, autonomy, fairness, meritocracy, inclusiveness, and respect inspires and produces the best results.

Pursuing a Noble Purpose

The purpose of life is not to eat. We need to eat to survive, but hopefully our life's purpose is more meaningful. Similarly, the purpose of business is not just to be profitable. Organizations have to be profitable to survive, but hopefully the business purpose is more inspiring.

Having authority and a title is not in itself leading. That's managing, and people are simply following orders. An inspiring noble purpose that galvanizes everyone into action is crucial. That's why current business leaders such as Ray Dalio of Bridgewater Associates, Charlie Kim of Next Jump, Larry Page and Sergey Brin of Google, Howard Schulz of Starbucks, Satya Nadella of Microsoft, Paul Polman of Unilever, John Mackey of Whole Foods, Chris Forman and Nora Dashwood of Decurion, and Bob Chapman of Barry-Wehmiller have made it a priority to develop and operationalize inspiring purpose and values in their business organizations.

As I said earlier, the primary purpose of life is to be fully alive, awake, and present. How about pursuing audacious dreams, making a difference, contributing and serving unconditionally—aren't these supposed to be our purpose, you might ask? Yes, of course, but you have to first start from a place of being fully awake. Only then can you truly discover your calling, your purpose, your gift and the contribution you can make to the world. This calling has to come from deep within; we engage in it because it nurtures the soul. This calling is not governed by personal ambition or the dictates and desires of our ego.

When we identify our noblest of intentions, highest of aspirations, boldest of dreams, and deepest of yearnings and pursue them with passion, we experience peace and contentment. It is a mutually reinforcing cycle—presence leads to our purpose and pursuing our purpose leads to presence. This process naturally leads to higher performance and fulfillment, which we all seek in business and in life.

When you are in the top 10 percent of all the banks in the country, and in the top 5 percent of all the banks started in California (in continuous quarterly profitability since inception), you would assume that the bank is driven by profit motive and it is their primary purpose, right? After all, business organizations frequently operate as if revenue growth and profitability is the sole purpose. Well, think again. Great leaders and organizations know that profitability is a means to an end or a happy by-product of a noble pursuit. Outstanding financial performance is a strategy to achieve the purpose. CEO Ash Patel began this approach at Premier Commercial Bank (PCB) and has now fully embraced it Commercial Bank of California (CBC).

I facilitated a discussion with Ash and his leadership team to share their personal dreams and professional goals. This was the first time in the ten years they were together that they had engaged in such a deeply personal discussion. Some members shared the dream to build a great organization. Others were looking forward to pursuing their personal passion, such as travel, charitable work, tend to a horse ranch, and own a restaurant after retirement. As they were sharing their passion there was a perceptible shift in energy, enthusiasm, and excitement.

I asked, "Do you show up with the same enthusiasm every day at work? Why not? You are the leadership team, you run this organization. Why wait 'til you are retired or 'til you achieve your dream?" The result was dramatic. It became obvious that they wanted to be a lot more aligned and collaborative than they had ever been. They felt that their financial performance could be even better if they trusted and held each other accountable. They challenged each other to show up fully at work, as if they were living their dream and pursuing their passion.

They decided to make their Organization a great place to work. They defined the noble purpose: our organization will become a vehicle to help its employees, customers, investors, and all of its stakeholders to realize their dreams. One executive shared the excitement he feels on Sunday evenings and Monday mornings about coming to work, much to the amusement of his wife. He truly feels, "Thank

God it's Monday," which is in sharp contrast to the normal Monday morning blues many in the workforce experience.

Successful business leaders are adept at generating shareholder profit. For too long, they have relied on getting things done by the carrot-and-stick approach to motivation. They set goals or assign tasks and reward people for achievement and penalize them for shortcomings. There is overwhelming evidence to prove that there is a better way, yet many leaders keep practicing this approach. The end justifies the means, they say, and argue "By increasing value, we produce economic prosperity for all stakeholders; investors get a good return and invest more, customers get quality products at competitive prices, employees make a decent living, suppliers thrive, and communities benefit." This approach seems to have run its course.

Great leaders keep the organization focused on achieving exceptional financial results while inspiring its people to give their best in pursuit of a noble purpose. They know that increasing shareholder value is not the greatest motivator for employees. They realize that fear, self-centered achievement, and greed motivate, but people don't give their very best under those circumstances. Studies in human nature and motivations suggest that we get deeply inspired by meaning—working for a cause or solution larger than ourselves—and mastery. Pursuing a noble purpose while staying focused on execution and the bottom line creates an exciting and fulfilling work environment.

Engaged and inspired employees who are driven by a larger organizational purpose help maximize results. They challenge each other to free the mind, open the heart, and unleash their spirit. Striving for excellence becomes everybody's job. People do not settle for polite mediocrity or dysfunctional teamwork. As individual productivity and teamwork take a quantum leap, so does creativity, innovation, and business performance.

The secret to unleashing greatness and unlocking organizational value is the pursuit of a noble purpose: Purpose drives performance, which in turn drives profits. Ever wonder why people work harder and smarter in transformative organizations such as Google, Amazon, Commerce Bank, Apple, and Southwest Airlines? It is a remarkable sign of the times we live in that companies such as Zappos practice "Delivering Happiness" as a path to profits, passion, and purpose; and Google has "Don't be evil" as the informal corporate motto!

The Value of Purpose

One of the challenges facing business organizations is the absence of a noble purpose to which people can commit. Revenue growth and profitability may get the owners and shareholders excited, but that's not what drives other very important stakeholders—employees, customers, suppliers, and partners. Employees are more interested in an open, inclusive, and authentic environment where vision and values are connected to and drive daily operations. This is exactly the environment that 3.0 authentic leaders create and nurture. In doing so, they appeal to the higher states of awareness and consciousness, such as the drive to contribute and serve unconditionally for the greater good and to make a difference.

Going to the next level means getting the whole person to engage—their heart, mind, and spirit. This 3.0 leadership inspires the highest level of performance and effectiveness from self, team, and organization. It transcends, and includes, the traditional motivational practices based on security, fear, and intimidation of 1.0 and the self-centered ambition or achievement of 2.0. Toughness without care breeds rigid conformance and mediocre compliance; similarly, care without toughness could lead to apathy. Neither of them is as effective as the tough love of enlightened authentic leadership.

This new breed of 3.0 leaders and their business organizations can be the role models for enlightened leadership and can become the agents for change that we want to see in our global socioeconomic organizations. They are driven to build organizations that actively seek to fix the disconnect between authentic living and economic success by integrating purpose and values with extraordinary performance. Let's talk about the four Ps of such organizations.

- **Purpose:** Pursuing a noble purpose creates an exciting and fulfilling work environment. Employees are inspired to give their very best individually and collaborate toward an inspiring common purpose. As individual productivity and teamwork takes a quantum leap, so does business performance and innovation to provide the best offerings to the customers. Let me give you a metaphor from life. We don't pursue happiness; our experience tells us that the more we pursue happiness, the more elusive it is. Happiness is a result, a by-product, of leading a purposeful and meaningful life. The same is true in business; profitability and stellar financial performance are by-products of working toward a noble purpose. We can say that profitability is a strategy to achieve a great cause, to fulfill a noble purpose.

- **Performance:** A happy and somewhat paradoxical by-product of pursuing a noble purpose is outstanding financial performance. Seen another way, outstanding performance is a strategy to achieve our noble purpose. In order to take this performance to an even higher level, we set internal benchmarks for ourselves to excel in serving all our stakeholders. We measure employee engagement, customer satisfaction, and community involvement because doing well here ensures superior financial performance. We also monitor how well we are doing in building trust and collaborating, resolving passive conflicts, making fast and effective decisions. These are the leading indicators that point to how well our performance is going to be.

- **Principles (Core Values):** Almost all organizations have nice sounding values. But the key question is: How effectively are they being followed in daily business transactions? Who developed them? Do these values reflect the aspirations of the organization? Do they fit the personality profile of the leadership team so they can practice what they preach? Is there an incentive for diligently practicing those values? Is there a consequence for flouting them? When these questions are successfully answered, it just doesn't feel good to practice these values; business performance improves dramatically.

- **Processes:** Having a purpose and values is good but is of no great value if they are not reflected in the daily activities and business processes of the organization. These values have to be demonstrated when you facilitate meetings, make decisions, resolve conflicts, and engage in negotiations. It is not sufficient to talk about values or hang signs everywhere. Engaged people, disciplined management, and operational processes are critical. You have to conduct your daily business this way and infuse service and excellence in the DNA of your organization. You have to hire and promote people that excel personally and professionally. The leadership team has to practice what they preach. In one of my most successful engagements, the president and the entire management team was engaged in learning, teaching, and practicing enlightened leadership skills. The president and his executive vice president were the best and most diligent practitioners. The president especially had a phenomenal hunger and aptitude for learning.

Galvanizing Business with Purpose

Success in life and business is about effective execution and spontaneously performing right action in real time. What is the purpose of business? This is not a trick question. I don't believe there is an absolute right answer. Your answer depends on your mindset, your state of awareness or consciousness, or even priorities.

If you are in a 1.0 mindset, basic comforts, stability, and security are what gives you happiness and fulfillment. In this case, a business organization's primary purpose is to create a profitable and stable environment so the investors get a steady return, customers can expect a dependable product or service, and employees earn a steady, lifetime paycheck. Conformance and compliance are more important than creativity and rapid professional growth.

If you are in a 2.0 mindset, the business environment's primary focus is growth and opportunities for professional development. Creativity, innovation, and intellect are rewarded even if they create stress. Investors expect high growth and returns, customers anticipate new innovations, and employees can look forward to professional growth and an intellectually stimulating work environment.

If you are in a 3.0 mindset, you want both professional excellence and personal fulfillment. You want to integrate and align your life's purpose with the purpose of your business, since you spend well over 50 percent of your waking time at work. In addition to stable employment and professional growth, business provides opportunities for personal fulfillment and mutual support by helping each person become the best they can be intellectually, emotionally, and spiritually. This allows head, heart, and spirit to flourish. Similarly, investors and customers can expect to be a part of larger shifts in making a difference while benefiting from exceptional returns and outstanding products and services.

Creating Purpose, Vision, Mission, and Core Values

Creating your purpose and vision is an important exercise that cannot be outsourced and shouldn't be taken lightly. It requires a deep understanding of oneself and aligning your core beliefs and values with those of your peers. One high-performance CEO said that he and his leadership team had spent hundreds of hours meditating, reflecting, and walking in the woods to get this right. An effective purpose—and vision if you choose to develop both—is one that is inspiring, that stretches you and your organization to consistently grow and give your best, and instills an owner mindset in everyone. Let us start by clearly defining each of the terms:

- **Purpose:** It is our why! This is the noble reason we choose to work here or to start or lead this organization. It is typically deeper and more profound than a vision statement, though some companies combine both and use them interchangeably.

- **Vision:** Vision is a virtuous dream; it inspires and provides directional guidance. It is a journey and does not have a destination as such. It is an ideal state or state of perfection that your business should be continually striving for.

- **Mission:** Mission has a destination and an endpoint. It is the overarching objective that is measurable and realizable. Completion of mission ensures that you are effectively pursuing your vision.

- **Core Values:** Core values are the values you espouse and commit to live by in your daily interactions in order to fulfill your mission and pursue your vison effectively. Our goal is to match the stated values with how we show up, how we behave, and how we interact with each other.

- **Core Operating Principles (COPs):** COPs provide more detail, clarity, and definition to how you operate your business and how you interact with each other and with all your stakeholders.

There is no right or wrong purpose. However, you must choose the purpose of your business organization deliberately in order to reflect your desired cultural mindset. A hierarchical business organization cannot rise above the development of its leader and its leadership team. If the CEO is at a 1.0 mindset, it is not advisable to have a vision and core values reflecting a 3.0 mindset. However, if the CEO is at a 2.0 mindset but is actively engaged in developing and evolving to 3.0, it is fine to pursue building a 3.0 organization.

A CEO cannot do it alone—business is team sport. It requires an empowered and aligned executive team whose center of gravity or tipping point is at about the same level as the CEO's. A leadership team that holds each other accountable can nurture an engaged organization. If the collective awareness of the organization is at 1.0, you have to pass through 2.0 on your way to becoming a 3.0 organization. As I said before, you can accelerate but cannot skip steps of personal, professional, and organizational evolution and development.

Product-Centric versus a People-Centric Approach

It is the people who develop, drive, and deliver products or services to their customers that underlie any organization. A 3.0 purpose is focused on making a contribution to the world by unleashing the human spirit at work. The approach is to create an environment where we will become the best version of ourselves. This is called a people-centric, as opposed to a product-centric, purpose.

People-centric organizations believe that the best way to make a difference and contribute in the world is by leading consciously and nurturing a culture where employees show up authentically. They help each other become the best they can be. It doesn't matter what product or service they offer, as long as they take right action: Treat each other with respect, care, and support while building sustainable and profitable organizations.

A rapidly increasing number of organizations, such as Decurion Corporation, Next Jump Inc., Bridgewater Associates, LinkedIn, Barry-Wehmiller, Morning Star, Sun Hydraulics, Valve, and FAVI manufacturing are focused on nurturing profoundly people-centric workplaces and engaging in peak performance principles. These companies operate inside out—in the reverse order of conventional businesses. They start with people purpose, which drives their principles, which in turn generates performance and profitability.

We don't all need to be designing next-generation products or manufacturing lifesaving medicines to feel a sense of accomplishment or to feel like we are making a difference. What can be more remarkable than showing up exactly the way we are, being fully present and authentic, and helping others be the same? When your primary purpose is to help one another become the best they can be, how can it not lead to enhanced productivity, creativity, and stellar performance?

No wonder people-centric companies are wildly profitable. Business now becomes the playground to express your highest aspirations and deepest yearnings. You unleash your highest potential and unlock the full value of the organization. Principles and values mean something; they are not just words on the wall.

If you want to build a 3.0 organization, you need a 3.0 purpose to steward and lead the organization responsibly. This means that the CEO and the executive team have to dig deep. In doing so, you uncover your purpose and passion in life, your dreams and aspirations, the beliefs and values you live by, your strengths and the natural gifts you possess, and the weaknesses, fears, and blocks that are holding you back from giving your very best. How do you accomplish this? I have found the following exercise to be most effective for achievement-driven, successful business executives and leaders:

- You share your personal story, your hero's journey—your greatest successes, joys, and thrills—as well as your deepest disappointments, frustrations, and failures.
- You identify and share the highest accomplishment that will make your life worthwhile and meaningful for you.

You cannot get to the core of your essential being without going through the process of sharing your journey. You cannot afford to skip or even rush this step. If you do, the journey is much slower and bumpier. This process is most effective when you are calm, present, reflective, and in an alert and wakeful flow state. This is not always a comfortable exercise, but it is a necessary step for you to show up authentically. It is also critical for building an aligned, high-trust, and mutually accountable 3.0 leadership team.

The next important step is to define the business vision that is in alignment with your highest aspirations. This is followed by the development of mission. Vision provides directional guidance whereas a mission is more tangible, practical, and can be clearly tracked and measured. When you make progress and accomplish your mission, you are on an accelerated path in your purposeful journey.

Finally, it is critical to carefully pick core values and core operating principles that are relevant for your business purpose, vision, and mission. You also must commit to live by these values and principles. These are the operational guideposts that help you stay true to your purposeful journey, pursuing your vision, and accomplishing your mission. They also help you become more effective in the way you communicate, decide, reward, incentivize, plan, and execute on a daily basis.

Purpose, Vision, Mission, and Core Values at CBC

At Commercial Bank of California (CBC), I facilitated deep discussions over several sessions that included the CEO and core members of the executive team. This richly rewarding exercise resulted in the following:

Purpose: Promote life wealth.

- It is about leading a full and fulfilling life which includes, but is not limited to, financial wealth. Life wealth incorporates: financial, intellectual, physical, emotional, social, and spiritual wellbeing for our employees, customers, and everyone with whom we engage.

Vision: Transform the way you think about banking.

- We will disrupt the industry by decentralizing banking. We will create an ecosystem of transformative financial products and services to enable our customers' businesses to achieve success with a purpose.

Mission: Be an organization with empowered employees, loyal clients, proud owners, and appreciative communities.

- Be in the top 10 percent in our segment of the banking industry in financial performance, customer satisfaction, and employee engagement.
- Mission 20/2020—Achieve $20 million income with $1 billion in assets by 2020.

Values: Embody gratitude, respect, integrity, trust, courage, compassion, and humility.

- We will track adherence to these values in performance evaluation of every executive and employee in the organization.

Promoting life wealth is a people-centric 3.0 purpose. By taking this bold step, CBC has joined the league of elite companies in the business community who are at the forefront of the socioeconomic shift. Business is no longer a place just to earn a paycheck and, if we are lucky, engage in intellectually stimulating work. It can and should be much more than that. It can be a place where we can bring and grow our whole self—intellect, emotion, and spirit.

Below are some of the statements that were considered in these brainstorming sessions:

- We help pursue the dreams of our stakeholders—employees, customers, investors, and partners—and enrich their lives.
- Everything we do and every interaction we engage in is an opportunity to fully unleash our talents, gifts, and creative genius. We help each other to be the greatest expression of who we are and bring out the best in all of us. We are on a purposeful journey to build an organization with inspired employees, delighted customers, proud shareholders, grateful partners, and an appreciative community.

Examples of Purpose, Vision, and Mission

Here are some examples of the type of noble purposes and missions embraced by successful product-centric organizations:

- **Google's vision:** To organize information and make it easily accessible and useful.
- **Apple's purpose as envisioned by Steve Jobs:** "To make a contribution to the world by making tools for the mind that advance humankind."
- **Southwest Airline's mission:** To connect people through friendly, reliable, and low-cost air travel.
- **LinkedIn's vision:** To create economic opportunity for every member of the global workforce (3 billion people).
- **LinkedIn's mission:** Connect the world's professionals to make them more productive and successful.

These companies do a very good job of taking care of their people. Some of them are exceptional, but it is not the core purpose of their business. Below are examples of people-centric vision and mission statements:

Microsoft: Our vision is "to help individuals and businesses realize their full potential." Microsoft's more recently stated vision and mission statements reflect CEO Satya Nadella's 3.0 leadership approach to inspire and empower (instead of command and control) and build a 3.0 culture of learn it all (as opposed to know it all).

Google (Original Motto): Don't be evil. When Google became Alphabet in October 2015, it had a similar code of conduct, "Employees of Alphabet ... should do the right thing—follow the law, act honorably, and treat each other with respect."

Starbucks: "Our mission is to inspire and nurture the human spirit—one person, one cup, and one neighborhood at a time."

Zappos: Our vision is "Delivering happiness to customers, employees, and vendors."

Barry-Wehmiller: "Make our employees' lives meaningful." This global manufacturing firm has taken the concept of caring for their employees to a whole new level.

Aligning and Engaging the Organization

A noble purpose and uplifting values are good, but not sufficient to keep the organization aligned, engaged, and inspired. As leaders, you have to fully "walk the talk," and demonstrate behaviors that are in alignment with these values. You have to be consistent in messaging and in your behavior. A 3.0 statement with 1.0 behavior is devastating for morale, productivity, and performance. As discussed in Practice 1, "Master Human Motivations," there are seven crucial mindsets that drive our fundamental behavior. You can achieve positive behavior change by working at the source and mastering these mindsets. You have to hold your peers accountable and then demand the same from the rest of the organization. In addition, you have to demonstrate action leadership skills (see Practice 6, "Engage in Action Leadership").

What is the most effective way to get the best ideas and buy-in from the leadership team? Present a well-thought-out idea as a first draft, then wholeheartedly invite input, comments, and feedback.

It is crucial for the leadership team to clearly communicate the vision and get buy-in from the whole organization. You have to effectively connect the vision to the needs and requirements of all your stakeholders and constituents so they can emotionally and viscerally relate to that vision. It has to satisfy their self-centered motivation to grow, and also appeal to their altruistic nature that seeks to make a difference and contribute. It plays out differently for different stakeholders. For example:

- **Executives:** You will shape the direction of this organization in alignment with your highest aspirations. You will create an environment that will push you to be the best you can be, and by example, you will inspire others to do the same.

- **Employee:** Your employer provides rapid growth opportunities and meaningful work in a collaborative environment that will inspire you to express your greatest strengths and gifts.

- **Customer:** The company's product/service makes your life and/or business more productive, effective, and exciting. By engaging in a genuine win-win relationship, you help us make a difference.

- **Owner/Investor:** You will get an exceptional return on investment and be a proud partner in contributing to the change we wish to see. The business and its leadership will be role models for running high-trust and high-performance organizations and institutions.

Instilling an Owner Mindset

When everyone in the organization feels like, "This is my company and I will do what whatever it takes to fulfill our mission and live our values," greatness and high performance naturally follow. A powerful way to get buy-in and instill an owner mindset is to give everyone the opportunity to shape the vision and values of the organization. This can be practically accomplished by sharing a well-considered draft that has been developed by the executive team, and requesting input from anyone interested. Each senior executive will conduct this exercise with their respective departments, taking the time to ensure that any doubts, misunderstandings, or misgivings are addressed.

How did CBC accomplish this? We started with a small team of eight senior executives, including the CEO, and went through the exercises thoroughly to come up with a framework for purpose, vision, mission, and core values. We made sure that all good ideas and thoughts were included in this framework. After further discussions, culled it down to a first draft. We then invited other key executives that reported to the CEO and COO to review the draft with us. We explained the process, got their input, and finalized the first draft.

We discussed implementation ideas and decided that we should visit all our branches and departments and, once again, explain the process, present the draft, and solicit their input and buy-in. There were understandable concerns that if we opened it up to everyone there would be too much input, and some people would be bound to be disappointed. I reminded them that the key element in this process was that we should first thoroughly explain our rationale for this draft, answer all questions, and sincerely consider all input.

Using this process, we made some really good tweaks and edits before finalizing our statements and values. As expected, there were no major changes because our process was thoughtful and clearly explained to everyone. We announced the plan at the company's "all-hands" meeting and then visited all locations and departments individually. This way, everyone felt included and engaged. As a result, CBC got a lot more in return for the time we invested in this process.

Achieving High-Trust and High-Performance

An inspiring purpose and vision by themselves do not guarantee exceptional results or a smooth path. You must have the courage to not be discouraged by the doubters who consciously or unconsciously place obstacles in your path. If you are not careful, you can be overly consumed with responding to the cynics who are close-minded, as opposed to focusing on skeptics who are open to change and nurturing the "always on" transformers.

A 3.0 organization is a high-trust and high-performance (HTP) organization. Achieving high-trust and high-performance requires practically connecting noble purpose and vision to daily operations and execution. You have to create the environment for the values to be practiced, tracked, and rewarded. This is a leadership job and is a struggle for many. According to an Ernst and Young and Oxford University study, only 37 percent of business leaders who believe in a higher purpose know how to accomplish it.

All business organizations perform the same fundamental tasks such as communication, decision-making, strategy planning and execution, performance evaluation, and compensation. How you administer and implement these crucial functions vary significantly from a 1.0 to a 2.0 to a 3.0 organization and determine your ability to bridge the gap between purposeful intent and real-time impact.

A grand vision without an execution plan is a pipe dream, and execution without a vision is dull.

Consider the methods for conducting meetings, which are an important form of communication in every organization. In a 1.0 state, belonging and being accepted by the team is most important. You take pains not to hurt others in the team. You believe that what they think of you is more important than sticking to facts and providing your true opinion. Issues don't get surfaced, problems and challenges don't get resolved. There is no accountability to complete tasks.

In a 2.0 state, you are driven by the desire to get the job done. You are direct and blunt and are not focused on collaboration. You neither care nor or aware of how the team is feeling or how the direction is being received.

In a 3.0 state, you go beyond the ego's need to belong, to be liked, and to grow and be recognized. You want to get the job done of course, but not at the expense of teamwork and core values of the organization. You listen to other ideas, opinions, and objections and achieve buy-in. We used to think that this skill was necessary only for social leaders who are bringing about socioeconomic change. This is now a mandatory skill for a business leader who wants to create a 3.0 organization.

Action Leadership Skills

Demonstrating action leadership skills directly and positively impacts execution, productivity, and performance of the organization. Detailed in Practice 6, "Engage in Action Leadership" and Practice 7, "Bake Mastery into Your Organizational DNA," these are authentic communication, proactive conflict resolution, empowered and accountable decision-making, energizing and effective meetings, inclusive and and dynamic strategy planning, conscious budgeting and goal setting, tracking the three dimensions of performance, objective performance evaluation, fair compensation and incentives. As a 3.0 leader, you must manifest the rare and paradoxical skills of openness and assertiveness, humility and self-confidence, care and toughness, professional excellence and personal fulfillment.

Vision Inspires; A Roadmap Delivers

A noble vision inspires us, but it does not deliver the result unless we have a clear game plan and a roadmap. That's what CBC did next. We identified the five key activities that were necessary to pursue our vision and fulfill our mission. Each activity had a cross-functional, inclusive, and diverse team that was responsible for developing the plan and delivering the results. The five activities included the following:

- **Customer excellence and customer experience:** Will provide exceptional customer service and cutting-edge customer experience.

- **Product innovation and data analytics:** Will ensure that the company is in the bleeding edge of technology and that data is effectively utilized to serve employees and customers.

- **Employees first—great place to work:** Will create an environment to make this company a meaningful and exciting place to work.

- **Leadership development and alignment:** Will make sure

that the leaders are walking the talk and holding each other accountable.

- **Superior financial performance:** Will implement steps to ensure that financial performance and efficiency ratios are among the top 10 percent in the industry.

As a leader, you have to mentor, coach, and train your respective departments, divisions, and teams. You have to infuse these mastery skills into the DNA of organization. This is a journey of professional, personal, and organizational mastery!

Trust and Mutual Accountability

Ash continues to be remarkably passionate, vulnerable, and courageous in his effort to become a facilitative, conscious leader. In a recent conversation I told him, "You're driving all the time. Instead of asking questions and trying out people's ideas, you're always pushing and telling them what to do. That works up to a point, but you need to develop your relationships further."

Exceptional teams give each other permission to tell the truth, give honest feedback, and hold each other accountable to best serve mutual learning, personal growth and awakening, and achievement of a shared noble purpose.

That was a little hard for him to hear, but he accepted it and said, "Why don't you come over to my executive meeting today?" That was pretty brave of him, so I attended. Once there, he told the assembled colleagues, "Sudhir is here because he thinks I can be more effective, and he will give us some tips."

The meeting started and he was doing his thing. After a while he asked, "How's it going Sudhir?"

I responded, "You have the most passion in this room, and you're telling people what to do. I know all of these folks are very driven and passionate, but it's not showing up. So, if you ask them questions and invite them to get involved, the outcome could be better for everyone."

The only problem with that idea was that the team had been used to his style for so long that when asked to contribute, none of them stepped up. At that point I reminded them about how a team needs to be aligned, and they responded, "We're already aligned." I responded, "Yes, you are aligned, but you're just following your CEO's instructions, and you're waiting for him to give you the answers and solutions. The alignment we're talking about, and what your CEO is interested in, is that he wants you to contribute your ideas and to challenge his and each other's ideas. He wants to listen to different perspectives and make sure you do that with each other, holding each other accountable—not only in terms of strategy and business direction, but also the values you espouse and live by."

Another executive said he was confused and wondered if the CEO was trying to create a conflict between him and his colleague. We clarified by explaining that polite indifference with each other had resulted in a conflict between members of their respective teams. This could have been prevented and could now be addressed more effectively because the executives (and the leadership team) were on the same page and communicating the same message.

Mutual accountability can happen only when there is trust. Trust can be developed only when you are authentic and vulnerable and share your hero's journey, your highest goals and achievements, and your deepest disappointments and failures. You have to be vulnerable to be authentic.

The Benefits of Noble Purpose

Why is it so hard to develop a 3.0 purpose? It is this anxious force within and people around telling us that the sole purpose of business is to make money. When business makes huge profits and increases shareholder value, everything else will fall in place. Making profit is the only purpose, nothing else really matters. Low engagement and high stress is a necessary price to pay. Business is not a charity and it should not worry about the well-being of its stake-holders. That's not what capitalism is about.

Back in 2011, when Ash Patel and his team at Premiere Commercial Bank (PCB) decided to make their organization a great place to work, he made sure it was a place where employees, customers, investors, and all stakeholders could realize their dreams. He led his bank to become the Small Business Administration's Lender of the Year and received an invitation to the White House. Its leadership team and inspired employees further raised the bar on their financial benchmarks to be among the top 1 percent in the industry.

Walking the Talk

As a 3.0 leader, you always should demonstrate positive behavior change to inspire your team. You and your leadership team have to make a specific effort. You can begin by asking your stakeholders and the leadership team how they sincerely think that you are progressing with your own behavior change. Your leadership team then becomes your accountability partner, helping you to move forward. At the same time, the entire team acts as accountability partners with one another, furthering the behavior change within the organization. (I delve deeper into this in Practice 5, "Bridge the Intent-to-Impact Gap.")

There's no rush to work on purpose, vision, and values if you're not willing to demonstrate 3.0 behavior change, beginning with yourself. Moving from 2.0 to 3.0 takes time and effort. In my experience, significant shifts take about a year to eighteen months. Once we taste success though, this becomes a lifelong practice. It is not easy, but we don't want to live and lead any other way. Organizational transformation takes several years and can be significantly accelerated by implementing these seven practices.

So how does a CEO who has developed enlightened 3.0 principles transmit those same values to the organization? One way is to inspire through one's own actions. Live and work in a 3.0 enlightened way, and you will be an inspiration to others. As a 3.0 leader, you listen more and encourage those around you to speak more. You embolden and inspire others to come up with solutions rather than you providing them. This shift will take time, just like accomplishing your fitness goals take time. Having a plan and diligently following through guarantees progress, but it is not always smooth and steady. There will be bumps and setbacks. This where your team comes in handy to help you get over the hump.

At CBC, we have worked hard to create an environment where the executives could point out to Ash whenever he slipped back into his old habits. It took a while for them to get used to this approach, but, once they did, Ash and several other senior leaders made rapid progress. This led to even more remarkable improvements. Several people noticed that Ash would dash past the front entrance when he arrived at work, often talking on his phone. One of the executives pointed out that it would make a big impact to the general morale if he would greet them warmly. Ash listened and took action, greeting everyone, especially the staff at the front desk, when he arrived at the office. This, in turn, gave Ash the moral authority to point out similar issues with other executives on the team. The impact now is much more powerful than using position or rank to direct change. A change that comes from within is a lot more impactful and long-lasting.

Another common challenge for successful leaders is the tendency to get into problem-solving mode immediately. Many leaders have an open-door policy, which is wonderful. However, this can create more trouble if you don't watch out. Some people take advantage of the open-door policy to play victim and complain about someone without first trying to address the issue directly. Others bring in operational and customer complaints without first routing them through the appropriate people in the organization and giving them an opportunity to resolve the issue.

Sometimes, in your noble intent to do the right thing, you might end up creating more tension. You might feel sorry for the person accusing or complaining about a colleague or a manager. You immediately call the other person in, your body language already making them feel like they are being pronounced guilty without being given a fair shot. From then on, it can spiral downward if you don't appropriately engage and involve all the parties and allow them the opportunity to succeed. If you end up intervening and driving without giving them a chance, the problem may be temporarily resolved, but morale and productivity are affected. Nobody learns how to communicate authentically and resolve conflicts on their own. And worse, this becomes the new cumbersome, inefficient process to solve future challenges.

The bottom line is that you shouldn't automatically jump to conclusions and start giving orders. Encourage employees to explore the situation, and ask the principals to speak to one another and come back with a solution. The following process is simple and works beautifully:

1. Person A walks in to talk about Person B.

2. Check if A already spoke to B about this. If no, send him or her back.

3. If yes, ask why B is not here. If the answer is B doesn't know I am here, send A back.

4. If the answer is B knows I am here and is good with it and we both need help, it's time to engage in a conversation.

5. The next important step is to become a coach and help them solve the problem. Do not solve the problem until you have exhausted all options to facilitate a solution.

6. Listen deeply, ask the right questions. See if they are able to resolve the challenge. If they are unable to do so, provide a win-win solution that serves as a template for the future.

7. When a similar challenge occurs in the future, have them or others refer to this template to resolve conflicts and communicate directly and constructively—authentically.

8. Make it a habit to share these events—both successes and lessons learned—in the organization.

Ultimately, leadership is manifested in the way you conduct yourself and the way you relate to your colleagues every day. The values you wish to espouse will be evident by the manner in which you interact with those around you. Be an authentic leader and manager. Be up-front with the rest of the organization about the journey you're making and let them understand that you're not there yet. This makes you more believable and trustworthy to the people around you. It's pretty inspiring and very powerful.

It all comes down to this: Be the change you wish to see. Then your words carry more meaning, and your life becomes your message, transforming the environment around you.

Practice 4: Assess Current Reality

"Reality doesn't bite, rather our perception of reality bites." — Anthony D'Angelo

"We don't see things as they are; we see them as we are."
— Talmud

"**A**ndy," a hard-charging CEO, was disappointed. We have been on this culture change journey for more than a year," he told me. "How come I keep hearing complaints from our employees about stress, lack of work-life balance and unrealistic expectations from management?"

I had to tell Andy the bitter truth and spare him from the sweet lies he had been hearing from others and telling himself. This situation was not a surprise to anyone who had been observing with an open mind. The main issue was that Andy was not walking the talk and was sending mixed and inconsistent messages about empowerment, flexible hours, and work expectations. It wasn't that Andy wanted to send mixed signals—he was simply not mindful of the disconnect between his talk and actions, even though his intentions were sincere. It happens to the best of us. Why did this happen to Andy, and why was he the last one to know about current reality, the actual state of culture, at his company?

- Andy got preoccupied with numbers and the hardcore issues of targets, profits, revenue growth, market share, and company acquisitions. He did not participate in leadership development and culture initiative.
- Since he was not involved, Andy did not grasp what it would take to make the shift from a dysfunctional culture to an excep-

tional culture. Besides, he would frequently pull his senior executives out of meetings dedicated to these efforts by giving them "higher priority" business actions.

- Andy became impatient and restless with the slow progress of the cultural transformation effort. He had never been a part of such an endeavor. The goal had sounded exciting to him, but he did not know how—did not have the patience and discipline required—to get there. I reminded him that companies such as Southwest Airlines, Bridgewater Associates, Starbucks, Next Jump Inc., and Whole Foods that are known for their culture have been at it for years with the CEO leading the charge. I guaranteed Andy that he could get there much faster if he prioritized the cultural initiative for him and his executive team and demonstrated the same passion for it as he had for short-term revenue and profitability growth.

It has been said that you don't see things the way they are, but you see them as you are, conditioned by your unique filters and perspectives. It requires a high degree of personal mastery to rise above this conditioning. In Practice 1, I noted how Peter Senge, systems scientist and senior lecturer at the MIT Sloan School of Management and author of *The Fifth Discipline*, a classic on learning organizations, has stated that mastery is continually learning how to see current reality more clearly. I would add to this and say that mastery is the ability to convert your noble intentions to consistent actions. In order to do this effectively, you have to accurately assess how you are currently showing up. What is the gap between your noble intention and practical impact?

The Prerequisites for Assessing Current Reality

Freedom and autonomy are good, but they have to be deployed skillfully to be effective. It is a necessary, but not sufficient, condition in order to feel engaged and fulfilled. You need meaningful work and relationships based on authentic communications and trust. You have to help each other stay present, contribute, serve, and make a difference while unleashing the best version of yourself. This is true in life and in business. You have to assess current reality against those prerequisites. You may not like the answers, and the picture that is painted may not look pretty, but that is not a reason for not assessing current reality. It is better to face reality and take action than to ignore it and hope it will go away.

As Americans, we are always assessing the approval rating of Congress and the President. The numbers don't look pretty and are actually depressing to a lot of people. No wonder presidents age rapidly on the job because no matter how hard they try, a significant percentage of people will think you are doing a lousy job. If you are living in a different country, you might think "Wow, America is really screwed up. There's something wrong with it." Of course, you may be oblivious to your own problems simply because current reality in your country isn't being assessed with the same transparency, or at all. There may be bigger issues and challenges, that you are ignoring.

That happens in business situations too. People who start the process of assessing current reality have to go through the painful process of getting feedback that might not be pleasant, or hear comments that they're not walking their talk or are sending mixed messages or not building a meaningful organization. It comes with the territory, and a leader has to manage and master the situation.

Which aspects of current reality are important to know? The hard numbers such as revenue, earnings, growth, and market share can be accurately determined. However, they are lagging indicators—they are what they are whenever you track them. You need to know the leading internal indicators that affect these results. These leading indicators—leadership behavior, leadership alignment, customer satisfaction, and employee engagement—affect the bottomline of any company. The current reality here is leadership behavior, which in my experience (and confirmed by Zenger Folkman research), has the most significant impact on the culture, development, and profitability of an organization. (I discuss leadership behavior, alignment, and employee engagement in Practice 6, "Engage in Action Leadership," and Practice 7, "Bake Mastery into Your Organizational DNA.")

It is not easy to accurately and objectively determine the current reality in any organization. At the same time, it is an extremely important first step; building a great organization requires you to know where you are, where you need to go, and the aspirational gap that exists between the two. Creating transformational change in an organization has to begin with changing yourself. By focusing on strengths alone and ignoring weaknesses, you can achieve significant success. However, if you want to fully unleash your potential, you have to identify and overcome obstacles that are getting in the way of unlocking your greatness. Great leaders are open to identifying their blind spots, have the self-esteem to accept the gap between their intention and action, the self-confidence to admit their shortcomings, and the self-discipline to relentlessly work on inner development or self-leadership.

Operating in a 3.0 state with a high degree of personal mastery is one sure way to determine how you are showing up and how effective you are. You will know when you are there, and the personal development assessments indicated below will confirm that. Since business is a team sport, it is not enough for the CEO alone to operate at 3.0 leadership. You want your executive team to be on the same page.

What can you do to make sure that you are getting accurate assessment of current reality of leadership development?

- Many organizations use personality (psychometric) tests. They are useful, especially in a 2.0 environment, but don't give the full picture of a leader's development and effectiveness.

- Personal development assessment is a more complete and comprehensive way of determining a leader's development and effectiveness.

- I use a three-step assessment process that has benefited CEOs and their executive teams. This is a combination of self-inquiry, stakeholder feedback, and master coach perspective, as explained in detail below.

Truth-Telling

Unless you are operating at a conscious 3.0 state where you have the natural ability to see the things the way they are, it is very difficult not to have a personal filter attached to your perception. Taking the time and establishing the process to understand reality is critical. To achieve this, establishing an environment of truth-telling is very important. Unless there is an open, transparent environment where everyone can speak their minds, it's very hard to accurately understand the current reality. Of course, this still requires you to have the courage to take advantage of the environment, speak up, and be bold and vulnerable.

Whenever I hear this (and I hear it a lot), "I don't want to throw him or her under the bus," it means that they are operating in a judgmental environment with no tolerance for mistakes. People in such places share only news of growth and achievements. No mistakes are pointed out or admitted to. They work very hard to put a positive spin or inject awkward humor rather than deal with the issue directly and constructively.

That's why I spend a lot of time on the importance of an environment of truth-telling and the importance of what you need to do to establish that. How do you and your executive team members set an example of truth-telling, holding each other accountable, and being able to call each other out? You need to be vulnerable, authentic, and direct. As I describe in Practice 2, "Lead with Self-Mastery," this means being open with your colleagues about your strengths, weaknesses, and doubts as you strive to become a better person and leader. Everybody in the organization needs to practice this, and it requires you to be vulnerable and honest, accepting and discussing the gap between your intentions and your behavior.

A high degree of mastery and personal development is required to joyfully accept what you do not know and engage in intense exploration to know.

Ray Dalio is one of the great investors and entrepreneurs of our time. He founded Bridgewater Associates in 1975 and built it into the world's largest hedge fund. *CIO* magazine has called him the Steve Jobs of investing. According to Bloomberg, Bridgewater has made more money for investors than any other hedge fund in history. Dalio's secret sauce, which he shares freely in his book *Principles*, is creating radical truth and radical transparency in the organization.

Bridgewater Associates is one of the three companies featured in Robert Kegan and Lisa Lahey's *An Everyone Culture*. These organizations have taken a breakthrough approach where people's development is woven into the daily fabric of working life and the company's regular operations, daily routines, and conversations. People development is focused on being yourself, speaking the truth, and constantly learning to become radically transparent and passionately authentic.

In such an environment, mistakes are treated as learning opportunities. Mistakes are a natural consequence of pushing the envelope. It is inevitable that you will fall and make mistakes in this process, but that is how our greatest growth comes about. So why wouldn't you want to foster an environment where mistakes are not only tolerated but treated as learning opportunities? Here it is okay to make mistakes, but it is not okay to hide them. You will be rewarded for owning your mistakes and working on preventing them in the future. This is how learning organizations are built. The key is to make sure that your emotions of fear and anxiety don't take over when you first discover a costly mistake. In a learning organization, you not only work on your own emotional mastery, you help each other to accelerate the journey.

Personality (Psychometric) Tests and Personal Development Evaluation

Everyone's brain is wired differently. Some of us are more left-brain thinkers—logical, analytical, organized planners. Others are predominantly right-brain oriented—emotional, artistic and creative storytellers. There are several psychometric tests such as Myers-Briggs Type Indicator (MBTI), Workplace Personality Inventory, DISC (Dominance, Influence, Steadiness and Conscientiousness), and Team Dimensions Profile which accurately define our personality traits, characteristics, and tendencies. These are attributes such as being a creative, visionary, big picture thinker versus a task oriented, attention-to-detail implementer; a driver and a domineering type versus an amiable and social person; other personality profiles such as *advancer, executor,* and *flexer* help you determine the right roles for different people. You can match people's strengths with the appropriate job function, so together you can thrive and succeed as a team.

In Part One's "Claiming the Next Level in Leadership" I discussed the ancient limbic system of the brain which controls emotional responses, including the amygdala hijack and the neocortex, which is the seat of planning and higher-level executive decisions and functions. There is your higher, conscious self that is calm and collected, driven by the reflective executive function of the neocortex. There is also your lower, subconscious emotional self that goes into fight, flight, or freeze mode, driven by the limbic brain. I introduced them as the *higher essence* and the *lower ego.* They are the higher you and lower you. The higher you is altruistic, driven by unconditional service to make a difference. The lower you is focused on survival, self-centered growth, and achievement. Your mindset is dependent on your personal development. This is the reason I find personal development to be crucial and even more important than personality traits, especially for leadership positions.

To shift from a successful leader to a conscious leader, from a good team to an exceptional team, from a profitable organization to a purposeful (and profitable) organization requires you to operate at 3.0. This is Maslow's self-actualized state, or Kegan and Lahey's self-transforming state. If we want to get even more granular, this will be Level 5 to Level 7 in Barrett's model (see "Claiming the Next Level of Leadership"). This development is also a function of spiritual intelligence (SQ). When you are operating at this higher state or advanced mindset, you naturally demonstrate the "and" behavior: creative and analytical; visionary big picture and detail-oriented implementer; humble and confident; open and assertive. This is most important for a transformative leader.

The typical psychometric personality tests do not get to this level of personal development detail. If you are a visionary leader who can see the big picture but your lower ego is in the driver's seat, the results can be disastrous for your organization and your executive team. Even if you have an operational manager to take care of the details, you will not give them enough latitude or respect for that person to succeed.

Similarly, if you are a leader who is action-oriented but at a lower developmental stage, you might not value and respect vision and strategy. This is why I recommend a personal development assessment. I introduced several good ones in Practice 2, "Lead Thyself With Self-Mastery," including Barrett's Leadership and Values Assessment test, as well as the Kegan-Lahey-based Washington University Sentence Completion Test (SCT), and the Subject-Object Interview (SOI), all of which take thirty to sixty minutes to complete. Another useful self-assessment test is the SQ 21 by Cindy Wigglesworth.

Typical Mistakes You May Make Now

What are the typical mistakes you make as a leader and professional, and why is it so hard to change those behaviors? Consider the following causes:

Mistake 1: Working at the Surface Level of Behavior

Perhaps you try too hard and will yourself to change without understanding the internal dynamics of human nature or the mechanics of human behavior. It is like going on a diet to lose weight. It works well for a while but is hard to sustain. Unless you work on the root cause, you will have limited success. It helps to understand the underlying reasons for our behavior. Why do we do what we do? What beliefs and values drive us? My blind spot was judgment. I used to have difficulty forging trusting relationships with hard driving, achievement-oriented successful leaders that I was supposed to be helping. I was trying really hard and not making much progress until I realized that I was judging them harshly with unrealistic and idealistic expectations. And, no surprise, I was doing that to myself too. Once I identified the root cause and worked diligently to overcome it, life became much lighter. I developed some exceptional life-long relationships with my clients besides helping them become inspiring leaders.

Knowledge of what you should do does not necessarily translate to consistent action. You go to a lecture on weight loss, physical fitness, or emotional mastery and hear all the success stories and learn the steps to take. You then need to rigorously back it up with consistent practice. For example, Alice is an intense and deep leader with a sound theoretical knowledge of emotional intelligence. She also has a good grasp of personnel issues of her team. This gives her a false sense of security and superiority. As a result, she is not as diligent in her own practice and falls into the trap of being shut out from her own blocks and blind spots. She is focused on fixing the team for problems that were unconsciously created by her. I see this movie play out with many analytical and brilliant people. Alice was disappointed with her key VPs for not being able to resolve their conflict without recognizing that one of the primary reasons for the strife was the contradictory direction they independently received from her. They in turn were resentful of Alice for pontificating and not practicing what she preached.

Mistake 2: Inadequate Follow-Through

Following through is also key to bridging your intent-to-impact gap. Richard is the CEO of a manufacturing company. He is a classic old-school command-and-control leader. He is high-strung and struggles with trusting and empowering competent people. He got to this position because his previous bosses were similar, not because people were inspired to work for him. He was getting burned out with this approach. He did not find fulfillment in his work, the stress became unbearable, and he was also seeking medical help. Richard realized he needed to make changes to his style of work and leadership.

To be fair, Richard made the effort initially. He followed my suggestions and guidelines, and the results were encouraging. His direct reports and colleagues noticed the change, but Richard couldn't maintain it. He became inconsistent and regressed—his old habits came back—and he went into fits of rage. He did not communicate or meet with me as regularly. He was struggling with being held accountable. In private moments, he broke down, but he was unable to open up and describe where and why he was struggling. He could not and did not want to dig deeper. That's how far he could go for now.

Mistake 3: Conflicting Priorities

More than twenty years ago, a young lady from a conservative Indian family was getting ready to go to the United States for higher education. In the weeks building up to the big journey, she got plenty of advice, mostly unsolicited, from uncles, aunts, and friends on how to adjust in a more open culture. (This is much less of an issue now in modern India.) As she was waiting with her dad at the airport, it suddenly dawned on her that her dad never gave any advice. She asked him and all he had to say was, "Don't let your secondary goals come in the way of achieving your primary goal." She went on to build a remarkable career as the founding president of a respectable non-profit organization.

You can be serious about behavior change but still may be unconsciously and blissfully unaware of another internal priority which conflicts with it. One of the CEOs I partnered with was really energized to change her behavior and become a more patient and compassionate leader. She was getting tired of packing her calendar with back-to-back meetings and discussions. She was inspired by Warren Buffet's simple and effective practice of leaving several blank spaces and free times during the day. This sincere desire, however, conflicted with a higher priority to please her chairman. It was easy for her to fall into that trap because they were both type "A" personalities—hard-charging and hard-driven. Her team members were getting discouraged because she was not making any serious effort to demonstrate that she'd changed. She would get disappointed in her team because they did not appreciate her genuine intent to become more patient and less volatile. As the British scientist and spiritualist J.G. Bennett said, "We tend to see ourselves primarily in the light of our intentions, which are invisible to others, while you see others in the light of their actions, which are visible to you."

It's not that the CEO did not want to change. We all have the best of intentions when we declare, "This New Year, I am going to exercise and meditate every day." However, we may have a higher, often subconscious, priority to not rock the boat. We don't want to appear to be different from our hard-charging colleagues or our drinking buddies or a spouse who does not share the same commitment and passion.

Mistake 4: Negative Emotion and Lack of Trust Hijack Your Best Intentions

Lance is a CEO I worked with closely. He is dedicated to becoming a calmer, more patient, and present leader. One of his biggest professional challenges was his senior VP, Vince, who brought out the worst in him. Since Lance is an action-oriented go-getter, he is not the best at involving everyone and keeping them informed, though it is never deliberate or manipulative. Vince points out this problem at every opportunity and does not stop others from making the same observations. To make matters worse, Vince engages in similar behavior himself.

I facilitated a few difficult conflict resolution sessions with Lance and Vince. I shared the following insight to help them and set the stage:

> Your enemies bring out your blocks and worst characteristics that your friends and family suffer in silence and that your soul longs to overcome. Therefore, you should be grateful and thankful to your enemies for helping you unlock your limitations that are stopping you from unleashing your greatness.

Lance was appreciative of this point and acknowledged the difficulty he was having. Vince, on the other hand, did not display the same awareness and maturity. Both are high strung and struggle with managing their emotions. Lance embraced his problem and practiced meditation, but Vince did not own his challenge. This is also an example of how following the right process objectively isolates the problem person.

This process works best when everyone in the team is committed to holding each other accountable. Thanks to Lance's willingness to be transparent, I was able to include Vince's colleagues in the conflict resolution exercise. They were asked to listen objectively and present their perspectives. They had a much better appreciation for their CEO as a result of this exercise. They said that the process allowed them to assess the nature of the problem firsthand and directly clarify misunderstandings. It also gave them an opportunity to help resolve the challenge for the benefit of the team and the company.

Mistake 5: Ego Gets in the Way

A very bright and successful senior executive once asked me, "Don't you think you need ego to be a strong leader?" I find this to be a valid concern as well as a cause of confusion for many leaders. It's also something that took me a long time to overcome. Many old-school leaders have come up the hard way in a competitive, self-interest-driven, zero-sum approach and see the world with those filters even if the environment is now different. They believe that their ego has saved them from being taken advantage of. That is valid for that environment, but ego does not serve you well when the goal is to be authentic, to build trust, and to be purposeful.

Ironically, and not surprisingly, I find leaders with large egos have a hard time engaging in direct, assertive, and authentic conversations. They do not take the tough and courageous steps necessary to effect real behavior change because their fragile egos cannot handle constructive confrontation. Malcolm is a classic case. He frequently loses his cool and engages in shouting matches, but his bark lacks bite. He does not confront or take action for poor performance. He micromanages people and makes them dependent on him. They do not make any decisions. They are used to being yelled at but do not have to worry about any serious consequences. The vicious cycle of mediocrity and mutual dependence continues. I find this often with aggressive bosses. They operate from fear and have knee-jerk reactions and do not constructively and directly confront the problem or the person. When you bring inclusion and humility to your drive, you become a lot more direct, assertive, and effective. This can happen when your ego is in service of the goal but not in the driver's seat.

Assessing Development

When you are at a certain level of development, objectively seeing reality is extremely helpful. The most popular assessments that are used in the business world, such as the DISC® and Myers-Briggs personality tests, focus primarily on the external nature of the person. (Are you gregarious, extroverted or introverted, more domineering, a driver, or more sociable influencer, people pleaser, etc.?) Those are popular and helpful for understanding the different personality types and helping to communicate a little better, but they really don't address the fundamental development level of the person taking the test. One can have any of those attributes but still be at a lower or higher development level.

While it is interesting and somewhat helpful to know personality types and external behavior characteristics, what really moves the needle in building effective relationships is understanding the development level and addressing the root cause of the behavior. If the person is, for example, at the 2.0 developmental level and self-centered, then it could be really hard for this person to see reality the way it really is. This is why it took Andy so long to see that the organization was not as engaged and the leadership team was not aligned as he assumed or hoped. Once he recognized the problem, he took quick corrective action.

The Three-Step Assessment Formula

In one of my projects, some folks were complaining that things were not going well, saying, "It's a lot of work." Others were supercharged, excited ambassadors for change. And still others were somewhere between those two extremes. An executive leader may have trouble seeing reality the way it is. You might get swayed by listening to one or two or critics and assume that the project is doomed. Being able to accurately assess development is important.

How do you go about assessing development level? I utilize a three-step assessment process that works very well. It includes self-assessment based on self-awareness and self-inquiry, stakeholder feedback, and master coach perspective. That gets you very close to an accurate assessment of development level.

1. Self-Assessment

Self-assessment is a good option, especially if you are self-aware, but by itself, it is not enough. You have to be able to see yourself and your blocks, which is not possible unless you're operating at a high state. A combination of self-assessment and stakeholder feedback from people who are interacting with you regularly and consistently, can give you a more helpful perspective.

I recommend that you begin self-assessment by going through your biography and recalling times when

- you were in a happy flow state;
- your actions felt natural and effortless;
- you were frequently asked for help and advice in that area; or
- you received unsolicited compliments.

You can now identify your gifts and strengths.

Now, recall times when

- you were under a lot of stress;
- your work and actions were laborious and painful;
- you were chastised and reprimanded for your behavior and actions; or
- you received unsolicited criticism and judgment.

You can now identify your weaknesses and blocks.

You can now capture your foundational values and the state of your mindset. This is not an easy exercise since you are now facing your weaknesses and blocks. Can you confront your limitations and take corrective action? When you do this for yourself, you will be a lot humbler, empathetic, and confident.

Next, ask about eight people that know you very well and have seen you in your best, worst, and in-between moods (boss, peers, subordinates, spouse, a close friend, even a critic) to articulate your gifts and strengths and your weaknesses and blocks. The "ask" should be sincere, humble, and not defensive. How you ask makes all the difference. (See Practice 2, "Lead with Self-Mastery," where I describe the self-assessment process in detail.)

2. Stakeholder Feedback

In my early days in the corporate environment, I used to always seek feedback from my employees and subordinates even though it wasn't required and was not common practice. Initially, it was difficult to hear negative feedback. At the same time, I discovered how you can easily live in your own bubble, oblivious to the opinion of your subordinates and peers and the true impact you are having on them. I found this unfiltered information to be extremely valuable.

You show-up differently depending on whom you are interacting with. You are usually on your best behavior with your superiors, highlighting strengths and hiding weaknesses. YOU may be doing the same with Your and peers if you feel the pressure to show that you belong. It is easier for your less evolved, arrogant side to come out with your subordinates. You might be conditioned to put on a tough exterior and be an old school leader who "doesn't let them see you sweat." Encouraging others to provide authentic input without fear of reprisal is extremely valuable information for your development as an inspirational servant leader. You might discover like I did that you are not really fooling anyone more than the "man in the mirror." It requires humility from the boss and courage from the subordinates to create and thrive in such an environment.

Get input and feedback from people who know you best and interact with you in different environments and catch you in different moods—best, normal and worst. Again, I talk to anywhere between eight and twelve stakeholders. Choose people who interact with you closely and who also have a vested interest in your development. This is a simple, objective, and effective way to get a clear picture on your behavior and actions. Marshall Goldsmith, whom Forbes magazine called one of the five most respected executive coaches has built a thriving coaching practice based on this stakeholder-centric model.

3. Using a Master Coach

When you thoroughly grasp the full spectrum of human motivations, you can accurately evaluate your own and others' developmental levels. A master coach who has taken the personal development journey can conduct an accurate assessment of where you and your colleagues stand in your evolution to becoming 3.0 leaders. I do this frequently. By observing people in executive meetings and conducting 1:1 sessions where I ask penetrating questions and listen deeply, I can assess the developmental level with a high degree of accuracy.

You also can use a standard measurement tool that provides a rigorous analytical, unbiased, and objective result. Examples include Richard Barrett's Personal and Leadership Values Assessment and Cindy Wigglesworth's SQ 21. I find Barrett's assessment particularly useful since it builds on Maslow's hierarchy and comprehensively defines levels of human development. (See the discussion of this model in Part One's "Claiming the Next Level in Leadership.")

I discuss the benefits of using a master coach in greater detail in Practice 5, "Bridge the Intent-to-Impact Gap."

Converting Feedback to Success

In my experience, many successful leaders are self-aware enough to know when they are stuck. They are willing to acknowledge and uncover the mental blocks and emotional barriers that are holding them back and preventing them from unleashing their greatness. Looking at your shadow side with compassion and without self-judgment and self-flagellation requires a level of personal evolution and self-mastery. Besides, this is not something which can be easily shared with another person unless there is a high degree of trust in their maturity, skill, and competence. Being a successful leader can be lonely and emotionally draining. This is where an experienced coach can be an invaluable partner.

Following are profiles of some of the CEOs I have partnered with who are on their memorable journey from success to greatness. They received this input from their respective stakeholders. You might see yourself having many of the same strengths and weaknesses.

1. **Strengths:** Entrepreneurial driver, tireless worker, deep knowledge of the industry, loyal, kind-hearted—gives second chances and roots for the underdog, sharp intellect, not quite sure if treating with care and giving away trust is a strength or weakness.

   Obstacles: Impatient, sends mixed messages, top-down decisions, emotional, slow to hold people accountable, gets stressed and creates stress, black and white—finds it difficult to navigate in gray areas of human motivations and emotions.

2. **Strengths:** Brilliant mind, strategic, driven to make a difference, aspiring servant leader, articulate, hands-on, charismatic.

   Obstacles: Avoids conflict, reserved, judgmental, does not direct and teach, slow to delegate and empower, focused on hard work but does not easily see smart work.

3. **Strengths:** High IQ, functional expertise, calm, even-keeled, and strong work ethic. Obstacles: Slow and steady—corporate, manages more than leads, separates personal passion and dream, checks emotion and spirit, avoids constructive conflict and authentic communication.

4. **Strengths:** Strategic thinker, articulate, collaborative team player, service-oriented, humanistic, win-win approach.

   Obstacles: Weak mindset—nice guys don't win, have to sell out to be successful or drop out to be happy and fulfilled, it's a dog-eat-dog world, does not own beliefs and values, afraid to pursue passion, tentative, and timid.

5. **Strengths:** Hands-on, ambitious, hard negotiator, financially driven—knows his numbers, functional knowledge, and expertise, loyal.

   Obstacles: Micromanager, emotional and volatile, low trust, critical and judgmental, focus on what's wrong, penny-wise but pound-foolish, insecure, win-lose negotiation and approach, does not hold people accountable.

You can see how leadership behavior plays a direct and strong role in establishing the company culture and environment.

No Holds Barred: 360-Degree Feedback

Following are some of the representative examples of no-holds-barred 360-degree feedback that leaders received from their stakeholders. For the sake of illustration, I purposefully selected some of the harshest comments. You can clearly see the confidence required to seek such feedback, the humility necessary to accept it, the courage to act on it, and the commitment and discipline to stay with it. Mind you, these comments were directed at some of the most financially successful CEOs and executives.

- **Focuses is on what's wrong and on minutiae:** Comes from a place of no-trust. Claims he is into "trust but verify"; however, no one is really fooled. Does not focus on strategic issues. Nitpicks on small stuff and minor expenses.

- **Does not listen.** Decisions and opinions are pre-determined: Is resistant to a logical decision and presentation. Not open to listening, has good insights and could be right many times. Uses old-school techniques. Comes with guns blazing, will test people by pushing them and see if they can push back.

- **Micromanages and does not hold people accountable:** He is too involved and has his finger-prints all over. He is not organized, conducts ad hoc meetings, and gives the same task to multiple people.

- **Win-lose negotiation, no deal is final:** The approach seems to be that we know we have a good deal if the other person is seriously upset. We sign contracts without proper due diligence and then renegotiate. No wonder we do not have trusting, win-win relationships.

- **Critical, explosive, and judgmental:** Some reaction and feedback is warranted but not in the manner it is done. Publicly attacks and criticizes. People can't share bad news. Gets easily frustrated and writes people off if they are not detailed. This approach breeds mediocrity; good people leave and the ones that stay are paralyzed.

Not All Feedback is the Same

In the daily whirlwind of frenetic activity and frequent changes in internal and external conditions, staying positive and enthusiastic is the only thing that guarantees progress. Whenever we take up a path-breaking transformation program, it is only natural for many to be skeptical or jaded. The overly sensitive leaders take cynicism and negative feedback from an outlier or only from poor performers as a broad-based critique. I have to remind CEOs "The best leaders in the world today are practicing what you have been doing with your team. Just because your cutting-edge work is not being appreciated by some people doesn't make it wrong or unnecessary. Don't ever doubt that!" You have to pay attention to who is being critical and respond accordingly:

- If it is a cynic who is closed-minded and not onboard, you can't be wasting your time with this person.
- If it is a skeptic whose mind is open, you should take the time to listen, understand, and clarify.
- If it is an enthusiastic change agent who is onboard, you should be concerned and take extra care to understand her critique and determine what and how you can do better.

"Marsha," the CEO of a new media company and the leadership team, was going through a particularly stressful time of organizational change prompted by business challenges. I helped her conduct an open and authentic conversation with all her top executives. Her strengths were fairness (to a fault) and transparency. However she was overly sensitive to critical and well-meaning feedback. She needed to be reminded and reassured that they really were touched by her sincerity and integrity.

I told her, "The participants were genuinely touched by your authenticity and vulnerability. They trust you and that's a big deal! Earning the trust of employees is one of the most prized and difficult tasks of a CEO. They want you to be more patient, understanding, and be a good listener. Key areas to work on are patience and listening. You don't have to worry about fairness, because an overwhelming majority of people trust and believe in you. It is only a couple of people who brought up the issue of fairness because they did not want to admit to and own up to their poor performance."

I continued, "By taking this courageous action, you have created a whole world of opportunity for the team and yourself. I am also delighted to see you convert your anger, frustration, and disappointment to assertiveness, self-confidence, and right action. When you know what you want, the world will conspire to make it happen for you."

We then implemented a nine-month intensive program for Marsha to work on patience and listening. She would actively engage executives in conversation by asking probing questions and get them to think and help find answers. This was an extremely difficult discipline since she was wired to and used to be the one with all the answers. She would tell and give directions and was dearly loved by her teams over the years. However, they wouldn't collaborate well with each other and rarely held each other accountable. That was the price she paid, but figured it was worth it. She thought this was much better than the alternative of chaos and indiscipline.

Marsha then discovered the superior third option, the best of both, and enthusiastically embraced this discipline. We would debrief and at times I would participate in the discussions to get a first-hand objective read on the situation. How do we know if she is making progress? We are not the ones to make that decision; we track progress by checking with her stakeholders, the executives, every month. We would act on the input and make adjustments. She made significant progress on a behavior and habit that had been hardwired for more than twenty years. The best part was that the verdict came from the people who faced the brunt of this behavior directly.

Identify the Intent-to-Impact Gap

Now that you have an accurate picture of how you are perceived by the people who matter most in your life and business, you can assess the practical impact you are having. You can then begin to establish the degree to which you and your colleagues are currently "showing up" and identify gaps that need improvement. Below are steps to help you identify your "intent-to-impact" gap.

1. **Consolidate information.** Consolidate the information you receive from all sources, including self-evaluation, stakeholder feedback, and your master coach's perspective. Reconcile conflicting messages by establishing the context and relationship. For example: A subordinate might say that the leader is not open to other perspectives, which may not be obvious to the leader's superior or peer. This is another very good reason why an experienced master coach is crucial to this process. She will be able to integrate different feedback into a coherent set of messages.

2. **Identify greatest gifts *and* obstacles.** By focusing on strengths alone and ignoring weaknesses, we can achieve significant success. However, if you want to fully unleash your potential, you have to identify and overcome obstacles that are in the way of unlocking your greatness. Accept limitations and unconscious blocks without feeling limited. Identify root causes for weaknesses, obstacles, and the gap. Discover the noble intent behind actions and behaviors that do not make sense. These obstacles are often unconscious and painful to face.

3. **Identify the gap between desired state and current reality.** Pick one primary behavior that, if improved, will make a significant difference and impact your performance. Typically, we all have a major block that comes in the way of unleashing our greatest gift. For example:

- **Gift:** A natural gift for resolving conflicts and ability to appreciate multiple perspectives.
  Block: Judgment of people who do not.
- **Gift:** A brilliant, strategic, and incisive mind.
  Block: Inability to accept other points of view.
- **Gift:** A caring and inclusive approach to tackling challenges.
  Block: Overly sensitive to direct feedback and criticism.

- **Gift:** A noble quality of helping the underdog and giving opportunities to succeed.

  Block: Taking a controlling and top-down approach. Develops a mutually dependent relationship and stifles independent growth.

Undiscovered Obstacles to 3.0 Leadership

Most of the assessment tests out there do not catch some of the less obvious obstacles to your success. Instead, they sugarcoat them and provide a general response. For example, Mark is a hard-driving, fast-talking, operations expert who keeps a close watch on the numbers and manages the bottom line well. At the same time, he can do a better job of listening and getting buy-in by accepting other perspectives. Everybody knows this, including him, since he is fairly self-aware. A typical self-assessment profile like DISC will identify this aspect of his personality; especially if other inputs are concerned and suggest he work on improving to become a more effective leader. However, two key things are missing in this assessment: (1) What is the root cause for this behavior? What mindset, belief system and values are driving it? (2) How can he fix this in a critical business function that matters?

Here are some other examples of obstacles to 3.0 leadership:

- Robin is the owner of a large conglomerate with a need for respect and recognition. Jennifer, the group CEO, is stuck at the same level. They wield enormous power, resulting in an organization with moderate financial success, but with low trust, poor employee engagement, and high stress.

- Jamal is a CEO who wants to be liked and loved. Relationships are important to him—so much so that he takes criticism very personally. He compensates with a short temper, top-down direction, and arrogance. At other times, he does not give tough love when needed.

- CEO Martina likes to give underdogs a chance, provides a long rope, and at the same time does not immediately squelch dysfunction and demand for control from her C-Suite. She has to overcome that.

- Steven is an entrepreneur CEO who came up the hard way, by lifting himself up by his bootstraps. He now runs a large company but does not mentor or coach. He identifies the surface problem without delving into the root cause and waits too long to come up with a solution. In the meantime, he does all the work, thereby bordering on burn-out while his executives are wondering why they are not being given the opportunity to grow. He is suspicious of and has a poor opinion of managers in the field, which fuels the conflict.

A skilled master coach who is operating at a higher level can help uncover the root causes of your obstacles. How do you fix these habits that have been ingrained for many years? I encourage these CEOs to call each other out on these behaviors while conducting business—in key meetings and conversations, strategic and decision-making deliberations, project planning sessions, etc. When I am facilitating or observing in these sessions, I highlight this point and drive that discussion. With Mark's permission and enthusiastic participation, I coached him not to be directive and squelch conversation. Instead, he presented suggestions, encouraged debate and authentic communication, and facilitated conclusions and decisions.

The Engagement Disconnect

Most leaders do one of two things when assessing current reality. One, they assume everything is fine and don't do enough to get feedback and understand what's really going on. The other extreme is asking passive questions that can lead to complacency and a false sense of achievement. Unless you watch out, it can often even encourage whining and complaining without any personal accountability. To successfully assess the state of affairs in your organization, you need to have everybody actively participate in the process of making your work environment purposeful and engaged.

Earlier I mentioned the Gallup poll that showed only 30 percent of people are engaged, and that 20 percent are actively disengaged. Given these numbers, think about what it would be like if you got 60 percent of your people engaged. It would be amazing! This phenomenon is actually a great example of what's happening in the current political and socioeconomic scenario of our country. A significant number of bright, well-meaning people are discouraged, disengaged, and disillusioned by the functioning or lack thereof, of our democracy and capitalism. A democratic system is supposed to offer freedom and autonomy. They don't seem to be experiencing that freedom and autonomy. This raises some deeper questions. Does the democratic system the way it is being practiced offer everyone a voice that truly makes a difference, or can democracy be hijacked by special interests? Are freedom and openness sufficient, or are these only the first steps in keeping the citizens engaged and inspired? Perhaps the country needs a noble purpose that galvanizes its citizens.

These are not easy questions to tackle. However, as a leader, you can address them in a business context because the challenges are similar. You can be the change you wish to see! For example, it is very rare to see people and their representatives who are aligned to one party engage in a direct and constructive dialog with members of the other party. We rarely hear anyone say, "Let me try to understand your view. Perhaps you are right. You and I have the same goal; we want to see our country prosper. We have different perspectives on the path to get there. I want to learn more about your view and why you think it is a good solution." This challenge is true in any team, family, business, or nonprofit organization. We usually stifle open discussion in family or business organizations. In my humble opinion, we do this because we cannot handle the emotions and do not have the skill to facilitate an authentic conversation. Our excuse generally is that it is time-consuming and dysfunctional—both are true only if we don't know how to train ourselves and our people to articulate confidently and listen respectfully.

As a business leader, you can and should create an environment where people are free to express a different perspective constructively and engage in civil conversations to find common ground. You will have a significant competitive advantage. You can develop superior strategies, improve morale, engagement, creativity and speed of execution. Until recently, this type of culture was more prevalent in consumer and retail organizations such as Southwest Airlines, Whole Foods, Patagonia, Starbucks, and Zappos. Now, innovative CEOs such as Satya Nadella of Microsoft, Bob Chapman of Barry-Wehmiller, Ray Dalio of Bridgewater Associates, and our own Ash Patel of Commercial Bank of California, as well as those of more traditional organizations in technology, manufacturing, and finance, are driving this transformation, seeing the bottom-line benefits of an inclusive, transparent, high-trust culture.

When you see the current socioeconomic scenario from this deeper perspective, you don't have to feel gloomy and paralyzed, nor do you have to swing into reckless action in the opposite direction. Neither of those reactions will solve the problem. In fact, they only exacerbate the situation. The need of the hour is to understand the challenge and the root cause with a cool head, incisive mind, and an open heart in the spirit of collaboration. When we demonstrate this skill, we inspire our families, teams, communities, organizations, and countries to take right action!

Understanding Reality is Critical

You need courage, commitment, and conviction to walk the distance from current reality to future possibility or aspiration. You can't fix a problem if you don't know about it or don't think there is one. When an issue occurs, you can only provide a band aid unless you dig into the root cause of a problem. Physicist Albert Einstein said, "If I had an hour to solve a problem I'd spend 55 minutes thinking about the problem and five minutes thinking about solutions." That's exactly why assessing current reality is an important practice along your CEO Mastery Journey.

Operating at 3.0

While you can attain material success operating at 2.0 (even 1.0 in some situations), it is not possible to achieve greatness, fulfillment, alignment, and full engagement unless you consistently operate at 3.0. While your intentions reflect 3.0 characteristics, your actions can sometimes be all over the map. For example, when you are in a good mood or during an offsite retreat, you operate at 3.0. During planning and review meetings, you may revert to 2.0, and drift off to 1.0 when dealing with everyday stresses and conflicts. This is an important root cause for the gap. Unless you address the root cause, you are only using ineffective band aids and quick-fix measures that feel good temporarily but do not have a lasting impact.

We know from research and common sense that organizational transformation is not possible without personal transformation and personal behavior change. I have dealt with way too many people who say or believe that behavior change is not possible. They become their own worst enemy as they engage in an unfortunate self-fulfilling prophecy sometimes consciously but mostly unconsciously.

I was training the executive team of a technology company when the CFO asked a question which may sound familiar: "I have been to many leadership and teamwork sessions," he stated. "Some of them are really good. You learn a lot, you behave a lot better during those few days, but it does not take long to revert back to old patterns. You are genuinely excited to take action, but you don't stick with it. Why is that?"

One critical reason is the environment. In an offsite training session, the mood is relaxed and the environment safe. When you get back to work, exposing your weaknesses and being vulnerable are not common practices. Your best intentions can be hijacked when emotions run high in real-life situations. Another key reason is a lack of consistent practice when you get back to real life. You have a business to run and life to live. You typically don't make the effort to integrate the new learning and practice into your life.

Leadership alignment and collaboration are crucial to fulfilling audacious goals and pursuing noble purpose and grand vision. Operating as a high-performance team is mandatory. It is not enough for the leadership team to just perform well; it is imperative that the teamwork is exceptional. The key to making this shift from good to exceptional is behavior change. The higher up we rise as leaders, the more critical it is for us to demonstrate impeccable behavior.

I was working with the leadership team of a large private company with the noble purpose of exhibiting servant leadership and making a difference to the lives of their stakeholders. As individuals, their functional expertise, commitment to the company, and work ethic were exemplary. However, they were struggling with teamwork. It wasn't bad by normal standards, but it was not at the outstanding level they desired. The team members were open with each other and identified the areas of weakness and obstacles that were holding each of them back. They were particularly frustrated because intimate knowledge of each other's blocks did not result in change. I reminded them that is exactly the point. It is wonderful and necessary to identify our blocks, but that is not enough. They needed to take consistent action and shift their mindset that was preventing them from changing.

While being frustrated with your and your colleagues' slow behavior change is understandable, it is neither logical nor reasonable. Why? Behavior change takes months and sometimes years of consistent effort to manifest in consistent behavior. It is simple but not easy. Just as we cannot get physically fit until we exercise regularly, we cannot shift our behavior until you build your emotional muscles.

Channel your frustration and use it as a fuel to take action. There is a process and structure you can follow to achieve lasting behavior change. That's what it took for me and many other leaders I have worked with over the years. Even now, I am constantly working on my behavior. I can't afford not to. You owe it to yourselves to do the same—behavior shift is a game changer and a life changer. It is the gateway to greatness. As I've repeated throughout this book, *organizational transformation is not possible without personal transformation*. There are two major misconceptions about adult behavior change:

1. **It is not possible.** Be vigilant of this internal mindset. If you think it is not possible, then you will make sure it won't happen. If we think it is difficult but possible, you will be better equipped to work towards that shift. Remember, we are always right!

2. **Knowing what I need to do will magically shift my behavior.**
This is the reason you get frustrated with yourself and your
colleagues because you know your issues, but they have been
lingering for months and years.

Leadership and Teamwork

Getting an executive team of smart and knowledgeable achievers to
be aligned and mutually accountable is one of the toughest challenges
you will face. Working toward a common goal certainly helps. It gets
a little better when the common goal is a purposeful pursuit that stirs
your heart and soul. But even a noble purpose does not guarantee full
alignment. Great minds and philosophers have for thousands of years
pondered over the best form of leadership. Operating at a higher level
of personal development, with a high EQ and SQ is the only guarantee for full alignment.

The more developed a leader and her team is, the easier it is for
them to collaborate and push each other to be the best they can be.
When you are operating in a higher state, this is natural and practical;
otherwise, it is just a good intent and theory. Operating in a 3.0 state
means that you are focused on making a difference and actualizing
your purpose. You are naturally comfortable cooperating with others
for mutual benefit and fulfillment. It is much more difficult to achieve
this when you are operating at a lower state of development focused
on personal needs and achievement only.

It makes sense for a leader's development state to determine the
type of leadership that is most suitable. Traditional notions of autocratic, democratic, and benevolent dictatorship take different mean-
ings when we consider developmental levels. A 3.0 leader is more
likely to be benevolent than destructive even when he or she has too
much power or authority. By contrast, power is dangerous with a 1.0
leader, and too much power with 2.0 leader is risky. Our focus is 2.0
since that's where most successful professionals and leaders in the
knowledge economy operate. In this state, tapping into the collective
intelligence with thoughtful debate and discussion to achieve buy-in
is most effective.

However, when the leader is at 3.0 and many others are in 2.0 and 1.0 states, it is not very effective to engage in too much debate. As a leader, you have to ensure that there are no unhealthy debates going on between someone with acknowledged expertise and another who first needs to listen and understand before challenging a decision. Otherwise, conversations become less productive and even dysfunctional. Leadership is situational and contextual. For every situation, it is helpful to clarify who the teacher (or expert) is, who is a peer, and who is a student independent of their position and title. This instills fairness, objectivity, and meritocracy. This is what I pay attention to when I am facilitating and guiding a leadership team and recommend the same to CEOs.

Once you recognize the limitations of the command-and-control approach, you will be open to a newer way of getting things done and take your effectiveness to the next level. It helps to be cognizant of the following stages of evolution:

- **Stage 1:** Recognize your limitations without feeling limited or defeated.

- **Stage 2:** Be vulnerable and admit to weaknesses. May think that is enough, causing frustration to self and others with slow progress.

- **Stage 3:** Actively work on resolving weaknesses and include your team and stakeholders in the journey by inviting closer scrutiny.

The journey from 2.0 to 3.0 leadership is the quest from success to greatness. Admitting your weakness is a commendable first step.

Practice 5: Bridge the Intent-to-Impact Gap

"In theory, there is no difference between theory and practice. In practice there is." — Yogi Berra

Once you have identified the gap between noble intent and practical impact, between aspiration and ability, you can bridge it. To do that, you have to resolve the challenge of converting your great intentions to tangible achievements and outcomes.

Simply knowing your gap does not magically solve your problems. Action does. You know that ignoring these hurdles will not make them go away. Unless you proactively manage your awareness, these blocks or hindrances rear their ugly heads without warning at the most inappropriate times. You must hold yourself and your team accountable to take consistent action that produces results. You have to decide if you can do that by yourself, or whether you want to select an accountability partner. If you choose the latter, whether he or she is a colleague or a master coach, you will need to define the characteristics required in that person and evaluate the advantages and disadvantages of working together.

Understanding how to modify your own behavior while connecting with others at a deeper visceral level requires you to be comfortable dealing with your emotions as well as others' emotions. It requires you to listen and appreciate different perspectives. It also requires you to be authentic and vulnerable. This requires you to have a lot of humility, courage, and the ability to manage your ego. In short, it requires you to operate at a higher state of awareness or consciousness. This is the 3.0 state; while you might be able to easily understand 3.0

behaviors, only a few people operate at that level consistently. Still, you have the innate capacity to get there. And that is why this practice essentially is about the mechanics and process of engaging in 3.0 behaviors.

The Keys to Successful Behavior Change

What are the keys to successful and lasting behavior change? What are the key dynamics that you should be aware of?

Remember the way your mind and ego work: You are always right, and you try to be right. You have cognitive biases that you want to prove right by taking appropriate actions. If you think behavior change is impossible, you won't even get started and resist all attempts. You may have a cognitive bias which tells you that a particular behavior change is not possible and/or too painful. So, you start reluctantly; you will not put your heart and soul into the effort and quickly lose momentum. You only see examples of failure and arm yourself with information to prove this right and justify your self-fulfilling prophecy.

John is the executive VP of a technology company. An upright, hardworking professional, he is overly suspicious of salespeople, especially if they are good communicators. Carlos has a reputation of being somewhat of a slick sales leader. He is articulate and pursues creative deals, but within legal and ethical boundaries. Over time, he has embraced openness and authenticity and further reformed his approach. John still didn't trust him and couldn't let go of Carlos' past reputation. He did not believe Carlos had changed because his father told him a leopard never changes its spots. His cognitive bias became a self-fulfilling prophecy. He was not willing to change his rigid ways and wouldn't pursue sales opportunities that Carlos and his team brought to the table. He would find reasons to shoot them down outright or go through a laborious due diligence which usually resulted in a slow and painful death. He gave up even before he started.

Carlos wasn't blameless either; he easily became impatient and irritable with John's reasonable questions to qualify the opportunity. Their CEO asked me to conduct a conflict resolution session between them since he believed that John was being overly cautious and Carlos too aggressive. When we combine the best of John and Carlos, we have the right balance. And that's what we did.

You don't have to be a slave to your tendencies and nature and blame it on your genes or your upbringing for your short temper, impatience, or restlessness. You just have to work a little harder than the average person to channel that to an inspiring, results-oriented drive.

Scientists used to think that our intelligence and memory would stop growing after a certain age. We now know that our brains are not fixed; we can rewire and rebuild neural circuits at any age. Scientists call this neuroplasticity, and the bottom line is that we can improve our brain power, intelligence, and memory with effort. I have personally experienced this phenomenon with meditation and chanting of Vedic mantras from memory in Sanskrit—my analytical and memory skills are better now than when I was going to college three decades ago. You might be thinking, "Well that's easy to do when you start low". I humbly accept that. A study published in the January 2018 *Scientific American* offered a most interesting conclusion that "rigorous memorizing and chanting of verses from the ancient scriptures in the Sanskrit language helps a person's memory by increasing the size of the brain's regions that are associated with cognitive functions."

I have taken the same approach to enhance my physical, mental, and emotional state. It is liberating, mind-bending, and exhilarating when we go beyond self, beyond social or culturally imposed barriers. My work on "how to" lead a self-actualized life and a self-actualized business organization is exactly that. We don't need to have the right genes (though it certainly helps) to become a self-actualized, servant leader. It is more about making progress, learning, and growing than reaching an exalted end point. It is the mastery journey we care about. Progress is guaranteed and results will come as long we stick with the program!

Work at the Source for Maximum Leverage and Impact

Your beliefs and values drive your thoughts. Your thoughts, in turn, drive your emotions and behavior. It is much more effective to reflect on and inquire into the reasons behind your actions and work at the source, meaning your mindset, beliefs, and values. Everybody thinks that their actions are justifiable for a noble cause. Even the worst social and criminal offenders have a justifiable cause in their mind. But you don't have to go there. The challenges in business are relatively tame, though it doesn't seem that way when professionals get locked into their positions resulting in lack of trust and alignment.

There is always a noble intention even behind a seemingly annoying and irritating action. The problem is it never gets surfaced, you get fixated on the outward action and the pain it may be causing you without pausing to understand the root cause. In spite of all his wonderful qualities, Dennis was having trouble leading his team. Some of his loyal executives who had known him for years were considering the unthinkable—work elsewhere. His impatience and bouts of temper were causing serious stress and frustration for the team members. To make matters worse, meetings and strategic communication between Dennis and the team had become increasingly sporadic, thus adding to their concerns. Fortunately, I knew Dennis and his team intimately and recognized the source of the problem.

Dennis strongly felt that they were sitting on a fabulous but short window of opportunity for the company. He wanted to act quickly. He assumed that his team would trust his judgment and would be as inspired as he was in diligently pursuing the goal. He made assumptions without getting their buy-in. When that didn't happen, he became frustrated and wondered why they didn't get it.

When I met with the team, their stress level was so high that the first order of business was to connect, empathize, and calm them down. I reminded them that the key to their happiness is with them; don't give it to anyone else. I told them, "We love Dennis, but the key belongs to you; don't give it to him." We then explored the possible reasons for the behavior they were witnessing from Dennis. This turned out to be a remarkable and rejuvenating discussion. The team was inspired to help each other and their boss. Dennis appreciated the gesture and recognized the mistake he made in taking them for granted. It required humility from Dennis and courage from the team members to make this work!

Unearthing the root cause and noble intention requires us to slow down and go within, something we don't normally do in an intentional manner. One CEO, Al, faced a virtual mutiny by his team. He was caught unawares when they confronted him about his micromanagement. He had a competent team that was fully capable of handling the integration challenges with a new acquisition. But in his anxiety to make them look good (note that he did not have a selfish motive), he came across as second-guessing their every move. Once they got over the pain of Al's action and became curious about his intention, things changed. Similarly, I had to work with Al to move him away from feeling attacked by his team to understanding their anguish. It requires humility and courage to look under the hood and solve the source of the "problem."

When you engage the leadership team in this process, it significantly enhances camaraderie, trust, and alignment. A beautiful side benefit is that each of them develops a much better understanding of their gifts, blocks, passion, and purpose. We all encounter situations where actions based on good intent could negatively impact others. It is best to spend the time clarifying intent rather than arguing over the effect.

Drive Behaviors With Beliefs and Values

You don't need to change your beliefs and values to change your behavior. By shining light on them you are bringing more clarity for your self and relevance to the context. This action simply allows you to become more conscious of your behavior and makes it easier to change, and for the change to stick. You identify internal and subconscious reasons to resist change. For example, Marcie believed in rewarding loyalty and supporting the underdog by providing colleagues with the tools and resources to succeed. Her view was that if someone in the family was struggling, you don't fire him. Instead you provide him the support and guidance to succeed. Mind you, Marcie was not one who let people coast with mediocre performance. She was a go-getter known for her work ethic and mastery in her field. She had an interesting challenge with her executive VP, Daryl.

Daryl was struggling to keep up with technological changes and his department's performance was suffering. Daryl decided to fire an employee and Marcie discovered that the employee was not being given much of a chance to succeed. She intervened and suggested that the employee be given more training or be placed in another position better suited for her skills and talents. Daryl felt undermined and accused Marcie of not practicing the empowerment mantra she preached. This infuriated Marcie, and she was deeply hurt. Their poor relationship was harming the leadership team and the company. This became obvious to all the key people in the organization, including members of the board. Marcie was given the go-ahead by the board to let Daryl go. However, Marcie decided to take the difficult but courageous approach of working with Daryl and giving him another chance.

I facilitated the conflict resolution session and reminded them to be "direct about your perspective, position, and pain (feelings and emotions), and curious about the other's intention." As they each explained their perspective and the other listened with intent, the tension between them eased and the stress in the relationship declined. It was comforting for Daryl to know where his boss was coming from. Marcie, on the other hand, was relieved by the realization that Daryl was attempting to please her by improving efficiency and reducing costs.

As this example demonstrates, there is no need to change or apologize for your values. You determine your noble intent behind your current (perceived) difficult behavior. As a result, it becomes much easier to change

Tap into Innate Desire and Deep Yearning

Behavior change is not for the faint of heart. It takes patience and consistent effort. You have the intelligence to reflect and to inquire "Who am I? Why am I here? What is my purpose? Why am I suffering? How can I liberate myself from my suffering? How can I achieve my purpose?" This higher intelligence gives you the free will to change and to overcome your limiting beliefs such as, "I am incapable of changing, it is okay not to change, nobody changes anyway, I am set in my ways and it is best to stay that way."

You can strengthen your emotional and spiritual muscles to make shifts in your thinking and behavior. The nineteenth-century Indian mystic, Sri Ramakrishna said, "Do not seek illumination unless you wish to seek like a man whose hair is on fire seeks the pond." When you are driven by a grand vision or an intense deep passion, you are more likely to put forth your best effort to do what it takes, including changing your normal way of doing things.

I can vouch for this myself in my own passion to master organizational effectiveness. I learned so much about human nature and my own blocks that were getting in the way. I underwent major behavior changes which required me to push beyond my perceived limits and fall many times. Deep listening, authentic communication, not making negative conclusions, and being curious rather than certain about other's intent did not come naturally to me. It took intense practice to attain this level of proficiency and mastery. I continue to hone my skills at every possible opportunity, and so do the humble and courageous leaders with whom I work.

Mastery is the ability to consistently convert our noble intent-to-impactful actions.

Mary Ann is one of the most selfless leaders I have ever met and partnered with. She is the epitome of servant leadership and sincerely wants to empower her leadership team. However, she says "yes" to too many interruptions and provides answers when her team comes looking for one (instead of sending them back). She does not like conflict and is also unaware that some of the conflicts in the team are caused by her unintended miscommunication. Mary Ann gets frustrated with conflicts in the leadership team and disappointed when they aren't resolved internally. When I asked her why she doesn't help resolve the conflicts that are seriously affecting the performance of the organization, she said "I do not want to solve it for them … I want them to learn and figure it out for themselves."

Upon further inquiry, I realized that Mary Ann came up the hard way, lifted herself up by the bootstraps, and took the time and effort necessary to get the job done on her own. She expects the same "work hard, go solo" attitude from her team. I pointed out that her example was commendable but there are other ways to achieve excellence too. There is no harm in them seeking help and working smarter. Besides, it is not very efficient to learn to do everything on your own when the organization has grown significantly from the entrepreneurial venture it was many years ago. I added, "Life is too short to learn everything by personal experience alone. This team is stuck and they can use your guidance and direction. There is no harm in you offering help. After that, you can set clear expectations and goals for them to work on."

This was an "aha" moment for Mary Ann, and the shift in her was quick and dramatic. She met with the team individually and together. She directly addressed the issues, listened intently, and provided guidance. You could see the cloud of uncertainty and confusion lift from the team. They were energized and inspired and this in turn soon reflected in the business results and performance. Mary Ann herself began to work smarter, delegate more, and ask the right questions instead of providing the right answers. Her day is a lot less crazy and lot more effective—she slowed down to get there faster!

Focus on One Major Behavior Change

One of the keys to successful behavior change is to keep it simple, focused, and consistent. You have more than one area to work on, and in your excitement to accomplish more you are tempted to tackle a few behaviors to improve. But that is not wise; you do not want to dilute your effort and miss out on the joy of making progress. When you make progress on behavior change, that gives you confidence. When you don't, you can easily give up or not try as hard as necessary.

It is best to focus on one behavior change at a time. Usually there is one primary block that holds you back from realizing your full potential. You are wise to zero in on that unless you want to start with an easier secondary block or weakness to gain a quick win and get more confidence. Here are two specific examples that I used successfully with a CEO and an executive VP:

- **Improvement goal to overcome primary block:** I am committing to becoming a leader who will guide and coach, rather than direct and provide solutions to implement.
  Improvement goal to overcome secondary block: Improve listening skills.

- **Improvement goal to overcome primary block:** I am committed to getting better at "being with" others, to being less controlling, to being more open to others' ways of doing things.
  Improvement goal to overcome secondary block: I am committed to improving my non-verbal communications with others—facial expressions, hand gestures, posture, and tone of voice.

It is fascinating to recognize what we all have in common: A unique gift that comes naturally to us and a block that holds us back from giving unfettered expression to our gift and realizing our full potential. It is amazing how clear and direct your colleagues and friends can be when you sincerely ask for their feedback on a behavior you need to improve. I believe that your friends suffer in silence, which your detractors are eager to critique about an aspect of yours that needs work. Bottom line: The world has a way of letting you know repeatedly what you need to work on to effectively pursue your purpose. You just need to pay attention and take action.

Overcoming Blocks and Obstacles

When you create the right environment of transparency and trust, you can make remarkable progress. What's the big fuss about denying and hiding your blocks anyway, when you know they exist? When you don't label behaviors as good or bad and simply face them for what they are without judgment or feeling inadequate, you experience heartfelt, authentic, and extremely effective conversations. You uncover aspects of your own and your colleagues' behavior or attitudes which you were afraid to acknowledge and address.

These sessions with leadership teams are immensely rewarding. Not only do you identify areas to work on, but by just going through this process you experience a big weight lifting off your shoulders, and your block has a lot less debilitating effect on you. You are now ready to take focused action to overcome your blocks. It takes a lot of courage to face and work on tough feedback regarding your behavior, but the rewards are irresistible.

In my work with leadership teams, the following are representative blocks and obstacles, gifts and strengths which we identified to help with behavior change:

- **Blocks and Obstacles:** Impatient, disorganized, critical, judgmental, arrogant, cold—not empathetic, self-centered, micromanager, overly sensitive, emotional, stubborn, hard-headed, aloof, perfectionist, passive, poor listener, blunt, aggressive, autocratic, paternalistic, focuses on what's wrong, low trust, insecure, defensive, disorganized, no accountability, win-lose negotiation, poor communicator, sends mixed messages, does not acknowledge and recognize contribution.

- **Gifts and Strengths:** Driven, visionary, results-oriented, fabulous work ethic, brilliant, fair, knowledgeable, well-connected, caring, compassionate, inspiring, loyal, strategic, entrepreneurial, down-to-earth, collaborative team player, hands-on, generous, respectful, honest, transparent, authentic, trustworthy, straight shooter, provides real-time feedback, decisive, focused, engages in win-win negotiations, empowers, and holds accountable.

How do you address these blocks and obstacles so you can fully express your gifts and strengths? This takes us to the next point.

Regular and Consistent Effort

Regular, consistent effort is the key to successful change. Set reasonable expectations and stay with the practice. This is no different than working on physical fitness. The rules of the game are the same, except you are working on strengthening your emotional and spiritual muscles instead of your physical ones. You need to overcome years of conditioning and unconscious behavior patterns. Your biggest challenge is the inner critic who frequently reminds you that change is hard or even impossible. When you are weak internally, you let external events, people, and forces drive your agenda and derail your progress. This is where an experienced accountability partner is very helpful. Change is a natural aspect of your life and paradoxically you seek the thrill of change but fear the uncertainty of change. You have to be consistent in your practice and stick with the program.

Behavior change is a process, a journey. There will be ups and downs, periods of slow change; sometimes, you will take a step back, and at times, a big leap forward. You have to course correct when necessary and always stay consistent. Any change, especially behavior change, is difficult in the beginning, messy in the middle, and rewarding and liberating at the end. In my experience with individual leaders and leadership teams on behavior change, I notice major shifts in the nine–to twelve-month timeframe depending on the people, context, and intensity of the effort. First, you will feel and experience real-time changes internally. You feel and think differently right away and can experience the results based on your actions. Th key is to maintain this momentum consistently when changes are not as dramatic or obvious. When you stay with the process and put in committed effort, I have seen results 100 percent of the time.

I have had the pleasure of facilitating and participating in major shifts and breakthroughs with CEOs and leadership teams. Let me share two representative experiences: One involved working with a CEO, and the other included the CEO's leadership team. In both scenarios, a major shift was required: Both CEOs were at a turning point in their lives and were wondering if they need to drop out or pull back and do something entirely different. They were on the verge of burnout while still only in their forties and fifties. Work was not fun anymore, but they had many more productive years ahead of them. They were financially successful, professionally ambitious, in good physical health, and had a tremendous work ethic like most of the people I work with.

They decided to confront the problem head on—lack of passion and purpose! Initially their focus was on external triggers, events, and people that seemed to have conspired to create this crisis for them. We engaged in practices to shift inward and take stock of how personal actions and behaviors may have also contributed to the problem. The final liberating shift was to take control of their actions and their responses to events. The change needed was in mindset, proving the adage, "When you change the way you look at things, the things you look at change."

When we do this, we shape our future and destiny while being fully cognizant of the uncertainty of future and unpredictability of events. Our adversaries and antagonists now become our collaborators and co-conspirators in our mastery journey. What seemed to be debilitating problems now become blessings to help unlock our greatness. These leaders stayed committed and consistent with regular check-ins and conversations and experienced dramatic transformation. The passion, purpose, and performance all came back. They both stuck to their knitting and decided against changing careers and industries, which both were seriously contemplating. They became role models for professional excellence and personal fulfillment. They are continuing the journey and realizing their full potential personally and professionally.

Reward Positive Behavior and Penalize Poor Behavior

All organizations have a set of values that they profess and intend to abide by. However, there is rarely any significant incentive provided for adhering to those values (positive behavior) or penalty for not living your values (poor behavior). The result is that most organizations engage in good enough, legally acceptable behavior and fail to reap the tremendous productivity advantages of collaborative, authentic, and empathetic behavior. The common complaint you hear if you care to listen, "We talk a good game, but we don't walk our talk. Scott is a jerk but there are no consequences since he brings in tons of business." When I heard this from the executive VP of a company (about his peer getting a pass for poor behavior) I was consulting, I had to share it with the CEO confidentially.

The new CEO directly addressed the issue which had been the elephant in the room for five few years. Now, two years later they are all working together and have embraced authentic communication and radical transparency. Remember, the 2.0 mantra is "what gets measured gets done." Celebrate and reward good behavior, reprimand and have consequences for poor behavior. Incorporate behavior just like other metrics as a key measure in performance evaluation—this can be objectively determined by polling a cross-section of people who interact with the employee. This encourages and forces 3.0 behaviors.

Behavior change is a quest, a process, and a journey. One of the keys to the successful pursuit of any goal is the opportunity to gauge and experience progress. Research indicates that a sense of progress and forward motion is even more important than reward and recognition to inspire us to keep going. It is like saying that the pursuit of happiness is best served by the happiness of pursuit. How do you measure progress? This can be accomplished by establishing lead measures that you can track more frequently. For example, if you want to lose twenty pounds in six months, that is a lag measure. Lead measures could be to exercise three times a week, eat dinner before 7 p.m. every day, and eat salad for lunch four times a week.

I like to incorporate the same rigor and objectivity in tracking behavior change. One of the leadership teams I worked with rated themselves a 6 out of 10 in team work and alignment. They wanted to be at 8 in six months and decided to proactively engage in constructive conflict resolution to move the needle. We met every two weeks for thirty minutes with two agenda items: How did you do in engaging in constructive conflict? What will you commit to in the next two weeks to initiate and participate in authentic conversation and constructive conflict resolution? These lead measures kept them on track to accomplish the goal in six months.

We take it up another notch with my advanced practitioners. For example, reduce judgment or enhance gratitude. Lead measures might be: Meditate at least twenty minutes a day. Engage in self-inquiry before bedtime—How did I do today? Why did I do what I did? What were the triggers that tripped me up? You have to do the same thing with critical goals such as increased revenue, reduced expenses, and improved profitability.

You can't afford not to understand, improve, and track your actions, perceptions, and motivations!

Creating Accountability for Change

Now that you know the steps to take to effect positive and lasting behavior change, how do you ensure that you take consistent action and make progress? As I noted earlier, making progress and forward motion in real time is critical to meeting your goals and bridging the gap between where you are and where you want to go. You also require practical ways to track your real-time and short-term progress —you need a roadmap and process steps.

Who will hold you accountable? Can you do it alone? Why do you need an accountability partner? What are the characteristics of an ideal accountability partner? These are important questions and you will tackle them in this section. There are basically four options: (1) Do it alone, (2) Leadership Team Member, (3) Stakeholder, (4) Master Coach.

Doing it Alone

It is certainly possible to do it alone. This requires a strong will, self-discipline, and keen awareness of how you are showing up and how people are responding to you. A big portion of this work is about understanding and dealing with your emotions and thoughts that lead to action. Self-inquiry and deep contemplation or meditation are powerful practices that help you reach higher states of awareness and performance. We all have the innate ability to inquire within and dispassionately observe the thoughts and emotions that drive our behavior. It can certainly be done through advanced practices of self-inquiry and meditation. Not to be facetious, but Buddha did it!

Very few of us have reached the exalted state of recognizing, accepting, and fixing our blocks. The key is to overcome negative emotions by analyzing the source of the problem. This can be done through self-inquiry and by dispassionately observing without critiquing or judging negative emotions through meditation. With patience and self-discipline, you can engage in these practices to make quantum shifts.

It is my experience that the answers reside within you if you take the time and discipline to seek sincerely. You can then test them out in the school of life. This is how I discovered the deeper nuances of human psychology, human motivations, productivity, leadership performance, organizational alignment, and engagement.

While I was fortunate to connect with realized masters, I had to do the heavy lifting myself. They pointed the way and were there to offer support during uncertain and difficult times. The best lessons can come from pushing the envelope and persisting—learning from both successes and failures. Adversity and failure are outstanding companions on the path of learning.

Enlisting a Teammate as an Accountability Partner

Exceptional teams give each other permission to tell the truth, give honest feedback, and hold each other accountable to best serve mutual learning, personal growth and awakening, and achievement of a shared noble purpose. Therefore, this could be a powerful option with a seasoned team that has the necessary trust, experience, and maturity. When the whole leadership team engages in this practice together and holds each other accountable, it makes a powerful impact and turbocharges alignment and trust. The advantage of this option is that the leadership team can help and push each other to get better. Everyone already knows the business and organizational issues intimately. Leading by example, you send a compelling and persuasive message for the rest of the organization to emulate.

The same model can be used for all teams below them and across the board. The disadvantage, of course, is that personal and organizational effectiveness is not their area of expertise. It is critical that the team is already at a high level of trust and emotional maturity for this option to work well. Another practical challenge is to carve out the strategic time and discipline to meet regularly in the middle of tactical storms. Finally, being part of the same organization may make you too emotionally invested to make the calls and changes necessary.

It is critical that your accountability partner has at least the same level of EQ and SQ as you and that he or she is in the same pursuit. Otherwise, they will not be able to relate and support you adequately. If teams choose this option, they will need guidance by an experienced coach who can help set the guidelines and expectations and process steps. On rare occasions when organizations commit to a long-term change process, I become part of the leadership team and guide this process from "within the team."

I did this with CBC where Ash and I were accountability partners. Similarly, other C-level executives and heads of departments paired up. Ash is a caring and compassionate person but some see him as a hard charging, almost insensitive leader. I am very execution- and performance-driven, but to compensate for him, I tended to talk more about passion, purpose, care, and compassion. We both believe that toughness without care leads to mediocre compliance without buy-in.

Similarly, compassion without passion and care without tough love can lead to apathy and indifferent results. You must help each other be in balance so the organization receives a consistent message and experiences a consistent example.

Using a Stakeholder Partner

Your accountability partner could be one of your stakeholders, ideally someone who was part of the original assessment—a friend, colleague, or even a spouse. As you can imagine, this can be tricky. As friends and colleagues, these folks typically play the role of a sympathetic listener. They are your biggest supporters, even when you make a mistake. This is all some people want to or can give. Now you are asking them to step up and hold you accountable. It is a difficult transition for many. It is hard to be objective and call out your friend or spouse when you are emotionally attached. You are used to being there for them and being protective, perhaps overly so. Many of your close friends and others may suffer in silence with your blocks and missteps. By making one of them your accountability partner, you give that person permission to call you out. This can work if both of you are up for the challenge and could be very rewarding and liberating.

Coaching and Mentoring

As leaders, coaching and mentoring becomes a key aspect of your job. Let's face it—even the best among us have blind spots and emotional blocks. To be an effective coach, you have to help your colleagues see and overcome their blind spots. How do you do this? Not by telling them what their problem is. You know what that does to friendships and relationships. As a boss, you may get away with it in the short term but at a severe cost to your leader's creative engagement and commitment. A more effective way is to ask insightful questions and engage in deep, visceral, and non-judgmental listening. Many of us engage in silent and intellectual listening. You may not say anything, but you are mentally busy with your thoughts, analysis, and judgment. This is different from visceral listening which is deep, genuine, engaging, and inspiring.

It is very tempting to offer a solution, but a good coach knows that it will not be effective unless the person is motivated to seek and committed to act on the solution. This may sound simple, but it is one of the hardest things to do. You have all been in frustrating situations where you gave or received well-meaning but unsolicited advice that made the problem worse. A skillful coach guides the leader to discover the answer by asking questions, listening deeply, and offering perspective. If necessary, as a final step in the discovery process, the coach provides the solution by answering the question. You may understand this process intellectually but to consistently implement it in complex, emotionally charged real life scenarios requires wisdom and mastery, i.e., an integrated approach combining intellect, heart, and spirit ($IQ+EQ+SQ$), hallmark of an effective and enlightened 3.0 leader.

Working with a Master Coach

A leadership coach who has an in-depth understanding of human motivations and human nature, has mastery over emotions, and is operating in a self-actualized 3.0 mastery state, is a master coach. I work as a master coach, but I don't perceive my role as superior or exalted. In fact, I prefer being called a "partner to successful leaders in pursuit of principled and purposeful performance." In this partnership, there is mutual learning and respect. You bring different complementary skills and expertise to the partnership.

Our critics bring out our blocks and worst characteristics that our friends and family suffer in silence, and our soul longs to overcome.

A typical successful leader will have his or her moments of self-doubt which they are conditioned to mask. It is not easy for them to become vulnerable. Why do we care about this and what's the point in exploring this personal space? Because these underlying concerns and fears, unless they are fully addressed, will show up as impatience, frustration, perfectionism, win-lose mindset, autocratic command-and-control approach, and "my way is the right way." As a result, the leadership team is not aligned and collaborative, employees are not engaged, and innovation suffers. This leads to less effective strategy, execution, and decision-making; poor products, services, and customer care; and anemic profitability and revenue growth. How you show up has a direct impact on the bottom line.

As a master coach, my job is to pinpoint the root cause and communicate that authentically so the leader is inspired, not deflated. I have to delicately balance the needs and state of the human psyche. I have to respect the fragile nature of ego and show that I care and there is no personal agenda. I listen empathetically without judgment. This is crucial because in the early stages of high stress, the tendency is to focus the problem external to you. A master coach has to operate in a self-actualized 3.0 state where he or she is beyond praise and criticism. At the very least, he has to be conscious and willing to acknowledge when he becomes arrogant with praise and defensive with criticism. Only then is he in a position to mentor, coach, and partner a successful, confident, and humanly fallible CEO.

True Partnership: Master Coach and Conscious 3.0 Leader

A master coach partners with a successful leader who is willing to push the envelope and remove the blocks that are holding him or her back from fully unleashing the greatness within. As a true partner, he plays the multiple roles of a student, friend, and teacher as the situation and context demands.

The communication between a master coach and a successful leader should always be authentic. I define authentic as being direct and constructive. I follow certain communication guidelines diligently. I provide observations without judgment, explore root cause with curiosity, and offer recommendations with humility. When you take this approach, conversations are productive, rewarding, and liberating. The partnership is genuine.

Student–Deep Nonjudgmental Listening

In the role of a student, the master coach becomes a keen and curious student of the leader and understands his issues, concerns, hopes, and dreams. She listens deeply without judgment to fully grasp feelings, drives, and ambitions. This is a necessary first step to demonstrating that we care and open the channel for a trusting relationship and authentic communication. Several years ago, I was hired by the CEO of an organization to help him manage the operations and improve execution. I interviewed him and the leadership team and was about to present my plan of action when he recommended that I hold off on that. He instead requested me to be a silent observer in his one-on-one meetings with the leadership team.

After each of the individual meetings he would talk to me about their and his own strengths and weaknesses. He would then discuss his ideas with me about ways to resolve issues and improve teamwork and execution. He mentioned to me that my non-judgmental listening enabled him to see the situation clearly and allowed him to come up with effective solutions. All I had to do was to be fully present and listen deeply. The team members were struggling to do this because they were either intimidated or judgmental or both. That's how my coaching career officially began. I learned a very important lesson in coaching that day—to engage in non-judgmental listening.

The fact is that the entire leadership team was composed of bright, knowledgeable, and hard-working professionals. They all knew the market, their customers, and the competition. That was not the issue, it almost never is!

However, the leadership team was not aligned; its members had not taken the time to air their issues, differences, and concerns. Their personality conflicts did not allow them to objectively hear different perspectives and develop and implement a coherent strategy. None of them, including the CEO, took the time to make the effort to create an environment of non-judgmental listening. This kind of visceral listening requires empathy, calmness, emotional maturity, and wisdom and is the hallmark of an effective master coach. This is listening at its best—objective, dispassionate, and without judgment.

Wise Friend—Productive Inquiry

A master coach dons the role of a wise friend at times and helps you get unstuck. Let's face it—even the best among us have blind spots. This is typically obvious to everyone around us. However, some of your friends and family members are too emotionally attached to call you out. They let you blame the problem outside of you and allow you to play victim without asking you the tough questions and holding you accountable.

How does a wise friend help? Be empathetic, listen with care but do not let him go off too far with the victim mindset. Do not prescribe a solution; ask curious and insightful questions. Your goal is to help your friend stop blaming someone or something else and look inward to see how he may have contributed to the problem and how he can take charge of finding a solution. Let me give an example: Andy was complaining to me about his leadership team, "They don't make any decisions, don't have a sense of urgency, and come to me for all the answers. I am overwhelmed and disappointed in them." I knew all of them well enough to recognize that Andy was also part of the problem. However, unlike some leaders who like to be in this situation of central control and only complain when they cannot handle the whirlwind, Andy was sincere about delegating and empowering his team. But he made several execution mistakes:

- **Does not practice in real-time:** When Jason, his marketing VP, pops in for help to resolve an issue with operations, Andy does not direct him to Jane, the head of operations. Instead he provides the solution first and complains later when he runs out of time to tackle higher priority issues.

- **Slow to delegate and resolve a mistake:** Andy told Rob, his sales VP, to increase revenue and reduce expenses for the quarter. Rob in turn conveyed the same message almost verbatim to his directors and mangers. When Andy found this out, he conducted an exercise directly for them to go over the steps that needed to be taken on a daily and weekly basis to meet the targets. This could have been delegated to Rob with clear directions.

- **Impatient and directive communication style:** While Andy intended to empower them, his directive communication style suggested accountability without empowerment. He frequently stated, "I am upset with the slow pace, these delays are unacceptable. Why do I always have to be the one to solve problems?"

- **Inconsistent and unclear messages:** Andy does not pay close attention to the inconsistent communication he engages in with his team and unwittingly pits one against the other. Sometimes he asks two colleagues to perform the same task. He does not make the effort to keep everyone on the same page and clarify misinterpretation of information. In his anxiety to get things done quickly, he has the opposite effect and ends up taking an enormous amount of time to repair the misunderstandings and misinterpretations.

I obviously did not list these problems to Andy, nor was I anxious to offer a solution too soon. I could see him calming down as I listened empathetically. Then I asked him what he has done so far, how he would like to handle this situation going forward, and what the root cause could be. This led to a very productive discussion on where the bottlenecks were. He identified the first two problems on his own and said that he would work hard to avoid make those mistakes. Andy then asked, "What else do you see and what do you recommend I do?"

While it is very tempting to offer a solution, a master coach makes the leader see the block by being empathetic and asking the right questions, just like a wise friend would. By engaging in discussion and inquiry, he helps leaders unearth solutions from within and find their own answers.

It takes a high degree of personal and professional trust for a strong and successful leader to become vulnerable and ask for help. A master coach has to work with the dynamics of a CEO desperately needing a solution and the inability of their ego to clearly ask for it. This is something I learned the hard way after a few early mishaps.

Trusted Advisor and Teacher–Insightful Solution

It is very important for the coach to listen, learn, and ask the right questions as a student and wise friend. But that is not enough. There are times when the CEO needs someone who can be counted on to unburden and discuss the most pressing, conflicting, and complex personal, interpersonal, organizational, emotional, and spiritual challenges. This is not just safe confession, though that itself is of monumental help. A trusted advisor has the additional skill and capacity to either elicit or provide specific solution. The trick is to know when to do this. There are times when a CEO needs quick and direct answers.

In my own journey, I felt the insatiable hunger to discuss and brainstorm situations and solutions with someone who could listen deeply and provide helpful insights. I realized it is a rare and prized skill that would be of immense help to CEOs and leaders and decided to be of service by developing those skills. The master coach dons the role of a teacher who has the necessary expertise and experience to walk in their shoes and give compelling solutions with clarity. The key is to establish a trusting relationship, so a painful concern can be expressed and a question asked by the CEO. Both leader and coach work hard as partners to create a trusting partnership. It is not about hierarchy, ego, or power, it is simple common sense and physics. There is no flow of information unless you are humble, open, and curious.

In the case of Andy (see above), after answering my questions and having an interactive discussion, he gave me permission to guide him and provide specific solutions. I told him that he had identified his first two mistakes (not practicing in real time and being slow to delegate) correctly, but that he had missed the other two (impatient and directive communication style and inconsistent and unclear messages). I suggested that he share these with the team and invite them to offer input.

This approach usually leads the team to open up to how they can do better. If they don't, you can now ask them how they can contribute and take personal responsibility. You can encourage them to remind you in real-time when you repeat these mistakes. Now everyone works together and holds each other accountable. This builds trust and alignment, you resolve the problems much faster, and work becomes fun, light, and rewarding.

Instead of asking for timelines authoritatively, you can nudge team members to think through the important steps and actions needed to accomplish the goal. Your team works hard, but they are used to taking direction from you and have not developed the rigor and discipline to go through the steps before committing to a deadline. You will be surprised with how eager and enthusiastic your team can be in setting deadlines. Your role is to teach them and guide them toward the solution when they make a mistake, not to solve it for them.

When it comes to working with human motivations and emotions, sometimes a CEO doesn't know what he doesn't know. When I have the answer, I don't thrust it upon him. I ask myself, "How can I prod him into asking the right question so I can offer insights to tricky and complex problems and provide practical solutions?" One of the secrets of effective coaching is to make the person see the block and have him or her ask for the solution. You have to resist the temptation to offer an answer. Why will the person listen to your answer if they don't see the problem in the first place? This is very different from the manipulative style of "make it sound like it is their solution." The problem I have with this approach is you are giving in to their ego as opposed to helping them overcome the ego.

This is obviously not simple and requires skill and personal mastery. One of the most fascinating and enduring examples of this potent and practically powerful process is depicted in the 5,000-year-old Indian epic *Mahabharata*. Lord Krishna provides divine insights and practical wisdom on the battlefield to the most important questions in life faced by Arjuna, the greatest warrior of the time. The all-knowing Krishna only answers questions. Even though they share a deep trusting relationship, Krishna does not offer advice until a question is asked. Sometimes Arjuna asks a question, at other times he is simply stuck. Krishna then makes a subtle suggestion and skillfully nudges him to ask the right question. Only then does he provide the amazingly practical wisdom to the trickiest questions we all face. This treasure house of pragmatic insights is most relevant even today and is referred to by the greatest leaders in human history.

This dialog between a great warrior (high achiever, leader in modern times) and a divine guide (skillful, wise coach) remains a benchmark to this day for the ideal coach–coachee interaction. I do not mean to glorify or elevate the role of a coach to an omniscient divine guide. It is a partnership; there is no ego or hierarchy. In fact, Krishna and Arjuna were cousins and great friends. The point is to stress the importance of the process.

All of us intentionally or circumstantially play the role of coach and coachee with our professional associates, friends, and spouses, and it will certainly make the interaction more fruitful by following these guidelines. Remember the story of a seven-year-old boy who silently sat on the lap of an eighty-year-old neighbor who was in mourning after he just lost his wife of fifty years? After thirty minutes, the grateful man thanked the young boy for lightening his burden. We all have that power if we choose to exercise it.

Examples and Case Studies

As a coach I have to deal with egos and emotions very gently, especially when my clients are in a state of victimhood. When you face severe adversity and crisis, which everyone does at some point, the first reaction is to play victim and blame the world. You look for external reasons and other people to implicate in creating this crisis for you. You feel wronged for doing the right thing. You are convinced that you got a raw deal through no fault of your own. In short, you feel like an innocent or righteous victim. You are angry, frustrated, and disappointed that the world did not recognize your talent and brilliance. I have been there and am ever vigilant not to fall into that trap again. This makes you stuck and paralyzed in a state of victimhood. Unless you have attained exalted states of consciousness, this first reaction is natural and expected.

However, there is no reason to remain stuck there. You also have the capacity to come out of it. As you hone this practice, you reach a state where your default condition is to first look inward and take personal accountability. As Wayne Dyer said, "If we change the way we look at things, the things we look at change." How you respond and what action you take when you are confronted with adversity makes all the difference.

A Greatness Journey: Overcoming Victimhood and Rising Above Retribution

Some of us go deep into the rabbit hole and spiral into negative thinking and the gloomy self-talk sounds something like this: "This is a dog-eat-dog world; there is no room for honesty and integrity in business. I am considered weak if I express my emotions and listen to my heart. In business and in life, I have to be mean to win. I am stuck, I have nowhere to go. I lost out because I was not clever enough or conniving enough. I am too straight and transparent." This is the path of a victim who seeks innocence and feels powerless.

This is where Malcolm was when I started working with him. A highly successful award-winning president, he felt betrayed and treated unfairly by his partner and the board. Instead of encouraging and helping him develop into a solid CEO, he said that they stifled his growth.

The board was old-school and believed in command-and-control leadership and a hierarchical organization. Malcolm was the opposite; he was a maverick in a staid and conservative industry. However, he consistently delivered stellar results that far exceeded expectations.

He was convinced that their actions were malicious and intended to hurt him. Even if that was true, my role as his coach was to move him away from that slippery slope. It almost is never black and white; I knew they were doing the best they could. Their noble intent was to help the company become more successful. I see this game play out a lot: Professed results-oriented leaders make emotional decisions. Malcolm was deeply hurt; he was emotionally fragile and felt stuck. I knew that he was fundamentally a courageous warrior, and it would not take long to get him out of this. I shared the following perspective with Malcolm:

When something seriously goes wrong, and it invariably does for all of us at some point, and when it appears like you have done everything right and nothing wrong, and when it seems clear that certain people, events, and the world have conspired against you—you have a choice:

- **Do the obvious thing:** Get angry, upset, frustrated, disappointed, and take corrective action. Go on the offensive seeking revenge and redemption.

- **Do what is extremely difficult:** Do not blame anyone (including yourself) or any event. Fully accept and absorb the enormous physical and emotional pain.

When you choose the very difficult option #2, something magical begins to happen. The stress and pain melts away, giving way to an enormous sense of peace and lightness in your heart. You learn a lot more about yourself and others without judgment. You look at strengths and gifts, weaknesses, and obstacles dispassionately. You dig deep for the root cause of the conflict, take the high ground, and choose a noble response. Our anger and sorrow shift to appreciation and gratitude, the "tragic situation" becomes the catalyst for a life-changing transformation. Existing relationships get better and new doors open. Opportunities that you did not even dream of appear right in front of you and you perform at a higher level, at a new normal. You feel invincible yet humble, certain yet detached, passionate yet calm and flow through life acting on your deepest and truest yearnings and aspirations. Success seems imminent, but you paradoxically do not care since you have already tasted the greatest success— being fully present now.

Fortunately, Malcolm, like many successful leaders with whom I work, got it and shifted his mindset quickly. He already knew this; all he needed was a gentle reminder in his moment of heightened weakness and vulnerability.

Some of us take a different route. We pretend to be unaffected and declare premature victory over the crooks that are out to get us. We play the role of a righteous hero who is unshaken by the trauma around him. We internalize all the negative feelings and emotions and pretend to be unaffected. Not only do we put on this act to the outside world, we do that with our friends and family and even with ourselves. This is the path of a righteous victim who succumbs to paralyzing high stress. We can't work with these folks unless they accept the reality and are willing to deal with the pain.

When dealt with a devastating crisis, most of us tend to predominantly be in one or another state of victimhood. As a coach and accountability partner, how do I help people get out of this state?

The first step is to deal with their fragile ego and psyche. We have to demonstrate kindness, care, and compassion. Now is not the time for tough love or a pep talk asking them to snap out of it and to take personal responsibility. That will come later. You have to bring back a sense of stability and confidence in them.

I asked Malcolm to forgive, and explained that forgiveness does not mean he condone the perceived act of deceit, dishonesty, or duplicity. By forgiving, you will do not let anyone or anything come in the way of your wellbeing and leading your life in the manner you want. You take control of your emotions and actions. I then asked Malcolm to forgive himself. I knew that he was beating himself up for being naïve and for not seeing it coming. I told him "You did the best you could and the best you understood at that time. Hindsight is

20-20. It is not fair to judge your past with your current heightened state of awareness. We are supposed to learn and grow continuously. Let us learn from our missteps and become wiser. When we forgive ourselves, it is much easier to forgive others—and this approach accelerates the path back to our old state of confidence which we had temporarily lost."

The next step is to make sure that you have overcome your disappointments and are not harboring any thoughts of redemption and retribution. That will only slow you down and prevent you from staying focused on your goal. The goal now is to perform at a higher state. To accomplish this, you have to own your space, own your values, and stay focused on moving forward. We reexamine the values we stand for and reiterate our commitment. In Malcolm's case, the values he stood for and would not compromise on were fairness and inclusion.

When you don't fully own what you stand for, you lose because of yourself, not because of others. When you own and clarify what you stand for, it makes you strong. You are assertive yet calm, courageous yet humble. You stop looking at past events and people as villains. Instead, you view them as partners in your journey to stick to your values and unleash your greatness. This is a completely different way of looking at life and the people you work with. Malcolm was invigorated and got a new lease of life. He was clear about his vision and became even more committed to build a great, enduring organization. He was confident of achieving it because he believes in it fully and was ready to develop the strategy and action plan to get there.

A Leadership Secret: Humility and Confidence

Malcolm became increasingly confident with the board. He asked questions that made them testy and uncomfortable. In the past, Malcolm would be intimidated by that reaction, stay quiet, and move on. He did not back down anymore and persisted with his queries and insisted that they be answered to bring clarity. He was noticing that they did not like being asked and challenged in front of their peers. I checked with him to determine if he was feeling any need, however small, for redemption and retribution. He said that, thanks to my forgiveness exercise, there is hardly any of that need and he was staying on high alert to watch out for those emotions. He admitted to experiencing fear (driven by his perceived lack of expertise in some areas), but he does not let that stop him anymore.

Knowledge gives us confidence and courage, and, when we combine that with humility, we ask the right questions. Knowledge without humility leads to hubris and arrogance. So instead of worrying about insufficient knowledge, operate with confidence and humility. Admit what you do not know and ask clarifying questions like a wise and knowledgeable person would. You do not have an agenda and you do not want to show them up. You can put them at ease by being respectful.

Tracking Your Mindset to Function at Higher States

Malcolm was making remarkable progress, but he was neither seeing it clearly nor celebrating it. He would come with self-doubt and kept asking, "How do I know, and how can I tell I am making progress?" He would get impatient because he had not reached the goal of being fully present. He was at the stage of being unconsciously competent. My job was to make him conscious of his improved competence. I mentioned to Malcolm that we can track progress of our own state of evolution and consciousness. For example, he was able to describe his feelings and state of mind when he was communicating with the members of the board. In the past he would be intimidated and get quiet. Now he is a lot more assertive and a lot more aware of his feelings and emotions.

However, there is some internal anxiety which is making him stiff and he is compensating that with external nonchalance. He is conscious of this in real-time. As he becomes more conscious, welcomes, and participates in these situations, any remnants of judgment and anger will melt away. He will communicate more authentically and constructively. He will completely overcome the need to show the board up and become even more humble and even more self-assured. In this high performance state he will work with the other party's (members of the board) hidden emotions and concerns. He will be sympathetic to their fears and issues. He will ease them consciously by being respectful of their concerns while staying assertive with his questions. This is a peak performance paradox and the state of "flow" or "zone." It is a misconception that state of mind and our ability to show up and act with courage, confidence, and humility cannot be tracked. We can track our mindset and our state of operation when our awareness grows.

Channeling Stress, Conflict, and Adversity to Build Emotional and Spiritual Muscles

Stress, conflict, and adversity are a CEO's constant companions. The key to fulfillment and effectiveness is to not wish them away but to truly manage and even partner with them to unleash mastery. When someone's behavior and actions cause you stress, it is generally because of three converging reasons:

- His or her action is violating a value you believe in.
- You are not expressing your truth with conviction and authenticity. This may be because you are concerned the relationship will get worse, or you are afraid of being rejected.
- You are probably judging his or her actions without fully understanding them.

This situation is a remarkable opportunity for you to overcome one of the critical obstacles that get in the way of becoming an exceptionally conscious leader. What can you do to seize this opportunity and how do you need to show up?

1. **Gratitude:** Be grateful for the situation you are in. Gratitude and stress do not co-exist. This does not mean you ignore the problem.

2. **Empathy:** Go beyond your personal pain and try to understand the reason behind his or her action. His or her motivations may not be as selfish as you think, though we all have self-interest.

3. **Humility:** Be assertive and do so with humility and care. You cannot be intimidated by or fear something you love and care for. In this state, you will not have the fear of rejection and the need for recognition and respect.

Through these actions, you enhance your power. This is the paradox of peak performance and mastery. These expressions of gratitude, empathy, humility, care, and compassion will release happy chemicals, create bliss vibrations, and enhance the flow of life force within and around you. It has a systemic effect. This will make you solid as a rock—you will achieve emotional mastery and be unmoved and untouched by external catastrophes and crises. The Sanskrit word used by Krishna to describe this to Arjuna on the battlefield was *sthitaprajna*. Your whole being is aligned to fulfilling your purpose, and you will achieve a level of productivity and effectiveness that normal, successful people can't even imagine possible.

Own Your Greatness

As a leader, you must own your greatness. When you dedicate your life to a noble purpose, a cause that goes beyond your narrow self-interest, and when you are working tirelessly toward fulfilling it, you have a sacred duty and a solemn responsibility to share, express, and inspire all of your stakeholders in this momentous journey. It is neither hubris nor arrogance but a deep conviction and self-belief that come from a place of profound gratitude and humility. You have to own your greatness. It is thrust upon us as a by-product of pursuing a noble purpose and building an enduring institution.

My role is to help these leaders fine-tune the immense talent and unleash the greatness within to make an impactful difference on a larger scale. These successful leaders are ready for prime time to achieve legendary status in their respective industries. I see this as a noble pursuit and not a self-centered ambitious goal. It is a by-product of the desire to be a humble, conscious leader and build an empowered, conscious organization where people feel cared for and express their gifts and talents. There is nothing nobler than fully expressing your talent and making a difference to hundreds, thousands, and millions of people.

Patience and persistence are the key watchwords when it comes to the journey from success to greatness. I use the story of the Chinese bamboo tree when CEOs get impatient. You take a little seed, plant it, water it, and fertilize it for a whole year, and nothing happens. The second year you water it and fertilize it and nothing happens. The third year you water it and fertilize it and still nothing happens. How discouraging this becomes! The fifth year you continue to water and fertilize the seed and then—take note. Sometime during the fifth year, the Chinese bamboo tree sprouts and grows ninety feet in six weeks!

Life and business are much like the growing process of the Chinese bamboo tree. It is often discouraging when the goals are lofty. You do things right and nothing happens. But for those who keep taking right action and are persistent, shift will happen. Finally, you begin to receive the rewards. You are now receiving the rewards of seeds that were planted five years ago. Are you getting the results you want? If not, begin today to sow the seeds of what you want five years from now. Remember, if you keep doing what you've always done, you'll get the results you've always gotten. These experiences will help you achieve your goal of becoming a more caring, compassionate, and conscious leader and person.

Evaluating a Candidate

The key requirement for an accountability partner is detached objectivity and the skill to help the leader make a positive shift. You have the innate ability to self-inquire and dispassionately observe your thoughts and emotions that drive your behavior. However, even the best among us can use a partner or coach because you don't see your own swing. You need someone who is objective, authentic, courageous, and humble and has your best interest at heart.

What is the motivation for your partner to care for your progress and be genuinely excited for you? What is in it for him or her? That's exactly what Nancy, a skeptical CEO of a medium-sized company, asked me before deciding to hire me as her coach. "What's in it for you?" she asked. "Why would you be as desperate as I am to recover and become better than before?" She was just coming off an unsuccessful stint with another coach who she felt was not vested in her recovery and growth. Perhaps her coach was simply not equipped to deal with her complex situation. She had tried many people and approaches and had reached dead ends. Nancy was a co-CEO with her longtime friend. When I started working with her, she was at her lowest point, professionally and personally. The already fragile relationship with her friend and partner had hit rock bottom and got worse during the great recession when their business took a big hit.

Nancy felt she could not stay because her authority had gradually been taken away from her. Yet, she could not leave in her delicate emotional state. Where would she go? Her confidence was at an all-time low. She did not feel that she had it anymore to venture out on her own and start fresh. The ordeal took a physical, mental, and emotional toll on her. She was visibly distraught and in deep pain. She was advised to go on medication to deal with severe emotional stress and turmoil. Nancy did not want to take that route, but she was running out of options.

That's when I met her in what turned to be one of my most rewarding professional experiences and coach-leader partnerships. We connected immediately, and Nancy began to make steady, and at times, dramatic shifts. In a few months, she more than got her old spunk and energy back. We met every week for two years; after she made the shift, we tapered off to once a month and then once a quarter. A champion skier and tennis player, she is fully back, better than ever gliding through the slopes and life and experiencing peak performance zones on the court and at work. She rekindled her dream of building an inclusive, people-centric, service-oriented company, something she had shelved a while back. She said that her emotional and spiritual health has been better than ever.

Nancy confessed as to what made her hire me. She said that she liked the way I handled her skepticism about why a coach would be vested in her growth and well-being. I basically explained states of awareness and the purposeful life of a master coach. When you are focused on your growth needs, operating at higher states of consciousness, helping others fulfill their potential becomes a way of life. It is natural to be of service and to be deeply engaged in other's growth and wellbeing.

This is the 3.0 self-actualized state of mastery when your focus shifts from self-centered achievement to selfless service in order to make a difference. You will now have a burning selfless ambition to help other successful 2.0 leaders make the same shift to greatness. This drive is even stronger than pursuing your self-interest, and it is difficult for many people to comprehend this without personal experience.

In this flow state of mastery, you execute even better because you are fully aligned and have the support of the environment. You are operating at a higher state of awareness and presence. She is a master coach who is unconditionally driven to help others succeed!

Accountability Options, Schedule, and Timeline

The fastest and most effective way for you to move the needle on behavior change is work with an experienced master coach who is adept in dealing with human nature and is at a higher level of emotional and spiritual intelligence. This is no different from any other endeavor you pursue in life. You take help from a physical trainer who is fitter and healthier than you are. You go to a doctor when you are sick because she is trained to treat the ailment. You take the help of a teacher because she already got that degree and is trained to teach.

While there are several common themes and circumstances, no two leaders or CEOs are alike. I believe in customizing the program based on their needs, context, and willingness to put in the effort. The first step is the same. You get clear on understanding the current status, defining the gap, and choosing one or two areas you want to focus on for the next year to eighteen months. While progress is regular, significant breakthroughs involving hardwired habits and patterns happen only after consistent effort for several weeks and months. In addition, you have to ensure that changes and breakthroughs stay as a new, normal habit.

In my experience, you see major breakthroughs at around the nine- to twelve-month point. You then address the issues and challenges from this new mindset for the next several months to make this your new way of operating. Following are the different roles I typically embrace:

- **Advisor:** I meet periodically (monthly, bimonthly, or weekly) to evaluate status and current developments, discuss ways to get better, identify obstacles, and further accelerate progress. I role play and provide solutions to real-life examples.

- **Partner:** I attend critical meetings the CEO is a part of and observe her in action. I get the benefit of first-hand knowledge on how the leader is showing up. I will be able to pick up subtle nuances and patterns and provide specific advice and guidance. I also develop a good connection with her stakeholders, gain their trust, and enlist them in the process.

- **Facilitator:** In rare situations, I become part of the leadership team and on an interim basis. Under the right circumstances, this is a very powerful option. You lift the whole leadership team to a new level. I had some extremely rewarding experiences and breakthrough successes with this approach. Leadership teams experience real-time progress, participate enthusiastically, and get equipped to hold each other accountable.

Working with an understanding accountability partner makes the process rewarding, fulfilling, and liberating. Once you experience this, you wouldn't want to live any other way. It is painful only if you let ego get in the way. This is one of the secrets that propel successful leaders to greatness!

Evaluating Progress with Stakeholders

How do you determine if you are making progress in your behavior change goal? The simple and short answer is you will know. But then, even the most self-aware folks can use some help. Why not ask people who know you intimately and those who bear the brunt of and silently suffer your idiosyncrasies?

Even the most conscious and mindful among us may not be able to fully grasp the extent of change you are demonstrating and the impact it has on people around you. As I mentioned earlier, I recommend picking a good mix of stakeholders who get to see you in different settings where you are apt to demonstrate your best and worst behavior. This group should include your colleagues, subordinates, boss, peers, spouse, and friends. The more objective you are and the more honest you are about yourself, the better it is. This proven process works well when you stick with the practice consistently. As John Wooden said, "The true test of a man's character is what he does when no one is watching." Similarly, your true nature is revealed by your behavior with your subordinates where you have—or you think you have—nothing to lose. This is especially true in a command-and-control environment where the boss wields enormous power and authority. You tend to be guarded and on your best behavior with your superiors. I find it quite remarkable to observe people who unconsciously wear masks over their true nature and act very differently depending on the situation—with boss, peer, subordinate, friend, or spouse.

We celebrate your achievement and acknowledge the role your stakeholders played in this success. Having a group of stakeholders has many advantages: You get an objective assessment of progress, they become partners in your success, your relationships get strengthened, and you inspire them to do the same and undertake a similar mastery journey.

Stay Positive, Optimistic, and Enthusiastic

In the daily whirlwind of frenetic activity and frequent changes in internal and external conditions, staying positive and enthusiastic is the only thing that guarantees progress. Whenever you take up a path-breaking transformation program, it is only natural for many to be skeptical, jaded, and not fully "bought in." The overly sensitive leaders take cynicism and negative feedback from an outlier or only from poor performers as a broad-based critique.

I remind them to pay attention to constructive criticism from reasonable people but don't sweat over criticism coming from close-minded cynics.

The journey of greatness begins with personal transformation. It is simple to understand, difficult to practice, and extremely rewarding. As one leader said, "I don't want to be right and I am not attached to being right. I am no longer interested in imposing my will. As a result, I am more relaxed, my interactions are a lot more effective, and my relationships are more productive and fulfilling."

All of these processes and practices are deceptively and stunningly simple on paper. However, they are by no means easy, requiring uncommon common sense and unusual discipline. We all have the capacity for mastery. Isn't it fascinating that we allow ourselves to feel and be viewed as inadequate and incompetent?

Practice 6: Engage in Action Leadership

"Your actions speak so loudly, I cannot hear what you are saying." — Ralph Waldo Emerson

"Leadership is the most valuable commodity on the planet, and the rarest commodity we have." — Bob Davids

B usiness is a contact sport, and a leader is the captain. That person—you—leads by example. A point guard leads by example with points and assists, and a quarterback leads by example with passing accuracy and completions. A CEO leads with several key attributes of personal and organizational mastery. Earlier, I described the seven mindsets of personal mastery. Organizational mastery involves nine characteristics, as shown in Figure 6.1, which includes action leadership skills and attributes required to bake mastery into your organizational DNA.

Action leadership means first demonstrating and then demanding of others the skills of authentic communication, proactive conflict resolution, empowered and accountable conscious decision-making, energized meetings, and inclusive, dynamic strategic planning.

(The remaining four attributes further transmit 3.0 practices to the organization. These are addressed in Practice 7: "Bake Mastery into Your Organizational DNA.")

Action leadership in a 1.0 organization is "Just do what I say, and don't ask any questions." With 2.0 leadership, you get a bit more refined: "I want you to do this, what do you think?" In 3.0, you are inspiring: "What do you think we should do? How can I help you get better and achieve our common goal?"

Action Leadership Skills

1. **Authentic Communication**
2. **Proactive Conflict Resolution**
3. **Effective Decision-Making**
4. **Energizing and Empowering Meetings**
5. **Inclusive, Dynamic Strategy Planning**
6. Conscious Budgeting and Goal Setting
7. Tracking Three Dimensions of Performance
8. Objective Performance Evaluation
9. Fair Compensation and Incentives

Figure 6.1 Following these organizational mastery skills will put you and your organization on the road to greatness.

Authentic Communication

We tend to see ourselves primarily in the light of our intentions, which are invisible to others, while we see others in the light of their actions, which are visible to us. — J.G. Bennett

A core value for all of this is being authentic. This practice elaborates on how communicating authentically and performing these other functions well translates to improved business results.

Ash was genuinely concerned, "I love being authentic; that's who I am, but I get into trouble for speaking what's on my mind. When someone screws up, I don't want to sugarcoat it." It's just not Ash, one of the most successful CEOs in community banking. Many people I know, including thought leaders, get confused and conclude that it is neither appropriate nor possible to be authentic all the time. Several others believe that the price to pay for being authentic is to be perceived as being impertinent and impolite. I beg to differ.

The official definition of authentic is genuine, real, and legitimate. An authentic life is personally fulfilling. Authenticity is a highly desirable behavioral trait that enhances trust and inspires people to engage, collaborate, and align towards a common goal. It is therefore a critical and necessary quality for leading effectively in business organizations.

As long as your feelings toward yourself and others are positive and uplifting, it is easy and wonderful to be authentic. However, when the feelings are not positive and complimentary there is concern, confusion, and disagreement on how to act. Isn't it foolish and catastrophic to be authentic sometimes? These folks argue, why would we reveal our true inner feelings if they happen to be critical or negative? This is a genuine predicament, one that cannot be ignored or overlooked. I will present a way to overcome this problem and be authentic all the time.

Being authentic for me means satisfying two conditions—being direct and being constructive. We have to directly and constructively express how we feel about ourselves and others. Let us take a scenario where your friend, partner, subordinate, colleague, or boss has made a suggestion that you think it is a terrible idea. Worse, you may be angry, frustrated, or even fearful. You are now facing what my friend, Fred Kofman, calls, the "Quadrilemma." It is the concern that when you express what's exactly on your mind:

- You don't feel good about yourself
- The other person may be offended
- The relationship gets worse; and/or
- The issue does not get resolved and becomes even more complicated

It seems like you are stuck between two poor choices:

- Say exactly how you feel or what's on your mind. You explode. Is that being authentic? No, a better descriptor of that behavior would be blunt, tactless, lacking in empathy, insensitive, judgmental, and career-limiting. By being tactless and blunt, you end up engaging in a battle of wits and ego. Being right and winning becomes more important than finding the best solution.

- The other option is to sugarcoat your true feelings and stay polite on the surface but harbor resentment inside. You are clearly not being authentic. You implode. This doesn't feel right because you have compromised your values and integrity. You deny, ignore, or suppress negative feelings at your own peril. In doing so, your inauthenticity comes through, and you muddle through without resolving the issue. Worse, you blurt out concealed toxic thoughts at the most inopportune times.

Many people and teams alternate between these two poor and ineffective options, depending on the situation and context. Polite harmony on the surface among team members without addressing the underlying issues remain as passive conflicts and undermine morale, engagement, and productivity. Just imagine how much more effective teams and organizations could be if they engaged in authentic communication. The estimated loss of U.S. productivity due to poor engagement at work is $550 billion.

It doesn't have to be that way; there is a superior third option. But first, you have to recognize that there are people—a small percentage among us—who do not suffer from negative feelings about anybody or anything. When you are operating in a self-actualized state, this is a normal condition—to be always positive, grateful, complimentary, and inspired. However, many people do not operate in that state, certainly not consistently. This is an inspiring possibility.

A Superior Option

An even better option requires you to tackle your shadow or negative thoughts that lurk beneath your professional or civilized comportment. You have to take responsibility for your thoughts, actions, and behaviors. Do not blame someone or something else for your poor behavior. Instead reflect, go within, and self-inquire, "Why am I feeling negative and upset with this person?" Recognize that it is not about the other person. He only awakened a negative thought within you. Ask yourself, "What value of mine is being violated? Am I guilty of behaving the same way I am accusing this person of?" With this practice, you will be lot less bothered by people or events, and their stifling hold on you will be significantly reduced.

This is a good place to start and prepare yourself for a healthy conversation with the person whose words or actions offended you. You refine your toxic thought about the other person and approach them constructively. I say, "Don't get mad; get curious." We all have perspectives and opinions. It is impossible to operate without making assumptions and inferences, but it is dangerous to completely rely on them. Express your concern by focusing on observations and facts and share your opinion constructively. Ask with a curious mind and an open heart about the intention behind their action without taking it personally. Remind yourself that everyone has a good rational reason for what they do even when it appears crazy or incomprehensible to others.

If you dig deep enough, you will uncover the noble intention—even is misguided—behind people's actions. You cannot have an authentic conversation if you judge the other person's intention or if you fear conflict. You cannot have an authentic conversation if your goal is to be right. The purpose of an authentic conversation is to find the solution and engage in right action. Remember, right action is action taken in line with one's values and principles for the good of the team, without a personal desire to be right.

Articulating hurt instead of anger demonstrates vulnerability and humility instead of judgment. We do not allow our shadow to be in charge; it becomes subservient to our higher noble self. This doesn't make you inauthentic. I am not surprised but amazed to see so many well-intended hardworking leaders who are focused on advancing the common goal, yet fail to see that the other person is trying to do the same. Instead of confronting their action or position, they judge and demonize the person by attacking their intent. This happens between friends and spouses, in politics, and in business between partners, sales and operations, marketing and technology, CEO and CXO.

Since it takes two to have an authentic conversation, what if the other person is not ready or equipped to have one? You have control over your actions alone, not over someone else's actions, and certainly not on the outcome. There are no guarantees. However, by doing your part and staying in alignment with your values and beliefs, you may encourage the other person to participate, improving the chances of having an authentic conversation. If more people on the team engage in this practice, a tipping point of authenticity is reached.

By doing your part and staying in alignment with your values and beliefs, you may encourage the other person to participate, improving your chances of having an authentic conversation.

Remember what I discussed in Practice 3: In a 1.0 state, being authentic means that you must avoid hurting others on the team. In this case, belonging and being accepted by the team is most important. Saying what the other person wants to hear is more important than sticking to facts or your real opinion. In a 2.0 state, being authentic means calling it the way you see it by being direct and blunt without paying attention to how the other person is feeling or receiving. "It is about me, how I see it, and how I feel."

In a 3.0 state, you truly go beyond the ego's need to belong, to be liked, and then to grow and be respected and recognized even at the expense of the team. Being authentic means being factual, direct, and constructive by both sticking to the truth and delivering empathetically, with conscious awareness of others' feelings and receptivity.

Only in a 3.0 state can you fully grasp this and demonstrate the ability to communicate the same message to which people in all states can relate, understand, and connect. We used to think that this skill was necessary only for social leaders who are bringing about an evolutionary and revolutionary socioeconomic change. This is now a mandatory skill for a business leader who wants to create a 3.0 organization.

How can you be authentic when the chips are down and you are facing a crisis? Isn't it better for the leader to put up a brave front, don't let them see you sweat, and be less transparent? This is old school 1.0 and 2.0 leadership. Leaders build trust when they are transparent. If they lack courage or are easily overwhelmed, transparency hurts them. But these weaknesses will catch up with them later anyway. Leaders that are comfortable dealing with ambiguity and uncertainty—those who are self-confident enough to display concern or doubt—often seem more trustworthy and command greater loyalty. This is 3.0 leadership, which has a much greater chance of leading change and coming out of the crisis successfully.

For example, I facilitated a conversation recently between a CEO who was upset with his senior executive for not doing something which seemed like common sense to him. I spoke with each one individually, since their emotions were high, to prepare them for this conversation. I asked the CEO to be kind and gentle and reminded him to think about the times he may have missed something obvious. I requested his subordinate to not take it personally and pointed out that the CEO was struggling to communicate directly since "he has so much respect for your skill, ability, and character." This disarmed the executive. He took the lead and requested his CEO to be assertive and direct in his communication. He suggested that the CEO's emotional outburst without clarity of expectation was not helpful to either of them. In a touching gesture, they thanked each other for the honest discussion. There is a lot of anxious and restless bark in 1.0 and 2.0 leadership without the calm and self-assured bite of 3.0 leadership!

Authentic communication is easy to understand and difficult to practice, but is absolutely necessary to build trust and high-performance teams and to enhance organizational effectiveness. You have to become part of the problem and ask yourselves what role you may have played in creating this. You have to push the envelope and get uncomfortable. It requires courage—you have to be willing to be vulnerable by sharing your values and emotions. It requires you to be self-aware of your thoughts, intentions, and actions. You need a high degree of self-esteem to explore the discrepancy you exhibit between your thoughts, intentions, and actions. You need self-confidence to request and accept feedback on the impact your actions are having, and self-discipline to make a relentless effort for positive change.

In a Nutshell

Test your assumption of other's intention behind their behavior. Do not be quick to judge; be curious. Channel your anger and frustration by expressing hurt and concern. Do not fear conflict. Become part of the problem and focus on the solution and right action, not on being right. Suggest an alternate approach. If you dig deep enough, you will uncover the noble intention behind many seemingly crazy actions. There are no guarantees in business or in life, but we certainly have a choice to be authentic and that guarantees progress and peace of mind!

You are tested in your ability to engage in authentic communication when the power dynamic between two people is about the same as in business partners, co-founders, and co-CEOs. I find these opportunities particularly rewarding.

Developing Trust Between the CEO and CXO

The CEO and senior executives of an organization are ultimately accountable for its results. When the leader delivers results, professional trust in his or her ability grows. But results are a lagging indicator. Besides, good financial results can mask bad practices and poor short term results may make you overlook solid execution processes that have been put in place to ensure consistent results. How then does the CEO fairly evaluate the short-term performance of a senior executive (CXO) who is not directly executing tasks? More importantly, how does this CXO develop a trusting professional relationship with the boss, the CEO?

The issue gets even trickier when the boss is detail-oriented or used to be the CXO who moved up to become CEO and is now supervising his or her replacement. In both these situations, the boss tends to be hands-on and may understandably have difficulty letting go. This creates tension and frustration in the relationship which has to be handled with care.

Let us look at a worst-case scenario from both perspectives. The CXO feels unnecessarily micromanaged, and the toxic thought that enters his mind is that the boss will never let go. "She is always going to be looking over my shoulder." The CEO's toxic thought is," I can't trust the CXO to manage the details, he is too hands-off to catch critical issues early and we will pay for it later." If either, or worse, both of them, operate with certainty that their toxic assumption is true, their relationship and the effectiveness of the organization could be severely compromised.

This conflict creates a perfect opportunity for an authentic conversation. The CXO doesn't take his CEO's inquiry as a personal or professional affront and instead becomes curious about the intention. He may discover that the boss is being overly careful and only wants the organization and him to succeed. Ideally, the CXO will express his concern constructively and suggest an alternative approach—to focus both on process and results.

Similarly, the CEO tests her assumption that the CXO is not as passionate about execution. She converts her frustration to curiosity and inquires about the leader's approach to ensure execution is on track. She may find that the leader already has a process in place. If not, she suggests a more effective way to communicate and evaluate progress.

By following this process, the chances of achieving a mutually agreeable solution become much higher. It certainly goes a long way in making buy-in easier even if there is a disagreement. The CXO may have to accept to "agree to disagree" and abide by the final decision.

Your Peer Is Not Being a Team Player

A common concern many teams experience is when one member appears to not be a team player. Let us explore this situation further. What is the worst-case scenario? Your peer is deliberately holding back information to make it difficult for you and to get ahead of you. What is the best case scenario? He or she got really busy and thought this was not crucial or critical information to share. It may be that the organizational culture does not actively reward collaboration and sharing of information.

You don't know where the thought came from, but let's say the toxic thought that your peer is deliberately holding back information entered your mind. Shouldn't you check your assumption before you take action? Won't you compromise your personal and team's effectiveness if this assumption is not true? What do you do? You should refine your toxic thought and ask why your peer is withholding information. If open communication and inclusiveness are values you believe in and practice, then say so. Convert your anger and frustration to curiosity. In the depths of our heart, we are infinitely more noble than who we pretend to be. The key is to persist and explore the deepest truth.

If you have not made any attempt to check your assumption and did not request feedback on your own actions, do you have any right to complain? If this behavior is being tolerated in spite of your sincere efforts, why are you staying in such an environment? Culture starts with you and your leadership team. Your actions, not your words, shape the culture of your organization.

Proactive Conflict Resolution

"People aren't against you; they are for themselves." —Lao Tzu

The above quote is not some deep philosophical insight meant for a quiet monastic life in search of enlightenment. Conflicts are reminders and opportunities to work on aspects of our personalities to become the person we are capable of becoming. Conflict resolution gets us closer to that possibility. Why do I say that? Conflict is when you feel that an important value or belief of yours is being violated. When you reflect on your internal state before reacting to the external person who may have aggravated you, you will make a lot more progress. I find this awareness extremely valuable in resolving personal and workplace conflicts and disagreements.

What is a conflict? A conflict is a difference of opinion that becomes personal and negatively impacts a relationship. Conflicts come in the way of aligned teamwork and healthy collaboration, which in turn adversely affects outcomes.

Why do conflicts arise? Conflicts arise when you project your perspective is "right and true" and are unwilling to accept another perspective as viable and reasonable. In many cases, you may not even fully understand the other perspective—you let emotion cloud your reason and objectivity. As a result, many of the issues that you may actually agree on don't even get surfaced and discussed.

When you get an opportunity to express your opinion freely and disagree constructively, it is amazing how many conflicts can be avoided and resolved. This is the secret to developing alignment, collaboration, and excellence in execution. Great leaders, exceptional teams, and outstanding organizations follow this simple golden rule consistently.

Unresolved conflicts extract a heavy price. Relationships sour, social harmony is disrupted, countries go to war, organizational productivity suffers, and business performance is seriously compromised. Many business teams and organizations suffer from unresolved active conflicts and the "slow killer" (passive conflicts) that do not get proactively addressed. These internal conflicts are more damaging to businesses than external competitive threats and pressures. Careers get derailed, people don't trust each other, customers are not serviced effectively, decisions and product development get delayed, and revenue and profitability are affected.

I get concerned when I see teams that are polite on the surface but have issues that never get expressed openly. Many good teams and relationships suffer from this—they have passive conflicts that don't get acknowledged or resolved. They choose to live with them and accept a mediocre or "good-enough" performance or relationship. Why? Certainly not because they like mediocre performance. They simply don't know how to facilitate an open, direct, and constructive communication. So they squelch any uncomfortable dialog and discussion with an autocratic, top-down approach. Some of these leaders proudly proclaim that they have solid teamwork and don't have time for silly, irrational personality conflicts. They don't realize that they are losing precious time and productivity because disagreements don't get surfaced and people muddle through inefficiently, working around the issues.

The reason why most conflict resolution efforts don't succeed is because the root cause—ego—has not been addressed. Unless you fully and truly comprehend the other perspective, you cannot make a lasting change to the situation. This does not mean you are accepting the other viewpoints or positions, but you cannot connect, relate, and understand unless you master your ego. And, if you are of the belief that ego cannot be tamed, then progress is impossible.

I notice people sometimes tiptoe around the real issue with indirect reference or humor because they are concerned that they may be hurting the other person. This awkward dance ends up consuming a lot of precious time and energy without solving the problem. In some cases, both the problem and relationship get worse. Ego is automatically tempered at higher states of awareness (3.0) and is in service of a larger purpose, rather than driving its own fear-based, self-centered agenda.

What are some of the common and less-productive ways business teams and organizations choose to deal with differences of opinion?

- **Denial:** By denying there is a problem, they don't have to take any action now.
- **Avoidance:** They avoid dealing with the problem and hope that it will magically disappear or someone will take care of it.
- **Lobbying:** In dysfunctional teams and organizations, people covertly operate behind the scenes to lobby with colleagues and authorities to gain an upper hand in their conflicts.
- **Compromise:** In the rare situations they choose to address conflicts, these average teams and organizations end up compromising where they end up with a solution better than what they had, but a lot less than what is possible.

It doesn't have to be this way. Great leaders recognize that many conflicts are avoidable and others can be nipped in the bud. They know that having a process to prevent and resolve conflicts is a significant competitive advantage. How do they do it? What is their secret? They recognize that when we have a group of knowledgeable and informed individuals, different perspectives are natural and even necessary. They therefore create an environment to encourage and give expression to our natural and healthy differences of opinion.

We all have opinions that are shaped by our unique circumstances and lens with which we view the same events. Our perspectives of events around us are shaped by our DNA, the culture and environment we grew up in, and our personal effort and approach. We are born with certain biologically predisposed characteristics into a culture and environment that follows certain guiding principles, both of which influence our worldview. Our culture and the environment we grew up in includes language, ethnicity, religion, and country. While we don't have control over our DNA and the environment we are born in, we do have control over how we act and behave. This is where our personal effort and approach come into play. We have a choice to decide and act according to our free will. It is no wonder that two people with the same background and even from the same family can have different values, priorities, and approaches to life and business.

Effective business leaders are more self-aware. When you become more self-aware, you realize that your opinion and perspective are shaped by your unique circumstances. By closely examining the belief system and values that shaped your perspective, you can exercise your choice to change your position as opposed to forming an opinion unconsciously and sticking to it dogmatically. You then recognize that your opinion is your truth, but not necessarily "the whole truth." There may be other equally valid viewpoints. This recognition helps you to overcome the need to be right, which as you know, is one of the most difficult needs to transcend. By setting an example, great leaders ensure that right action is more important than being right. They actively monitor the environment to surface unaddressed conflicts and remove obstacles to resolving conflicts and achieving win-win resolutions.

While this concept is easy to understand intellectually, consistently implementing it is a whole different ballgame. Great business leaders recognize that it requires emotional maturity and wisdom to convert intellectual understanding of the reasons for conflict to consistent implementation. By becoming aware of how they are show-ing up, they take necessary actions to ensure that their intention to engage in win-win resolution is reflected in consistent collaborative behavior.

By understanding the underlying reason behind your truth and perspective, you will be in a better position to appreciate and accept, even if you do not necessarily agree with a different perspective. Having overcome the need to be right, they actively seek and achieve win-win resolutions to complex active and passive conflicts. They avoid the pitfalls of typical scenarios where people identify themselves with their position and "unconsciously" want to "win" more than get what they want. Great leaders recognize that when emotions take over, our best intentions are tossed, or, get tossed out the window and you end up causing serious, sometimes irreparable damage to teamwork and relationships. As a result, they work hard on mastering emotions.

Seven Steps for Appreciating Different Perspectives

Listening to and appreciating a different perspective came naturally to me. As a youngster, I recall being relied upon to mediate difficult conflicts and be a non-judgmental listener. I started paying conscious attention to the process I was following and also observed and learned from the best leaders and mediators. Over the years, I developed the following seven-step process to help resolve some of the trickiest conflicts and challenges involving individuals, teams, and organizations. Before beginning the process, however, you must look inward and then establish guidelines.

Reflect and self-inquire:

- What part of me is upset and uncomfortable?
- Why do I feel the way I do? What value or belief of mine is being violated?
- Am I projecting my internal conflict externally? Am I guilty of doing the same thing that I am upset about?
- What exactly do I disagree with?

Establish guidelines:

- Be prepared to separate facts from opinions.

- Commit to being open, curious, and non-judgmental.

- Look for the noble purpose. Do not mix intent and impact. Express and check assumption of each other's intent constructively.

- Channel desire to be right to seeking resolution.

Then start the seven-step process:

1. **Focus on the facts of the conflict.** Separate opinions and emotions. Establish the facts you agree on and identify those with which you do not agree.

2. **State your perspective with an example, share underlying beliefs, values, and reasons for your position.** Reveal your intent and noble purpose clearly. Express how you feel about the conflict. Disclose without holding back how you have been impacted—your feelings, thoughts, and emotions. Articulate the values and beliefs of yours that have been violated.

3. **Ask the other party to do the same.** Take the time to work through emotions. Stop only after both parties feel heard and acknowledged. We are not looking for agreement and resolution at this point. We want to create an environment of empathy and trust.

4. **Reframe the conflict.** Look at it from the other party's perspective. Engage in authentic conversation. Can you relate? Do you experience empathy and connection? Dig deeply and take it to the next level. Do you experience compassion, appreciation, and gratitude?

   - "A" expresses concern regarding specific behavior and action of "B." "A" details how both the business and they were personally affected.

   - "A" inquires about "B's" intention with curiosity and offers to share his or her assumption of the intention.

   - "B" summarizes "A's" concern and how it affected him

or her. "B" checks accuracy of understanding. Continue till "A" approves.

- ◆ "B" responds with his or her intention and the expected outcome.

- ◆ Reverse roles and follow the same process.

5. **Identify a shared purpose or goal.** Seek and confirm areas of agreement and differences. Separate your position or posturing from what you really want. Discuss each party's role in creating this conflict, either directly or indirectly. If you cannot become part of the problem, you cannot provide the solution.

6. **Act to resolve conflict.** Deliberate till agreement or consensus is reached. If not successful, escalate conflict to a person of higher position, authority, or an objective third party and to request decision. If all else fails, agree to disagree and move on. Commit to respect each other's perspective and to not rehash the same issue in the future.

7. **Settle the conflict amicably.** Abide by the decision. Victory is in resolving the conflict, not in determining how much each one gave in.

This conflict resolution process is a game changer and life changer for many. I have successfully applied this process to some of the trickiest challenges in board rooms and leadership teams, and even more emotionally demanding, personal and social challenges. Conflicts that had been simmering and lingering for months and even years are resolved and dissolve dramatically within days and sometimes immediately. Business leaders and executives I have worked with have said that the remarkable side benefit of this process is that in many cases their marriages and personal relationships prospered.

I have experienced some remarkable shifts and transformation in my own personal and professional life. By actively resolving difficult conflicts and proactively addressing those that are passive, I have developed some rich and rewarding relationships. Overcoming the need to be right and being unaffected by praise and criticism are highly developed states of mastery. It is one of the most important traits of the self-actualized state according to Maslow. Great leaders embrace challenges and relentlessly pursue this state by developing their emotional and spiritual muscles. They surround themselves with colleagues and advisors who are committed to this path and hold each other mutually accountable. When you master conflict resolution, you derive immense confidence, freedom, and fulfillment, along with an exponential rise in productivity and performance!

How to Make and Facilitate Effective Decisions

A CEO's decisions can make a difference to the lives and careers of hundreds and sometimes thousands of employees and stakeholders, not to mention the multimillion dollar impact on earnings and profitability. A pilot, fire fighter, or head of state's decisive action can be the difference between life and death. Your ability to experience a conscious and inspired 3.0 life, along with leading an effective and inspiring 3.0 organization, is determined by the decisions and choices you make.

Many of the leaders I work with place a premium on the value of quick and effective decision-making. One of the most successful and decisive corporate CEOs that I know humbly estimated his "hit-rate" on decision-making at 33 percent. How much is it worth for him and the company to improve on that? Another CEO told me that his rate is 30 percent to 50 percent and that's good enough. Is it really? Even though he has been successful, just think what he could do if he upped his average.

Sound judgment is not simply analytical or emotional but combines and integrates these two elements by being very clear on your purpose, principles, and priorities.

There are two key aspects of effective decision-making: individual decisions and group decisions. A conscious 3.0 leader excels in both—how she personally makes decisions and how she facilitates decision-making processes in the organization.

How to Make Effective Individual Decisions Quickly

There are two predominant views of effective decision-making.

- **Analytical:** The historical perspective that is embraced by many hard-driving professionals is the analytical model, which holds that good decisions can be reached by a logical step-by-step, rational process focusing exclusively on facts and data. This is the rational and logical approach.

- **Emotional:** Proponents of the opposing perspective argue that our experience in the real world demonstrates that good decision-makers rarely engage in this much rational analysis and decisions are made emotionally. This is the cognitive and visceral approach.

Consider some of the important neurological, psychological, emotional, and spiritual aspects of decision-making. People are wired differently, and most of us predominantly trend either toward the analytical left brain or the intuitive right brain.

The best decisions are made when we utilize both the thinking and feeling capacities of our brain. Sound judgment is neither solely analytical nor emotional but combines and integrates these two elements by being very clear on purpose, priorities, and principles. A CEO who is focused on profit and shareholder value can make quick and effective decisions to advance that cause. Another CEO who prioritizes purpose and stakeholder return similarly makes rapid decisions based on those principles. It is not about who is right or wrong; it is more about who is clear and focused. Emotional maturity and wisdom helps great leaders to filter their judgments with a clear set of principles, beliefs, and values. Outstanding decision-makers possess functional skill, sharp intellect, and demonstrate an uncanny ability to balance the thinking and feeling mind. This requires a high level of emotional and spiritual intelligence.

When your emotional intelligence (EQ) is high, you are not as distracted by fear, desire, and attachment. Neither do you shut down or block genuine feelings and emotions. Instead of being in a dysfunctional emotional state, you master emotions by being aware of and rising above them. Your logic and analysis work best when you are free, present, open, and conscious. Similarly, when your spiritual intelligence (SQ) is high, you care about the highest noble purpose, vison, mission, and core operating values. You are attached to right action and process while being detached from the result. This produces superior results.

Your intuition, also called spontaneous right action, works best when you are focused on the highest noble purpose and principles, free from fear and self-centered desire. When you are conscious and present, spontaneous right action is the normal mode of operation. Experience and expertise are seamlessly integrated with a value system of highest first, in this ascending order: Me > My family > My Team > My Organization > My Community > My Country > My World. At higher levels of emotional and spiritual intelligence, you become less me-centric and more team-, organization-, and world-centric.

You transcend (while being inclusive of) the lower survival and self-centered states to higher states of servant leadership and unconditional service to make a positive difference. It is important to recognize that all decisions including spontaneous, intuitive decisions have sound logic. A high EQ and SQ enhances logic and systems thinking. A low EQ and SQ makes you self-centered and emotionally immature with poorly developed logic, whereas a high EQ and SQ enables you to rise above narrow self-interests and demonstrate incisive logic that is grounded in inclusivity and higher purpose. 1.0 —Good IQ, Poor EQ; 2.0—Very Good IQ, Medium EQ; 3.0—very good IQ, and exceptional EQ and SQ. Decisive and effective leaders can logically and rationally explain their spontaneous decisions.

Decision-Making in a Team and Organization of Many Teams

In a team, everyone has an opinion and perspective. Some overanalyze and take too long to articulate their position. Some others are impulsive, not thoughtful, and are too quick to pull the trigger and say whatever comes into their mind. Some have a track record of objectivity and a stronger capacity to analyze and synthesize efficiently. All teams are made up of these different kinds of people. But not everyone likes to make decisions when they are held accountable. As a leader, you have to determine the best way to utilize these differences to make sound decisions and implement them effectively. The best decisions are neither autocratic nor democratic. A meritocratic approach is the right thing to do and inspires everyone who is committed to excellence to unleash their best.

You have to respect everyone's opinion and encourage them to participate enthusiastically. Then you have to make sure that the best opinions and suggestions carry much more weight. People who have a track record of success and have the capability to explain should have a bigger say in decision-making, independent of position and rank.

- **Autocratic:** Top-down with no involvement or input from people involved. Decisions can be quick, but what if the boss is not well-informed and is not the best equipped to decide?

- **Hierarchic:** Top-down with input and feedback from all concerned. This can work better but only if there is a culture of transparency and authenticity where people can express their true opinions, as opposed to what they are expected to say.

- **Democratic:** Majority-driven, everyone has an equal voice in a one-person-one vote. People feel vested and heard, but what if the majority is not well-informed and well-equipped? It could be like three wolves and a sheep deciding what's for dinner.

- **Meritocratic–Authentic:** Everyone participates and votes, but people with a stronger track record who are more knowledgeable, as well as those that are able to objectively analyze, synthesize, and explain get more weightage in the decision.

In business, you are dealing with new and ever-changing scenarios all the time. Obviously, it is unrealistic to expect people to have experience in dealing with all of them. Besides, many decisions are reversible; you don't have to aim for perfection. Instead, you have to encourage people who are able to analyze the situation, synthesize information, and explain their decision-making process.

Implementing Your Decisions

After making a quick and well-considered decision, you have to implement it. An important in-between step that you should not skip is getting buy-in from the implementers. Many leaders mistakenly assume or hope that has happened. Experience and human nature suggests that it is a not a very good assumption to make. You can, of course, pull rank and direct people to execute the plan. That gets you compliance but not creativity. They may not be willing to give their heart and soul to the effort.

A good solution is to involve implementers in the decision-making process. It is not always practical or efficient to involve everyone. In that case, share a well-considered draft and ask for input and suggestions. This is exactly what we did to engage the whole organization in developing the purpose, vision, mission, and values for CBC. Following is the summary of steps we took—and that you can take:

1. Start with a small team of people with diverse cross-functional backgrounds who together have the capacity and a track record of skills that involve the capability to see the big picture, analyze and synthesize information objectively, pay attention to detail, and have a sense of urgency.

2. Be clear with definitions and terminology. Provide accurate facts, data, and other information.

3. Develop a well-thought-out draft.

4. Share this draft with each member of the top leadership team. Get their input, buy-in, and finalize the draft.

5. Each senior leader now follows the same process with his or her department to secure buy-in. Now the whole organization is galvanized with a sense of purpose.

This process works when you make sure that people are allowed and even encouraged to air their concerns and doubts and engage in a healthy debate. As a leader, you have to remind them that being skeptical and open is normal and fine, but being cynical and closed is not. Once the decision is made, everyone has to work together to implement it successfully. In an open and meritocratic environment, reasonable people are okay if their views were considered but ultimately not implemented.

A 3.0 CEO puts the mission and values of the organization first. It would be wonderful to achieve exceptional results, but that is a by-product, not the goal. As I will detail in conscious budgeting and goal setting in the Practice 7, an accurate assessment of performance should include both process and results.

Energizing and Empowering Meetings

Meetings are often given a bad rap and treated as a necessary evil. You've probably heard comments such as "We have too many meetings," or "I am not getting anything done because I am always in meetings." What these statements are really saying is that your meetings are not productive. This is a shame because performing our jobs require us to interact and collaborate effectively. In order for performance to be fluid outside of meetings, you need to exchange information, surface issues, remove obstacles, and resolve challenges together while in them. There is no way around it. The irony is that human beings are social creatures who are wired to connect and interact. They love to share stories, exchange information, and have meaningful conversations. When you skillfully marry this natural tendency with common sense practical steps, you can engage in meetings that are effective, empowering, and energizing.

Isn't it ironic that people love to get together but hate meetings at work? The problem is not the meetings themselves, but how inauthentic and ineffective they are.

The true culture of an organization is determined by how we interact; communication with one another and how we treat each other—not just what we say we are. Therefore, how you execute as a company is connected with how effective your meetings are. What better way to evaluate your performance than observe how you act and interact in your leadership meetings? In well-run meetings, participants are more productive and effective than they would be individually. You make better and faster decisions, execute right tasks more quickly, and develop better strategies. Let's look at the breakthrough practices that exceptional leadership teams utilize to conduct effective meetings.

Well Begun Is Half Done

Starting the meeting in the best way is crucial. Most people enter meetings in a state of frenetic activity, with their minds occupied by events from the past or anxious about things that need to get done. When you are together, it is important that you are fully present—not just physically, but mentally and emotionally. You can't afford not to be; it is way too expensive! You have to leave the baggage of the past behind and not be distracted by the worries and uncertainties of future. How do you accomplish this, and how can you get centered? Here are some ideas:

- Observe a thirty-second silence.
- Do a three-breath check-in to focus on the present by letting go of the past and future.
- Review an inspiring quote.
- Read a document about meeting guidelines or about information needed for the meeting.
- Do a quick check-in with all the attendees.
- Conduct a two-minute gratitude meditation.

Establish Purpose and Agenda

Without a clear purpose and focused agenda, people get pulled in different directions and discussions veer off track. It is difficult to accomplish anything. It is important to establish or reiterate the purpose of the meeting. Similarly, set or confirm the agenda before getting started. Take the time to incorporate new thoughts and suggestions. Pause and get verbal as well as non-verbal acknowledgement from all participants.

Agree on Guiding Values and Principles

What does it take to get full participation and buy-in from the high powered, expensive, and bright minds in the room? Involve everyone in identifying the guidelines such as listening, respect, transparency, and mutual accountability. The trick is to adhere to these guidelines throughout the meeting. Catch yourself when you are not and give participants permission to call each other out.

Address Tensions

A great way to dive into addressing critical challenges and problems is to identify obstacles that are holding you back. The difference between a good team and an exceptional team has less to do with individual skill and work ethic and more to do with managing and addressing differing styles, opinions, and perspectives directly and constructively. Taking the time up front to pinpoint top concerns and tensions goes a long way toward improving trust and alignment. This sets the foundation for authentic conversations throughout the rest of the meeting.

Make Progress on Major Challenges

As a leader, your primary job is to address and resolve major obstacles. You have to tackle difficult personnel challenges, surface hidden and passive conflicts, and address concerns regarding areas of responsibility and accountability. It is essential not to get bogged down with minutiae and to avoid the natural tendency to start solving problems right there. Most functional and technical challenges can be delegated. This is not the place to solve all problems; instead you identify the steps and actions to take in order to make progress.

Be Decisive

This is one of the key benchmarks to gauge the success of meetings. When you don't make decisions, you don't make progress. There is no right or wrong way to make decisions—your focus should be on determining the most effective process for your team. Do you agree to a top-down or hierarchical approach? Do you like the majority decision to prevail? Do you like to empower the leader responsible? Consistent execution of the process you agreed to is the key here. You have to call each other out when you don't adhere to what you agreed upon. It is important for those in positions of authority to demonstrate humility and for subordinates to display courage if you want empowered and accountable decisions.

Do not force consensus by compliance. Encourage debate to express different viewpoints so that every member of the team agrees to support and vigorously execute the final decision. Facilitate skillfully.

Tap into the Collective Intelligence

You have to make sure to get the most out of the horsepower in the leadership team. You have to facilitate skillfully to make sure everyone's voice is heard. Some need to be reined in and others prodded to offer their opinion, especially if it is contrarian. This is worth the time and effort to get buy-in. Your goal is not to be right but get to the right solution. When you feel heard, it is amazing how unattached you can be to your perspectives.

Set Actions and Accountabilities

One of the most frustrating aspects of poor meetings is that you do not know what actions are being taken, when they are supposed to be completed, and who is willing to be held accountable. You do not have a sense of accomplishment or even progress. To avoid this letdown, maintain an action item list with clearly defined tasks along with due dates and responsibilities. This is an essential step and a good way to close a meeting is by finalizing this document. Make this an ongoing process. Update status and review action items in the next meeting.

Check Out on a High Note

You diligently followed through the process and had a productive session; you now need to close the meeting properly. You do not want to rush out but instead celebrate your success and work to get even better next time. Runners and athletes know the importance of stretching after a good workout. Similarly, you take your time coming out of deep meditation. Now is a good time to ask participants how they are checking out. Do they feel more energized, accomplished, and fulfilled as a result of this meeting? How can you improve and get even better? What worked and what didn't?

Mastery is a matter of having the discipline to follow through on these simple guidelines consistently. When you learn how to conduct and facilitate productive meetings, you have mastered the ability to align individual skills and strengths into a powerful cohesive force. This results in breakthrough improvement in productivity, performance, and profitability!

Guidelines for Engaging, Energizing, and Effective Meetings

- Have a stated purpose, agenda, and end time.
- Review action items from last meeting.
- Encourage, applaud, and celebrate transparency and truth-telling.
- Check your ego at the door. Your goal is to make a positive difference, not to prove how smart you are.
- Actively involve others and leverage collective intelligence. Focus on determining the right solution, not on "being right."
- Attendees should walk away with concrete next steps or action items.
- Every project or task should have an accountable individual (AI).
- Focus: Identify problem, make decision on solution process and assign an AI.
- Do not fall into the trap of solving problems unless you specifically want to do so.

Inclusive, Dynamic Strategy Planning

When we get an opportunity to express our opinion freely and we feel heard, it is amazing how unattached we can be to our opinion. This is the secret to developing compelling strategies and excellence in execution. Great leaders, exceptional teams, and outstanding organizations follow this simple rule consistently. Inclusive, dynamic strategy planning is critical. It encompasses all the elements of what it takes to build exceptional leadership teams and organizations. Every organization has to engage in this activity. Instead of defaulting to a reactive process, a proactive and enlightened approach will yield rich dividends. Most organizations engage in strategy planning sessions periodically.

Participants are senior executives, other top performers, and special invitees who, as one executive put it, have earned the right to engage in this exercise. The manner in which these sessions are conducted is very revealing of the culture and effectiveness of the team. In particular, pay attention to the following aspects:

- Is the collective intelligence being tapped? Are all voices and functions being adequately represented?

- Are all participants freely expressing their viewpoints? Are they disagreeing constructively? If you were to take an anonymous poll, would their opinion still be the same?

- Are there enough diverse opinions? Are contrarian views being expressed, encouraged, and considered?

- Are you considering the input from the implementers of strategy? How do you get their buy-in? How are they included in the process?

- Are you detailing various strategic options, and their pros and cons?

- Are you explaining and discussing the reasons, beliefs, and values behind a strategic option?

- Are you balancing both external conditions and internal situations? Are you considering internal skills and operational capabilities?

- Is there an explicit understanding of how decisions are being made? Is the discussion free-flowing or is it being dominated by a few?

The old strategic planning model involved an exclusive group of senior executives and thought leaders, some of them external experts, who met once a year and decided on the strategy for the troops to execute. That model is dead. The new approach allows for diverse perspectives from a cross-functional group of executives and employees that includes implementers of strategy. This means that you can formulate better, more practical strategies that have the capability and buy-in to execute faster. Also, with business, technology, and markets changing so fast, you can't afford to wait a year. The organizational structure and culture should be flexible to inspire real-time dynamic strategy planning and decision-making. You can accomplish this by distributing power and authority to people who are closer to customer contact and internal development. They can make strategic decisions on the fly and course-correct what has been agreed to in the strategic planning document.

Every aspect of action leadership that I've discussed in this practice supports one primary, basic truth—that exceptional teams pay close attention to the issues and embrace the following principles:

- **Align values:** It's about the process: They set the foundation for a robust discussion by establishing guiding values and principles such as openness, authenticity, collaboration, risk-taking, and are not attached to being right. They work hard to overcome narrow agendas and limiting beliefs and give permission to hold each other accountable.

- **Pursue full engagement and commitment:** They ensure everyone is fully engaged and committed to the process. They encourage quieter members to present their ideas. They work hard to overcome narrow agendas and limiting beliefs and rein in those who dominate discussions and squelch opposing perspectives.

- **Do not seek or force consensus:** They encourage vigorous debate and focus on analyzing the pros and cons of various strategic options. They do not force a top-down decision or seek the elusive consensus but make a meritocratic decision. They achieve operational consensus. Once a decision is made, everyone is whole heartedly committed to its successful execution.

- **Unleash full capability and unlock full value:** They don't limit themselves, and they avoid gaming the system by targeting incremental growth. They establish stretch goals designed to think and act outside the box and unleash their full capability. Even some large public firms such as Unilever have decided not to succumb to the quarterly growth expectations and instead focus on unlocking the full value over the long haul.

- **Execute and course correct:** They recognize that execution begins with people and planning. They plan meticulously and take the time to allocate and match capability with resources for implementation. They evaluate progress and establish the process for dynamic, real-time course correction.

Action leadership is about inspiring people to be the best they can be. It is not about making everyone temporarily happy. This requires them and you to get uncomfortable and involves pain. But it doesn't have to debilitating, and you don't have to suffer through it. I agree with the Japanese writer Haruki Murakami, who said, "Pain is inevitable, but suffering is optional."

Steve Jobs in his own inimitable style once said, "If you want to make everyone happy, don't be a leader—sell ice cream." I might add, the ultimate happiness is in being the best you can be and helping others be the best they can be. Any change, especially behavior change, is difficult in the beginning, messy in the middle and rewarding, and liberating at the end.

I have worked with many well-meaning, successful leaders and teams who struggle with the implementation of these common sense practices. Why? It requires a keen grasp of human nature, emotional mastery and spiritual wisdom, qualities of higher states of consciousness.

Exceptional leadership teams integrate business skills with the emotional and visceral qualities of spiritual intelligence, and they deliver consistently. Many organizations and their high-IQ leaders do a good job of articulating the importance of buy-in and collaboration, but it is the ones with emotional depth and spiritual wisdom that translate it to effective and consistent implementation. They remove the obstacles that get in the way and establish the environment to inspire full engagement and commitment. That is action leadership.

Practice 7: Bake Mastery into Your Organizational DNA

"Leadership is based on inspiration, not domination; on cooperation, not intimidation." — William Arthur Wood

"The most damaging phrase in the language is: 'It's always been done that way.'" — Grace Hopper

Now it's time to make mastery a way of life in your organization. Your true culture is determined by how you and your colleagues interact with one another, how you treat each other, how you evaluate, recognize, and reward your valuable human capital. Your culture is how you conduct your business—not what you say it is. This is what life, leadership, and CEO mastery is truly about. You will now put your knowledge and self-actualization to good use by baking mastery DNA into your organization.

It is wonderful and invaluable to have a noble purpose, grand vision, and core values. However, they alone are not sufficient to build a great organization and to propel a successful leader to greatness. Vision and values have to be directly connected to critical business functions, operational processes, and daily interactions.

Integrating Effective Business Practices with Peak Performance Principles

I had recently been introduced to Jay, the chairman and CEO of an organization he started twenty years ago. Soon we started talking about some of my favorite topics: business performance, leadership, alignment, employee engagement, and organizational effectiveness. Jay was concerned about the low trust and poor communication in his company and was wondering aloud if it could ever be fixed.

I wanted to see how ready Jay was and how personally accountable he was going to be. I said, "You know, Jay, you created the culture that you do not like. It may have been unconscious and unintentional, but the state of affairs in your company shouldn't be a surprise to you. Being entrepreneurial and impatient, you have always had an ad hoc approach. Decisions have been imposed top-down without input, feedback, or buy-in from the people who are involved in implementation. You have not established inclusive processes for planning and execution." Jay was intrigued but not defensive. Nobody had pointed this out to him in such an emphatic fashion. He appreciated the candor and clarity. He did not get to where he was without being accountable.

I elaborated further: "You have unconsciously and unintentionally created the culture that you do not like. Now we can consciously, intentionally, and deliberately build the culture you want. It takes effort and hard work of a different kind. You are used to working your physical muscles to stay personally fit, and your intellectual muscles to ensure that the organization is expanding profitably. Now, you have to work on your emotional and spiritual muscles to build trust and openness. That's what this system is about: integrating what already works—primarily professional mastery—with personal and organizational mastery."

In many companies, vision and values appeal to the higher 3.0 state of mastery and contribution. Key strategy and planning meetings reflect the 2.0 self-centered achievement state, while daily, pressure-packed interactions occur in 1.0 state of survival and belonging. This sends mixed messages, creating confusion, cynicism, and stress resulting in less-than-optimal productivity and performance. This is an unintended consequence for most leaders and organizations.

Similarly, all organizations set budgets and goals, measure and track business performance, evaluate individual and team performance, and compensate and incentivize people. What sets you apart and determines if you are more of a 2.0 leader and organization or a 3.0 leader and organization? In a 3.0 organization, you engage in conscious budget and goal-setting, objective performance evaluation, fair compensation; you track three dimensions of performance, not just financial. When you do this, you bake mastery or infuse a self-actualized way of conducting business in your organization. (See Figure 7.1.)

Action Leadership Skills: Baking the DNA

1. Authentic Communication
2. Proactive Conflict Resolution
3. Empowered and Accountable Desicion-Making
4. Energized, Effective Meetings
5. Inclusive, Dynamic Strategy Planning
6. **Conscious Budgeting and Goal Setting**
7. **Tracking Three Dimensions of Performance**
8. **Objective Performance Evaluation**
9. **Fair Compensation and Incentives**

Figure 7.1. These skills will help you bake 3.0 leadership DNA into your organization.

If you have not changed how you set budgets and goals, measure and track business performance, evaluate individual and team performance, and compensate and incentivize people, your 3.0 intent does not match your 1.0 or 2.0 realty. If your organizational infrastructure is functioning efficiently but you are measuring or evaluating in the old, incomplete way, you have a serious culture problem at hand.

How do great leaders and organizations overcome this quandary? They make sure that mastery is everybody's business and is infused in the DNA of the company. Action leadership is about walking the talk, which is primarily focused on leadership behavior, communication, decision-making, negotiation, and getting things done (see Practice 6). Action leadership and baking mastery in the DNA together determine the culture of the organization that you deliberately develop and nurture. None of us can do it alone—it takes an aligned leadership team and an engaged organization.

The word *culture* is derived from the early Greek term for "cultivation of the soul." Great leaders nurture an environment where everyone has the opportunity to let the mind shine, heart sing, and spirit soar. Total buy-in is achieved when employees are all-in with all faculties—mind, heart, and spirit.

Companies, families, groups, and even countries have shared experiences that forge perspectives. Culture is a double-edged sword: it simplifies expectations and actions but can also limit exploring new ways. For example, try Googling the "Five monkeys and a ladder experiment," in which a group of primates was conditioned to beat up on one of its members whose actions were viewed as negative for the entire group. In a 1.0 and 2.0 state, "belonging," and group thinking drive the approach. In a 3.0 state, we are able to rise above the primal behavior of "belonging" and group thinking prevalent in the earlier states.

Another challenge in organizations is the gap between what is said and what is practiced. Do these paradoxical behaviors sound familiar to you (Source: *Conscious Business*)?

- Keep others informed, but hide mistakes.
- Tell the truth, but don't bring bad news.
- Take risks, but don't fail.
- Beat everybody, but make it look as if nobody lost.
- Be a team player, but what really matters is your individual performance.
- Be creative, but don't deviate from rules.
- Express your independent ideas, but don't contradict your boss
- Ask questions, but never admit ignorance.
- Promise only what you can do, but never say "no" to your boss's requests.

- Think about the company, but protect your own people and department.
- Think long term, but deliver immediate results

Mixed messages and inconsistent behavior cause serious stress and organizational ineffectiveness. It is worse when you repress reality and pretend there is no problem. You can't even discuss and try to change the situation. This is a toxic culture. We overcome this kind of toxic culture by baking mastery in the organization. By definition and practice, mastery is about always learning, growing, and being open to change and new ways of mastering our craft.

For most companies, creating a good culture means engaging in social activities such as picnics, after-hour socials and celebrating birthdays, making life a bit more convenient and comfortable with flex times and remote work options; and providing onsite amenities such as gym, yoga, gourmet coffee, and laundry pickup. This certainly helps, but there are other powerful needs such as being heard and being treated fairly and objectively in a meritocracy. And there are deeper motivations to make a difference, contribute, serve, engage in meaningful work, and nurture meaningful relationships.

Conscious Budgeting and Goal Setting

The 2.0 way of setting financial goals and budget is top down. Leadership at the top imposes a revenue growth requirement influenced by the expectations of the shareholders or owners. There is not much thought or airtime given to the ground realities of internal capabilities and external conditions. Not just growth, but significant growth, is the goal, no questions asked. It reminds me of a strategic planning session where the leader of the team said that he was looking forward to a collaborative and authentic discussion. He then stated that 10 percent growth was non-negotiable. It was an unconscious statement that was unconsciously accepted. What followed was a predictable game of, "What is the right thing to say?" and, "What can I get away with?" The players, companies, or industries may change, but the plot of the movie normally doesn't.

If your true growth possibility is 20 percent, why would you bother sharing that? You will sandbag and offer 10 percent and emphasize that is going to be difficult. You will save the rest of the growth for later, even though there is no guarantee that it will continue. On the other hand, if your best hope is only 5 percent, you have to be even more adept at playing the game. You have to first vehemently complain and then accept an unrealistic target. You then have to constantly reinforce the message by sharing the challenges of reaching the goal. If real issues and problems are not accepted and addressed, you are forced to play the blame game and find people and events at which to point the finger. This may sound crude or harsh, but it is the unfortunate reality in many business organizations. Like anything in life, over time people get numb to the realities and accept that it is the only way to do things.

The 3.0 way of conscious budgeting and goal setting is different. The focus here is to do an accurate and thorough analysis of the realities of external conditions and internal capabilities. Consider the interests of not just shareholders, but all other stakeholders as well—employees, customers, and suppliers. When setting the targets, there is a higher degree of trust and empowerment placed with people who are closest to action. Companies such as Patagonia, Zappos, Morning Star, AES Corporation, and FAVI Manufacturing, all profiled in Frederic Laloux's *Reinventing Organizations,* follow such an approach. They do not want to limit or force unrealistic growth. Constant short-term revenue and profitability growth independent of external market conditions and internal capability are impractical and counterproductive for the health of the organization. This is just common sense.

Even some large public companies such as Unilever, led by its courageous CEO Paul Polman, have decided not to succumb to quarterly earnings pressure and sacrifice long-term growth and sustainability. Polman was clear that Unilever's approach might not deliver the highest profitability every year, but he promised it would deliver consistently, year after year. And it has. In response to a question about how he managed to overcome the market pressure, Polman was charmingly blunt: "I think it is a cop-out. Any CEO can decide that he shouldn't get paid too much. Any CEO can decide to think long term … I think it is courageous leadership that is missing. The excuse is that the market won't let you…

Definition of Business Growth and Performance Has Expanded

When *Good to Great* by Jim Collins was published in 2001, greatness was defined in terms of financial performance. Companies that earned the "greatness" tag outperformed their peers financially. It did not matter, and we did not measure how disengaged, stressed, and unhappy employees were or how fragile their supplier and business partnerships were. Our perspective today has been evolving from a shareholder-centric to stakeholder-centric approach. In *Firms of Endearment*, authors David Wolfe, Jagdish Sheth, and Rajendra Sisodia convincingly argue that the definition of greatness goes beyond outstanding financial performance. A great company is defined as one which excels in stakeholder return and earns the admiration of not just shareholders but also employees, customers, suppliers, partners, and the community in which they operate. We are seeking both, not just "either-or" but "and" solutions: personal fulfillment and professional excellence, emotional expansion and intellectual growth, consciousness and technology, purpose and profit, meaning and money, principles and performance.

Brilliant Jerks and Great Values

One of the pet peeves in many organizations is that they tolerate brilliant jerks. This means that as long as the employee is delivering financial returns, that person gets a pass even if he or she demonstrates boorish behavior and does not live the company core values. Some organizations such as Next Jump, Inc., whose mission is to change the world by changing workplace culture, put their money where their mouth is by setting targets that are based 50 percent on revenue growth (for a business development or salesperson) and 50 percent on adherence to core values. Commercial Bank of California is planning to set targets based on a 50-30-20 split for the regional vice presidents: 50 percent on revenue, 30 percent on leading indicators (right action steps), and 20 percent on adherence to core values.

Tracking the Three Dimensions of Performance

I have been grappling with the issues of fairness and meritocracy in business and in life for many years. The commonly accepted views, approaches, and measurements are not satisfactory and frankly are unable to explain many results and developments. For example, a popular practice is to set growth goals that are easily measurable (such as financial numbers), regularly track progress, and reward participants accordingly. This approach has worked well but is incomplete—it does not adequately address the root cause of the results. It rewards results rather than specific performances that have produced those results. However, results are a lagging indicator and depend on other external factors beyond our control. Results are easy to measure; performance is a lot more difficult to evaluate. As a result (no pun intended), we give too much credit to individuals and leaders when outcomes are favorable, and place too much blame when outcomes are not favorable. This didn't seem right, and I was in search of a more effective way.

Successful business organizations focus and measure hard numbers with consistent discipline. Similarly, successful coaches focus on wins and losses. But the exceptional and all-time great coaches, such as John Wooden the legendary coach of UCLA basketball, focus on performance and right action, sound technique, and fundamentals, urging team members to play hard and play fair. This generates extraordinary results.

Being an avid athlete myself, I always wondered about the situations when I played beautifully and lost the game or times when I was not at my best and still won. What is more important, winning or giving your best? What feels better? You have to find your own answers, but for me, the idea of being happy when I won and unhappy when I lost was painful. I wanted to feel the joy of playing while working really hard to realize my full potential.

When I was about 13 years old, I lost a ping-pong match that I should I have won easily. I lost because I was overly cautious and was playing not to lose. More than the loss, my defensive attitude stung me badly. That was a turning point in my life. I realized that I was doing the same not only in my favorite sport of tennis but also in the way I approached other important aspects of my life. I decided to play to win and not be overly cautious anymore. I made a commitment and still live by it—I will always give my best and play hard. That is winning in real time, which is guaranteed and is in our control. What follows later is the winning or losing on the scoreboard, which is not entirely in our control. That victory is a bonus to what you have already won. I credit my growth and evolution to this approach.

How do you evaluate leadership performance? If you are using only short-term financial results, you are not accurately and comprehensively evaluating a leader. Neither are you able to predict with reasonable accuracy if this leader is going to deliver. In business, sports, or any other endeavor, greatness cannot be stopped. In the long run, results will follow when right actions are performed. Spot that spark and talent early and give leaders and high-potential leaders the support and time necessary to excel. By keenly observing the body language and evaluating the mindset of the leader, you can determine how he or she is showing up and get a good read on his or her leadership capability.

Aligned leadership team and engaged employees drive exceptional results.

I am not suggesting that you bank your performance evaluation on mindsets and action leadership skills alone. When you combine the evaluation of personal mastery and action leadership with hard results, you get a more complete grasp of their capability and accomplishments.

What can business organizations do to deliver exponential and exceptional results? The answer is in its people. Business is a team sport. The leader's development and skill is extremely important since he or she controls significant decision-making power and authority in a hierarchical structure. However, that is not enough. There are two other crucial constituents:

- **Leadership teams:** Are they aligned, collaborative and mutually accountable?

- **Employees:** Are they engaged, inspired and do they have an owner's mindset?

Leadership alignment and employee engagement are the leading indicators and important metrics that drive business success. You can realize incremental success by being on top of one dimension—your hard numbers. You will accomplish breakthrough results by adding leadership alignment and employee engagement.

Figure 7.2 depicts the three dimensions of performance. One dimension is basically revenue and profitability—the usual numbers. A second dimension is engagement. How engaged is the organization? The third dimension is executive alignment—the level of trust

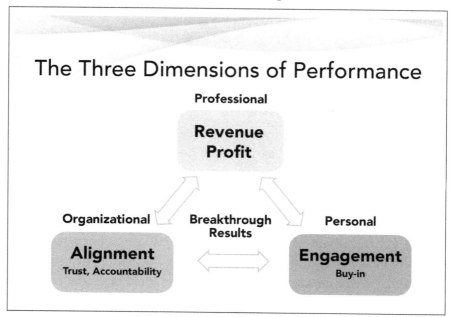

Figure 7.2. Tracking the three dimensions of performance can help create breakthrough results.

and mutual accountability. Monitoring those three dimensions can help you get breakthrough results.

Employee engagement and executive team alignment do not get as much attention as revenue and profitability. You need to focus on all three dimensions of performance as a leadership team and bring attention on them to the board level. Most organizations have not done that yet.

Executive team alignment is another critical factor for performance success that is seldom tracked or even considered. It is important for executives to not only to be aligned but to hold each other mutually accountable.

Alignment and engagement drive productivity and power performance. These are not as straightforward as the hard revenue and profit numbers but can be tracked fairly easily and accurately. Employee engagement can be tracked with software tools such as Tiny Pulse and Culture IQ. In Practice 3, I described an executive team that I had asked to rate their level of trust and mutual accountability. This is how I help executive teams determine how aligned they are and, more importantly, engage in exercises to help them be more real, authentic, and vulnerable. You will experience progress in real-time, and when you do this consistently, there is a significant improvement in alignment.

Active versus Passive Engagement Questions

I believe in active, rather than passive, employee engagement questions. Passive questions are those like "How happy are you?" or "How likely are you to recommend your place as a place to work for your friends and family?" These are the questions that most surveys ask. What I like to do is be more active by asking, "What are you doing to improve your engagement level?" or, "What suggestions do you have for making this an exceptional place to work? How are you contributing? How do you stay engaged? Why would you recommend (or not recommend) this company to friends and family as a place to work?"

Employee engagement, or any engagement for that matter, is a two-way street. The leader's job is to create the right environment so everyone can give their best and be treated fairly and objectively. Every individual has to take personal responsibility and accountability. You don't just sit back and wait for the right environment to show up fully. What are you doing to create the right kind of environment? How are you overcoming some of the obstacles? How are you providing solutions to the challenges and problems you're seeing? That's a very important aspect of building employee engagement.

At Commercial Bank of California (CBC), we have been very diligent and thorough in measuring and tracking the financial dimension. That is one important reason why we are so successful financially. However, we are not satisfied and we are not resting on our laurels. We are working hard to get better in the other two dimensions. I mentioned earlier how we evaluated trust and its connection to mutual accountability. We are constantly working to improve leadership alignment and pushing the envelope.

All senior executives, including CEO Ash Patel, have personal development "stretch" goals that will make them more inspiring and effective leaders. They will hold each other accountable to make sure that they are regularly taking the steps to which they have committed. Some of them have specific accountability partners and coaching guidance to accelerate the journey. We open individual challenges to the leadership team for their opinion in order to tap into the collective intelligence and push each other to improve faster.

Being a hard-driving entrepreneurial CEO, Ash is frequently concerned about the sense of urgency and attention to detail of his executives and doesn't waste any time in pointing that out. However, he asks a very important question which every CEO aspiring to build a meritocratic organization has to ask: "What if I am wrong? I want to make sure I get the benefit of collective intelligence and get their unbiased opinion." Obviously, this will work only if the trust in each other is high and people are comfortable expressing their honest opinion without feeling like someone has been thrown under the bus.

We use TINYpulse, to interact with employees frequently and solicit their input, along with feedback on leadership alignment, company culture, and of course, employee engagement. That is only the first step; we can't stop there. We engage the employees in an active manner and involve them in creating the right environment. We want to be an organization where employees give their best, are fully engaged, and demonstrate an owner's mindset. They are the ones to decide if we are on the right track.

We ask a series of questions and follow-up questions to determine the most important actions we need to take to make our organization an exceptional place to work. That is still not enough. We make the process easy by asking only one question every week. We make it fun and interactive by identifying the top priorities and responding to specific issues and challenges. We over-communicate and reinforce the message in department meetings, company-wide all-hands meetings, and in our regular strategic leadership team meetings. The point is to take the journey together, so everyone from the CEO to the frontline teller is pursuing the same goal. We improved trust and credibility when complaints about leadership behavior and lack of alignment were acknowledged and addressed.

Ash himself wrote a touching email to the whole organization accepting his mistakes and committing to leading as I discussed in "Taking the CEO Mastery Journey." This demonstration of disarming vulnerability and exemplary courage had the dramatic effect of creating a high-trust and high-performance culture. Even though we were not quite ready, we decided to participate in the "Best Places to Work" annual survey to gain experience and determine the gap between where we are and where we need to be.

Objective Performance Evaluation

Take the time to understand your people well, since nothing is more important for a business organization than its people. Professionals like to be treated, evaluated, and compensated fairly and objectively. This can be achieved in a well-functioning 3.0 meritocratic organization. What makes them come alive? What are they really good at? What is holding them back? When we focus on our strengths, we can do very well. However, if we want to excel, we have to uncover our greatest gift and overcome the most stubborn blocks that get in the way of performing at our best. This is how we dare to dream big and set audacious goals. In a normal business organization where the modus operandi is to look good and cover your weaknesses, you rarely, if ever, get this deep. You can achieve exponential results in business by helping evolve your people to be the best they can be.

Since you have already done this in Practice 2, "Lead with Self-Mastery," you can help your people do the same. You will find it personally rewarding and one of the best things you can do for the professional employee and for a business. Have authentic conversations in a trusting environment with the employee and several people who interact with him on a regular basis. Take advantage of the several wonderful tools I described earlier to determine personality traits, personal development, emotional intelligence, and spiritual intelligence.

One of the most important jobs of a leader is to evaluate performance objectively and accurately.

Ray Dalio, founder of Bridgewater Associates, more than any other business leader I know, made painstaking efforts to create a fair and objective meritocratic organization and offers excellent practical ideas and suggestions in his book *Principles*.

If you want to build a meritocratic organization, providing an accurate assessment of performance is the greatest gift you can give an employee. This should involve straight talk about strengths and weaknesses backed by specific examples. A deep and trusting relationship is impossible—personally and professionally—without straight talk and tough love. Toughness without love and care leads to broken relationships, and care without being straight and tough breed shallow and superficial relationships. Those relationships are not meaningful and you cannot count on each other to weather the storms that we all face in our journey of growth, learning, and achievement.

Help your people evolve to be the best they can be so they can give their head and heart, intellect, emotion, and spirit to your business, just like you do. This instills an owner mindset into your employees. To help this process, you have to first evaluate accurately. Probe, connect, and sync up by being honest, direct, and constructive. Objective evaluation means that you cannot allow your personal feelings, likes, or dislikes to get in the way of assessing someone's performance. Make sure that you have not assessed your subordinate harshly because you don't like certain personality traits. Similarly, make sure that you don't go easy on him just because you like him or you think she is a nice person.

It is difficult to give bad news about performance, and I see many so-called tough managers and leaders struggle with it. They do not want to hurt anyone's feelings. They try to soften the blow with attempts to be humorous or to sugarcoat the message. This awkward dance doesn't help either of you. Being accurate is more important than being soft. You can be kind, considerate, and compassionate in pointing out someone's weaknesses by providing specific examples. A reasonable person will accept and even appreciate it, even if it is a bit difficult initially. This can be an inspiring discussion and an opportunity to grow.

Providing feedback that is honest and constructive requires courage, humility, and mastery. It is worth the effort to do this right. I would even go as far as saying that, as a 3.0 leader, it is your moral obligation and responsibility to assess your people accurately. Take the time to get input from several other people who interact with the employee. Piece together a comprehensive and well-thought-out evaluation and accurately point out gifts and strengths, blocks and weaknesses with specific examples. Take the time to be thorough and detailed to provide an accurate performance appraisal. Don't slack off even if you have known the person for many years. People change and are supposed to evolve and grow. Make sure that is happening.

An accurate performance evaluation includes these three important dimensions:

1. **Results:** The scoreboard doesn't lie. What results has this person delivered? However, it is not as simple as that. As you go higher up the leadership ladder, your results are based on other people doing their job. How much credit do you get for that? How much of an influence did the external factors have?

Sometimes you get a lucky break even if you have not taken the right steps. Similarly, you could have taken all the right steps diligently, but the external market conditions and customer situation may have changed. That's the reason we incorporate two other dimensions.

2. **Process:** People who deliver exceptional results have a sound process they follow. It is worthwhile to understand and reward the right action steps being taken. In the short-term, right action and process may not match outcomes. It is important to see this and be more or less patient depending on how they are working to meet the goals. In the long run, greatness cannot be denied—right process will lead to the right results.

3. **Diverse perspectives:** To bring more accuracy and objectivity to performance evaluation, it is good to get other perspectives from people who closely interact and who have a track record of providing honest opinion without holding back.

These steps are necessary to realize the audacious goal of building an authentic meritocracy. It takes effort, but you reap exponential results personally and professionally.

If you see a gap in the value system—if the employee is not able to live up to the values and principles of the organization—that is a serious concern.

You can train someone for skills. Ability is tougher. You can't have a right-brain, creative person lead a large diverse team on a tight schedule. Similarly, you don't want a detail-oriented left-brain person lead a change effort to create innovative products and services. Skills are easy to learn, developing new abilities is a lot more difficult but happens naturally as we mature and develop into higher states of awakening. In a 3.0 state, you are naturally able to see the big picture and zoom in on the details; you are open and assertive, humble, and courageous.

Employees have opinions of their managers too. Make it easy for them and grant that opportunity to provide reverse feedback. You will disarm them and build trust. Ask for their honest opinion of your assessment. Try hard to connect and synchronize.

After providing a comprehensive, fair, and objective assessment, give the employee a sincere opportunity to improve. Provide the required tools and resources necessary to learn and progress. Training for skills is easy. Developing new capability is tougher and requires deep work and professional coaching. Help them explore their weakness and the pain that accompanies it, invite them to reflect and probe the root cause for poor performance. Determine if they are interacting with an open mind and heart and whether there is a willingness to learn and grow. It is inspiring when a message is delivered authentically and accurately. If they don't see it that way and if they are not open, they are probably not the right fit for the meritocratic 3.0 high trust- and high-performance (HTP) culture you are working hard to instill.

You can build a high-performance environment by not firing people. If they are not willing to get uncomfortable and go through the pain to grow, they will not be able to take the scrutiny and tough love; peer pressure will get to them. They self-select.

You can provide tough love and create a caring and compassionate environment. Charlie Kim, founder and CEO of Next Jump, Inc., treats his employees like family members. You don't fire your family members, he says. Ray Dalio of Bridgewater Associates has a different approach; he suggests that you train or remove people, don't rehabilitate them. He says, "cutting someone that you have a meaningful relationship with but who isn't an A player is hard but necessary for the excellence of the company."

The old 1.0 performance evaluation is boss knows best, and the boss evaluates the subordinate. In the last few years that has evolved into the so-called 360-degree analysis. This 2.0 approach includes input from peers, subordinates, and sometimes even some external customers. It is still up to the boss to effectively utilize this rich diverse input to provide a more objective evaluation.

The 3.0 performance evaluation involves frequent dialogue and real-time feedback for important tasks. When this is done correctly, the annual or semiannual review document will not contain any surprises. Some of the cutting-edge companies profiled in *Reinventing Organizations* have adopted a peer evaluation process. The employee shares his or her annual goals and targets for the year with the project team members. When the time comes, she will first self-evaluate her performance and recommend a merit increase. This is followed by a robust, interactive discussion, and team members help decide the final numbers. Here the role of the manager or boss is to facilitate, coach, remove obstacles, and provide the necessary resources and support. The conclusion is shared with HR who will then administer the details.

Incentivizing Value-Based Performance

Great leaders and organizations do not just hope that people will conduct themselves with utmost integrity, live by core principles, and run business operations by adhering to those values. That is not a practical approach. You have to assume that a large percentage of people act in self-interest and create conditions so that acting in their self-interest ensures and matches team and organizational interest.

You have to create an environment where fulfilling the job and communicating with others requires an employee to adhere to company values. How? You evaluate and reward people based, at least in part, on adherence to core values and operating principles. A noble shared purpose certainly helps and a small (and growing) percentage of people operate at higher levels independent of material rewards and personal recognition. But do not bank on that as a strategy for the company. That is simply not smart.

Rewarding and Penalizing Behavior

You have to nurture 3.0 behaviors by setting an example, rewarding right behaviors, and penalizing those that are inappropriate. All organizations have a set of values that they profess and intend to abide by. However, there is rarely any significant incentive provided for adhering to those values (positive behavior) or penalty for not living those values (poor behavior). The result is that most organizations engage in "good enough" behavior and fail to utilize the tremendous productivity advantages that come with actions that are collaborative, authentic, and empathetic.

How do you ingrain positive behavior change into organizational culture? Why not evaluate behavior too? What gets measured gets done, as they say! Celebrate good behavior and catch people doing things right. At the same time, do not ignore poor behavior. By taking appropriate action, you inspire people to do better and give tough love and an opportunity to shape up for those who do not. When you are making important decisions to promote, hire, and reward people, consider positive behavior a key factor. I recommend to the teams that I work with to incorporate (with significant weight) adherence to core values as a measure in performance evaluation. This can be objectively evaluated by polling a cross-section of people who interact with this person.

One of the most important jobs of a leader is to evaluate performance objectively and accurately.

Behavior change is a quest, a process, and a journey. One of the keys to successful pursuit of any goal is the opportunity to gauge and experience progress. Research and personal experience indicates that a sense of progress and forward motion is even more important than reward and recognition in inspiring you to keep going. How do you establish benchmarks to measure progress? Consider some tangible examples of goals, such as increased revenue, reduced expenses, improved profitability, or personal weight loss. You will know in six months or a year whether you achieved your goal or not. As I stated earlier in the book, that is is a lag measure which helps you focus, but it is not enough to inspire you to give your best every day and every week.

And how about following through on your commitment? You establish lead measures that you can track every day. For example, let's say that you want to lose twenty pounds. A lag measure could be represented by what you want your weight to be in six months. Lead measures could be exercising three times a week, eating dinner before 7 p.m. every day, and eating salad for lunch four times a week. I like to incorporate the same rigor and objectivity in tracking behavior change.

One of the leadership teams I worked with rated themselves a six out of 10 in teamwork and alignment. I had a couple of follow-up questions: Where do you want to be in nine to twelve months? What is one behavior you can incorporate that will help you move the needle? They said that they wanted to proactively engage in authentic communication and conflict resolution. They committed to meeting once in two weeks for thirty minutes, with two agenda items:

1. How did you do with your goal of engaging in authentic communication? Please explain.

2. What will you commit to doing in the next two weeks?

This level of discipline, along with the collaborative effort to push each other, resulted in noticeable progress. We made it a point to acknowledge and celebrate improvements, little wins, and achievements along the way to keep the momentum going. It also became obvious who was the right fit and who was struggling to function in this environment.

Here's another example of a similar process I use for more advanced practitioners. Let's say you want to show up in a more positive mindset. What is the one thing can you do that will result in demonstrating progress? How about reducing judgment and enhancing gratitude? Now establish lead measures: Meditate at least twenty minutes a day and engage in self-inquiry before bedtime by asking yourself, "How did I do today? Why did I do what I did? What were the triggers that tripped me up?"

As I stated earlier, you can and should track behavior change regularly! And, remember that your inner life drives your external behavior. You can't afford not to understand, improve, and track your emotions, perceptions, and motivations!

Fair Compensation and Incentives

Fair financial compensation is an important part of keeping your people and the organization engaged and inspired. Granted it is not the only compensation that counts to build a great 3.0 organization. Employees today view compensation holistically and the culture of the organization plays a big part. Total Compensation = Financial + Intellectual + Emotional + Physical + Social + Spiritual. However, you cannot afford to ignore a thoughtful debate and discussion on what is a fair, effective, and inspiring income gap between a top performer and an average performer, between a manager and a direct report, between peers who bring different skills and capabilities, between CEO and executives and frontline employees.

Let us start with what is not fair:

- Everyone gets paid about the same with a small gap between positions of higher and lower responsibilities and between exceptional and average performers. This is a big reason why socialism failed.

- A very large gap between top executives and others and between exceptional and average performers. This is why excessive, crony, or unconscious capitalism is failing.

Most people in modern societies appreciate that executives and leaders who add significant value and bear the burden of accountability need to be well compensated. We are motivated by this model to achieve and succeed as individuals. However, when the financial compensation gap is too large, it causes disappointment and disillusionment. You need to explore the right balance and also find ways to reward individual excellence and collaborative skill.

I say that socialism failed because of two problems. One is lack of meritocracy and accountability, and the other is the large income gap between the person(s) at the top and the rest. Modern capitalism has solved the first problem but has been unable to resolve the second. In order to solve the complex challenge of inequality, we have to dig deeper into understanding human motivations. We cannot ignore our quest for happiness, fulfillment, fairness, respect, justice, and our yearning to contribute, serve, and make a difference.

What is the right income gap? What is considered fair? What gap inspires everyone to give their very best? The best way to find out is to ask and have an honest and authentic discussion in your company. However, providing some context and research data is helpful to steer the discussion toward meaningful conclusion. A good dose of common sense and Maslow's hierarchy suggest that human beings have some basic needs of security, belonging, self-centered growth, and achievement that have to be met. After that what makes us truly happy, fulfilled, and inspired is to contribute, to serve, and to make a difference.

All reasonable employees expect an income gap in an environment of meritocracy and pay-for-performance. However, morale is impacted when the gap is unreasonably large.

According to a well-researched Princeton study by psychologist Daniel Kahneman and Noble Prize-winning economist Angus Deaton, that number is an annual salary of $75,000. We don't have to get hung up on the precise number since it could vary a bit based on factors such as the cost of living index, special needs for the family, etc., but you get the point. Inspired by this thinking and approach, Dan Price of Seattle-based company Gravity Payments, decided to cut his salary considerably in order to raise the minimum wage for all of his employees to $70,000 a year. Whole Foods has a salary cap policy which limits the total cash compensation that can be paid to any team member to nineteen times the average pay. This is in sharp contrast to market dynamics where the average CEO receives about 500 times as much as their average employee.

Just to be crystal clear, my interest is not based on morality and ethics. I am approaching this purely from a human motivation and productivity perspective. You have to figure out what works best for you. It is clear to me that we can do a lot better than the current market averages to reduce inequality in the workplace. Paul Polman, CEO of Unilever, could not have been more charmingly blunt: "Any CEO can decide that he shouldn't get paid too much. I think it is courageous leadership that is missing. The excuse is that the market won't let you … I think it is a cop-out."

Bill Gates and Warren Buffet have famously said that they need to pay more in taxes, even though they have paid enormous amounts of money in taxes already. Again, I am not taking a moralistic position here. I am merely presenting a common-sense observation. It is up to each leader to decide how they would like to contribute to reducing inequality and improving fairness in order to nurture a high-performance meritocracy. Every leadership team needs to have a thoughtful discussion about fair compensation and how it relates to their business model.

Let us contrast the business models of Walmart, a financially successful company based on the shareholder-centric model, and Costco, an even more financially successful organization that operates on a stakeholder-centric model, according to the research conducted for the book *Firms of Endearment*.

On average, Costco pays its employees 65 percent more than Walmart, and 40 percent more than Sam's Club. Its benefits are also much more generous. Yet, Costco generates significantly more profit per employee than Sam's Club. Costco achieves this by being more efficient and having very low employee turnover (6 percent in first year, compared to 21 percent at Sam's Club and 50 percent at Walmart.)

Costco designed a model that enables it to pay employees well, make good money for investors, have highly satisfied customers and suppliers, and generally be welcomed with open arms into every community it wants to enter. Here's what Costco CEO Jim Senegal says about why he is "overly generous" with Costco employees:

"Paying your employees well is not only the right thing to do, but it makes for good business. In the final analysis, you get what you pay for. Paying rock-bottom wages is wrong. It doesn't pay the right dividends. It doesn't keep employees happy. It keeps them looking for other jobs. Plus, managers spend all their time hiring replacements rather than running your business. You would rather have your employees running your business. When employees are happy, they are your very best ambassadors."

Costco's higher wages mean less money for recruiting and training costs and better relationships with customers. This leads to higher sales per customer and deeper customer loyalty. By contrast, Walmart reportedly hired 620,000 new workers in 2004 just to replace those who were let go or left.

Ironically, focusing intently on the bottom line alone often leads to poor bottom line performance. Placing shareholders far above all other stakeholders may be the worst long-term position a company can take. Shareholders gain more when their interests align with the interests of all other stakeholder groups. The merged businesses of Amazon and Whole Foods will be interesting to watch, since Amazon does an exceptional job of servicing its customers, and Whole Foods is among the best places to work for employees. They can combine the best of both and set the bar high for taking care of two of the most important stakeholders—employees and customers.

Income Inequality: Be the Change You Wish to See

Income inequality affects all of us, not just the top 1 percent or the ones at the bottom who are struggling to make ends meet. We enjoy social harmony and progress along with a decent quality of life for all when income inequality is dealt with seriously. As a business leader, you can set an example and be the change you wish to see. Capitalism has brought us remarkable progress, as detailed earlier. However, it should not surprise us to recognize that a model based on self-interest and self-centered achievement have helped create the challenges we are facing today both macroeconomically and within our business organizations. Focusing exclusively on shareholder return is proving detrimental not only for the well-being of employees, suppliers, and other stakeholders including communities and environment, but also to financial health itself. Now you can no longer afford to ignore the problem.

Many well-meaning and successful leaders actively care and contribute to social causes and non-profit organizations to make our community, our country, and world a better place. I know of many such wonderful people. It is time for us to dig deep and do more to instill fairness, objectivity, and meritocracy in our compensation structure within our business organizations and nurture an environment of excellence. Ash is doing both. He started a nonprofit foundation to help provide underprivileged children with education and better living conditions. He is also committed to building a transformative bank on the principles of fairness, trust, and meritocracy. A typically passionate and high-energy person, he is even more so when he is involved with the nonprofit foundation. I challenged him to demonstrate the same balance of passion and compassion at work. His direct reports say that he is making remarkable progress!

Purpose has to drive profit; unleashing your full potential should unlock the value of the business. This is the opportunity for 3.0 leaders to build purposeful and profitable organizations while nurturing an environment for the human spirit to soar. This is the exciting evolution we should all facilitate and accelerate: from self-centered capitalism to conscious, natural, inclusive, effective or inspiring capitalism. In doing so, we will help the twin engines of democracy and capitalism rise to their highest capability!

Infusing a Culture of Principled Performance

Infusing a culture of principled performance means that you want to build an enduring organization that excels in execution consistently. Some institutions which model this approach, such as the military and business organizations, get it only partially right, and they pay a price.

What do I mean? Military and armed forces have the advantage of a built-in noble purpose that is shared by all. Very few things are as appealing as the patriotic fervor of fighting for and protecting your freedom, liberation, and independence. That's great, but they also take a top-down, hierarchical approach with strict rules and guidelines. As long as you comply with these rules, you are assured of your job. However, there isn't much room for creativity, transparency, and most importantly, honest dissent—an opportunity to debate different perspectives constructively. Individual merit and drive is not adequately rewarded and recognized.

Creating a Circle of Trust

As I've discussed earlier in this book, great business organizations incorporate a noble purpose that appeals to human drives such as autonomy, meaning, and opportunity to unleash everyone's full potential. One of the most effective ways to achieve this is to establish a circle of trust at the leadership level and extend it all the way to the frontlines. This creates an environment for everyone to feel it is their company, and it is the best company they ever worked for.

How do you create that circle of trust where employees do not feel like they are disposable resources with no voice in the direction, decisions, and operations of the company? Some companies have a no-layoff policy. For example:

- Next Jump, Inc., extensively profiled in the pathbreaking book, *An Everyone Culture*, does not lay off employees for performance but trains them to improve. Founder Charlie Kim says that you don't fire your family members, you train them and fit them in positions where they can excel.

- Manufacturing technology supplier Barry-Wehmiller believes in heart count and not head count. They chose a pay cut for all instead of zero pay for some and successfully weathered one of their worst downturns and emerged stronger as a company.

Many enduring organizations such as Google, Netflix, and Southwest Airlines take the time to hire and train for culture fit. Companies such as Zappos take it a step further and offer to pay new employees to leave if they think this is not the right culture for them.

Ray Dalio of Bridgewater Associates has a different approach. He believes that you can earn the trust and loyalty of employees by evaluating them accurately and practicing meritocracy objectively.

Purposeful Parting

Baking mastery into the organization also involves a mindful approach to terminating employees. One of the most complex and rewarding conflict resolution experiences I had was with Meena, the CEO, and

Jorge, her key operations person. This was a difficult relationship, to put it mildly. They constantly butted heads in management and board meetings. The easy and recommended approach was to terminate Jorge and move on. That would then be followed up with a fairly vague and euphemistic company announcement about Jorge's departure.

We decided to do it differently and purposefully. I facilitated a conflict resolution session with not only the two of them but by also involved two other top executives. We wanted to make sure that the process was fair, especially to Jorge. He could have easily felt that Meena and I (her coach) were out to get him. Meena is a hard driver who moves fast and does not take the time to communicate with the executive team to get their buy-in. Everyone, including Jorge, acknowledges that there is no malicious or authoritarian intent on her part yet it causes grief. Jorge takes a confrontational attitude and to make it worse, he does not practice what he complains about with his own team.

They were bringing out the worst in each other. However, we pointed out that this conflict is an opportunity for both of them to overcome their weaknesses. We had several difficult conversations, and ultimately it did not work out. We ensured that the parting was purposeful and not bitter. We made an extra effort—Meena genuinely thanked Jorge by mentioning his specific contributions in the all-hands meeting. Jorge was visibly touched and appreciative of the noble and authentic gesture. I believe this prevented creating more bad blood between them. We transparently shared the situation with the leadership team and also included a couple of them in the conflict resolution process. This transparency stopped unnecessary speculation, water cooler gossip, and private conversations about what exactly happened and nipped possible conspiracy theories in the bud.

Finding Your Center of Gravity

Baking mastery into your DNA is not a spectator sport; it is an active endeavor where everyone participates in the culture you want. The trick in developing the appropriate culture is to determine the tipping point of leadership and center of gravity of the organization. Are there enough leaders on the team that can consistently practice and demonstrate stated values? Where is the collective awareness and expectation of the organization?

There is no right or wrong culture. While 3.0 is a more advanced or evolved state, earlier 1.0 and 2.0 states are not wrong—they are simply less evolved and less effective. Great leaders and organizations focus on consistency—actions match words. This means that everything you do is performed in alignment with your stated values.

You have to know the difference between your current behavior and expected behavior when you adhere to your purpose and core values. For example, even though your core values are authenticity, empowerment, and inclusive teamwork, you may not be currently pushing each other to have honest and direct conversations. You revert to hierarchical knee-jerk decisions and engage in top-down performance evaluation without taking input from other constituents. When you stay true to core values in your interactions, this discrepancy will be corrected.

What Makes an Exceptional Team?

Exceptional teams pay close attention to human nature and motivations with a high-SQ approach to enlightened conflict resolution and strategy development. This entails the following:

- **Focus on alignment of values:** They achieve full engagement and full commitment by clearly defining fundamental operating values and work hard to ensure alignment. Examples of these values are openness, honesty, collaboration, risk taking, and knowing that doing the right thing is more important than being right.

- **Clear and quick decision-making:** They do not rush or force consensus. Every member of the team expresses his or her viewpoint freely. Strategic options are thoroughly reviewed and everyone whole-heartedly supports and executes the final decision.

- **Prioritize, focus, and execute:** They ensure that the highest priority actions get addressed first. Focus is on completion before other less important items are addressed. They take the time to meticulously plan execution steps and allocate resources.

- **Keep commitments:** Action items with due dates and accountability are diligently executed. Team members pro-actively notify and provide an acceptable alternative if deadline is being missed.

- **Mutual accountability:** Team members take the responsibility to hold each other accountable to live up to espoused values and stay true to organizational mission.

- **Reward value-based behaviors:** Track, evaluate and reward behaviors that are in line with espoused values. Establish consequences for not walking the talk.

- **Proactive conflict resolution:** Proactively surface and resolve active and passive conflicts strictly on the merits of the case.

- **Objective evaluation:** Adhere to meritocracy and objectively evaluate performance with multiple inputs and perspectives.

- **Fair compensation:** Fairly compensate performance based on individual, team, and organizational goals.

I have worked with many well-meaning leaders and leadership teams who struggle with the implementation of this process. Why? Many of these practices are based on a keen understanding of human nature and behaviors that inspire extraordinary performance. Consistent implementation of these characteristics goes even beyond emotional intelligence. They require emotional mastery, wisdom, and spiritual intelligence.

Baking mastery in the DNA of the organization certainly requires an aligned, collaborative, and mutually accountable leadership team, but you need more than that. Typically, you engage a representative cross-functional team that is well trained and enthusiastic about your culture. This team helps identify the current status and the gap in becoming the company you can and want to be. They become key ambassadors and champions of change to create an environment where everyone feels it is their company and gives their very best.

I find this to be a critical piece in the organizational transformation work you are undertaking. Human capital initiative with the discipline of execution accelerates and enhances business performance. With the organization fully enlisted in your quest, there is no limit to how far you can go or how high you can soar on your CEO Mastery Journey.

Epilogue: Next Levels of Evolution

When we operate in a 2.0 state, low levels of employee engagement in business organizations, poor leadership, ineffective governance, and a polarized society are natural by-products. There is no point complaining or lamenting. Why not get to work and start with personal shift and transformation? You will then be in a much better position to affect change in our educational system and business organizations. The seven practices I have detailed in this book will help you operate in an awakened and conscious 3.0 state. However, if the collective consciousness of the leadership and employees is at 1.0 or 2.0 state, it would be very difficult to operate the organization with 3.0 principles and practices.

Meditation and Deep Breathing

You can take these practices further with meditation and deep breathing. In fact, they are among the most powerful exercises CEOs and leaders can engage in to enhance personal and organizational mastery.

Deep Breathing

A good way to ease into meditation is by calming down with deep breathing. Scientists say that on average a human being has 60,000 thoughts a day, 80 percent of which are mundane and repetitive. Our focus and productivity, not to mention our peace of mind would be a lot better if we could reduce these thoughts. The quality of our thoughts allows us to evaluate our state of personal development. If your thoughts are fearful, anxious, and based on self-preservation, you are operating at the bottom end. If your thoughts are focused on personal growth and achievement, you are operating in the mid-tier. If you are preoccupied with thoughts of universal wellbeing, unconditional service, and servant leadership, you are operating at the highest stages of human development. You are not what you say; you are what you think and how you act.

Controlling your mind can be like attempting to tame a wild, intoxicated elephant or a drunken monkey. Fortunately, there is an easier way. Your breath has direct connection to your mind. When you are anxious and restless, your breath is shallow. When you are calm and attentive, your breath is deep. So, the fastest and most effective method to slow down our restless, racing mind is to practice alternate nostril breathing, a 5,000-year-old practice called *Nadi Shodhana* in Sanskrit. One cycle of alternate nostril breathing involves the following:

1. Close your right nostril with your right thumb and breathe in slowly though your left nostril.

2. Hold for a few seconds as comfortable.

3. Close your left nostril with your right ring finger and breathe out gently through the right nostril.

4. Hold for a few seconds as comfortable.

5. Breathe in slowly through the right nostril by continuing to close the left nostril with your right ring finger.

6. Hold for a few seconds as comfortable.

7. Close your right nostril with your right thumb and breathe out gently through left nostril.

Meditation

Meditation is the royal road to operating at higher states of awareness and consciousness. It is a proven method to bring stillness to the mind, body, and spirit in order to realize your full creative potential. Meditation is distinctly different from the process of self-inquiry. In meditation, you become a dispassionate observer of your thoughts. Buddha said, "We are shaped by our thoughts; we become what we think." By observing your thoughts, you understand yourself better and have a much better appreciation for the rationale behind your actions. You also have a glimpse into your future direction which you can positively influence.

As stated earlier, we have positive thoughts, neutral thoughts, and negative thoughts. Facing our negative thoughts could be difficult initially because we come face-to-face with our shadow side. We can no longer deny this "unpleasant" side of ours. The trick is to not fight, critique, or judge those negative thoughts but to simply accept them for what they are. This is different from self-inquiry where we determine the root cause for why our thoughts are positive, neutral, or negative. When you dispassionately observe your thoughts, you will notice that the negative thoughts lose their intensity and grip over you.

You will strengthen your positive self and weaken the negative self. You will take responsibility for your actions and won't play victim by blaming others for your challenges. You will strengthen your resolve and purpose and weaken the thoughts that sabotage you from pursuing your passion and purpose. This is stunningly simple and feels too good to be true. But please persist and continue to meditate. With regular meditation, you will feel more alive, energized, and enthusiastic. You will develop a superior ability to deal with life's complexities and challenges. A CEO has no shortage of these! You will cultivate the discipline to prioritize and have more time to focus on and pursue your passion and purpose. This simple practice yields powerful results.

Consider this example of how meditation can result in a positive behavioral change. Let's say that you tend to judge and criticize your colleague's impatience. Obviously, your colleague resents and ignores your advice, even though you mean well, and your intention is to help him. You do not feel good, your colleague doesn't feel good, your relationship suffers, and the problem doesn't get resolved. Talk about a no-win, lose-lose-lose-lose situation!

During your meditation sessions, just observe your thoughts of judgment and criticism. You will notice you are gradually becoming less harsh and critical. You will also discover that you are being very critical of yourself, and you are upset with your own impatience. By accepting and observing these thoughts, you will become easier on yourself, and you won't judge your colleague as much. You are not triggered or overreact easily, you are calm. By accepting your impatience, you are paradoxically becoming more patient and are in a much better position to help your colleague in the process, too.

How to Meditate

Sit upright with your spine erect. This allows you to be in a state of restful alertness. Start with alternate nostril deep breathing exercise for about five rounds. This prepares you for meditation. Sit still and observe your thoughts dispassionately. You need an anchor to focus on, so you don't get sucked into or involved in your thoughts. A good anchor is to observe your breath. You can also choose to focus on an image or a mantra, a Sanskrit word like Om, or just silence and stillness.

You will alternate between focusing on your anchor and observing your thoughts. You might find yourself experiencing moments of stillness with no thoughts. Sometimes there are no gaps of stillness at all and the whole meditation session is filled with thoughts. This does not mean you are incapable of meditating or have not had a productive session of meditation. It is natural for us to have thoughts. By setting aside some focused time you are allowing the thoughts—especially those that are negative, repetitive, and unnecessary—to be released.

Just bring attention back to your anchor. This process frees the mind immensely, and you will feel less burdened by the thoughts as you go about your day. The gap between thoughts could be very short, sometimes there is no gap, and at other times fairly long. The longer the gap, the more peace and bliss you will experience.

But do not force anything. Let it come. It is during the gaps between thoughts that profound insights occur and answers to your deep questions come from within you. This is what we mean by "all answers reside within us." You could also call it intuition. The intuitive power works best when your mind is still and free from thoughts of fear, anxiety, and expectation. Through meditation, you can penetrate the layers of stress, ego, and ignorance, and connect with this omniscient source. Meditation has been the tool that has revealed answers to my deepest questions in life, leadership and mastery, including insights into authentic communication, proactive conflict resolution, accountable decision-making, effective meetings, objective performance evaluation, and fair compensation.

With consistent and diligent practice, you can develop the ability to turn your thoughts on and off at will and experience long periods of focused action or thoughtless stillness. Imagine the exponential increase in creativity and productivity when you develop the ability to focus on one task for long periods of time. It may take several years to get to that exalted state. This should not stop you from enjoying the immense benefits of the journey. Meditation, as we now know through scientific research, rewires brain circuitry, releases happy chemicals such as dopamine, oxytocin, serotonin, and creates new neural pathways. I have been meditating for more than 25 years and I rarely experience long periods of complete thoughtlessness. But every time I meditate, I feel more energized, more alive, and more enthusiastic than before.

Business and life are both fast-changing, uncertain, complex, and ambiguous. Great leaders are comfortable with the unknown and navigate with confidence by accepting their limitations. They master their thoughts and emotions, and focus on right action. They always show up with enthusiasm and give their best, even though there are no guarantees of outcomes. As Krishna said to Arjuna in the Gita, "you have control over your actions alone but not the results." Instead of chasing results, it is more effective to pursue your noble purpose, direct your destiny with self-assurance, and inspire everyone around you to do the same. By focusing on the process and right action, you will achieve exceptional outcomes.

The Butterfly Effect

My focus in this book has been on 3.0 business leadership and practices. They are equally applicable in educational, political, and socioeconomic institutions, but a lot more difficult to implement successfully without a rise in collective consciousness. Hopefully, we can learn from history and make this shift in a relatively smooth, less chaotic, and dysfunctional manner.

When caterpillars reach a certain stage of evolution, they become voracious monsters, eating everything in sight. They eat 100 times their own weight and can devour an entire tree. During this time, something happens inside their genetic makeup and special cells, called the imaginal cells, wake up and begin to cluster. These cells are in the minority, but when enough of them cluster, they become the caterpillar's genetic directors. The rest of the cells become the nutritive soup out of which the imaginal cells create the magnificent and amazing butterfly.

This is the opportunity we have in our business organizations where the evolved, conscious employees and leaders are the imaginal cells. The unconscious, self-centered individuals become the nutritive soup out of which emerges the promised organization that you are all seeking. The same phenomenon is applicable to socioeconomic institutions, communities, and countries. Edward Lorenz, an American mathematician, meteorologist, and a pioneer of the chaos theory, called this *the butterfly effect*.

Here's a remarkable biological fact: The genetic code that is responsible for the wings of the butterfly is the same one that makes the human heart beat. This is where love, compassion, longing, and your deepest yearnings reside. When you appeal to the higher states of human nature and reward those behaviors in business, you create high-trust and high-performance organizations. Similarly, when we collectively rise as a society, demonstrate exemplary behavior, and elect leaders who are operating at a conscious 3.0 state, we will direct our destiny and create prosperous inclusive societies and nations.

Index

Note: *Italic* page numbers indicate a figure. **Bold** page numbers indicate a table.

F

G

H

I

definitions, 188–189
Jobs, Steve, 193
Nadella, Satya, 193
summary of themes, 201–204
Integral Theory, 21, 123
integrated human nature self-
actualization model components
achieving organizational mastery,
59–60
achieving personal mastery, 58–59
high-trust and high-performance
operating system, 60–61
introduction, *55,* 55–57
personal transformation aspect,
57–58
intellectual intelligence, 57–58
CEO mastery, 75, 79, 80, 86, *86,*
132–134, 143–145
personal transformation, 57–58
intent-to-impact gap. *See* bridging
intent-to-impact gap (practice #5)
introduction
author's breakdown, 12–14
author's personal exploration, 9–11
author's professional disillusion, 7–9
author's search for a teacher, 10–11
author's upbringing, 5–7
Bhagavad Gita, 10
book's intended audience, 22–24
conscious thought leaders, 21
enlightened organization qualities,
19–20
Gandhi, Mahatma, 6–7
Goldsmith, Marshal, 10, 22
gratitude practice considerations,
12–15, 17, 18
Kofman, Fred, 21, 114, 275–276
Laloux, Frederic, 21
Maslow, Abraham, 6
meditation practice, 9–11
Natural Laws of life, 16–19
organizational mastery, 4–5, 10–11,
20–22
personal mastery, 4–5, 10–11
professional mastery, 4
questions driving personal mastery,
14

self-actualization, 3–4, 6–7, 10–13,
15, 17
Sthitaprajna state, 15
Swamiji, Sri Ganapathy
Sachchidananda, 15
vasudhaiva kutumbakam, 7
Wigglesworth, Cindy, 21, 131–132,
135, 212, 220
Wilber, Ken, 21
IQ. *See* intellectual intelligence

J

Jobs, Steve. *See also* Apple computer
engage in action leadership, 301
inspire with a noble purpose
(practice #3), 193
mindset, 115
purpose, vision, mission, and core
values compact, 193
Johnson & Johnson, 178

K

Kegan, Robert, 43, 210–212, 328
Kim, Charlie, 91, 174, 182, 319, 328
King, Martin Luther Jr., 3
Kofman, Fred, 21, 114, 275–276
Krishna, 10, 15, 17, 258, 265, 337

L

Lahey, Lisa, 43, 210–212, 328
Laloux, Frederic, 21, 308
Lao Tzu, 282
lead with self-mastery (practice #2),
141
master human motivations (practice
#1), 124
lead with self-mastery (practice #2)
assertiveness considerations, 162–
163
authenticity, 169–170
CEOs self-limiting examples,
144–146
direct link to business performance,
143–144
disappointment to inspired action
stages, 165–166

Credits

Publisher/Editorial Director: Michael Roney

Art Director: Sarah M. Clarehart

Copyeditor: Kathryn Abbott

Proofreader: Heather Pendley

Indexer: Karl Ackley

HIGHPOINT
EXECUTIVE
PUBLISHING

CPSIA information can be obtained
at www.ICGtesting.com
Printed in the USA
BVHW040108280219
541374BV00003B/8/P